Anchors
WORLDVIEW HANDBOOK

NANCY S. FITZGERALD

We are no longer to be children, tossed here and there by waves and carried about by every wind of doctrine... Ephesians 4:14

Published by
Anchorsaway®
13240 Old Meridian Street
Carmel, Indiana 46032
317-844-0381

ISBN 978-0-9771828-3-1

Dear Student,

You are about to embark on a journey that will transform your life and faith. I am excited to share with you some of what the Lord used to transform my faith into a living faith, that holds me firm during the storms of life.

My prayer for you is that your faith in Christ will mature and that you will desire to live passionately, think Christianly and love others unconditionally, to the glory of God.

Inside these pages you will learn that the Lord's purpose for all of us is to walk with Him, listen to Him, and obey Him, as we live our lives to the full. We live in a time when much of the world lives contrary to how God has called us to live. My challenge to you is to live in such a way that when the world sees you, they will see your God! My goal with this class is that you will be equipped with the foundation of the Christian faith, as well as an understanding of how to speak into other worldviews.

You are about to step out into a whole new world where you will meet people who live and believe differently than you. You are called to be an encouragement to them, and to share the hope and the love that the Lord has for them. I believe that you will be successful because you will be confident enough in your own beliefs to give a reason for why you believe. We are not about winning arguments, but in love, speaking truth with gentleness and respect.

Thank you for joining this journey. I pray that the Lord will bless you with a love for others and a life of impact for His kingdom. With a solid foundation and an excitement about loving others you will, I am confident, "no longer be like children, tossed here and there by waves and carried about by every wind of doctrine" (Ephesians 4:14).

Praying for your journey,

Nancy S. Fitzgerald

TABLE OF CONTENTS

Core Lessons

Elective Lessons

Appendix A – Resource Charts

Lesson 1: What Is the Christian Worldview?

Anchorsaway is a college-level Christian worldview educational experience targeting high school juniors, seniors and college students. Our purpose is to encourage each student's inner transformation through the working of the Holy Spirit and equip them to confidently live out their faith in every area of life, be it on the college campus or in the workplace.

The goal of Anchorsaway is for students to live passionately, think Christianly and love others unconditionally, for the glory of God.

Only 2% of evangelical students know why they believe. – Josh McDowell

The world will not listen to you until you demonstrate to them that you are consistently living out Christ in all areas of life. When people see you, they will see your God...and that is as close as some of them will ever get to church.

A. What is a worldview?

1. It is the way in which one views the world.

2. An understanding of how the world works and one's purpose in the world

3. The basic set of beliefs by which one explains the world, interprets circumstances and lives his/her life

4. The foundation from which one lives, views life, thinks and responds to the world in which he/she lives

B. All people wrestle with the Five Life Questions:

1. From where did I come?

2. Why is there such a mess in the world?

3. What hope do I have?

4. What is my purpose in life?

5. What happens when I die?

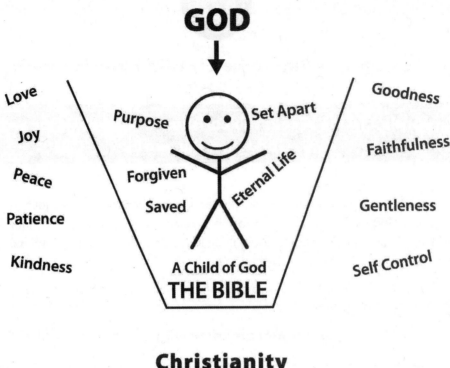

Christianity

Christianity rests on the belief in the God of Scripture who created the universe and everything in it. The Bible is the foundation of the Christian worldview. God has revealed Himself to man through the person of Jesus Christ. The person who responds to the leading of the Holy Spirit and believes that Jesus died for the sins of the world and rose again (proving His deity), is a Christian. When the Christian chooses to allow the Holy Spirit to guide him/her, the fruit of the Spirit (as shown above) will overflow in his/her life.

A. Key Characteristics of the Christian Worldview

1. The Bible is the inerrant, inspired Word of God and is the "handbook" for living the Christian life.

2. God created the universe and everything in it.

3. God is a personal Being who has revealed Himself to man (through the Bible, Jesus, and creation).

4. Man is sinful from birth, and therefore unable to be in a personal relationship with a holy God.

5. The relationship between sinful man and a holy God is only restored through the redemptive work of Jesus Christ (through His death and resurrection).

6. Salvation comes only as a gift from God, not through man's good works.

7. Because Christ died for us, we have the privilege of living for Him by imitating God, through the Holy Spirit, in all we do, say, and think.

B. How does the Christian worldview answer The Five Life Questions?

1. From where did I come?

"In the beginning God created the heavens and the earth" (Genesis 1:1). The universe and everything in it was created by the personal Creator, God.

"For you created my inmost being; you knit me together in my mother's womb. I praise you because I am fearfully and wonderfully made; your works are wonderful, I know that full well" (Psalm 139:13-14).

"So God created mankind in his own image, in the image of God he created them; male and female he created them. (Genesis 1:27) What does it mean to be made in the "image of God?" We have a soul, intellect and reason, a value system, choice, a purpose for living to glorify God, not self, by putting others first while loving others and receiving God's love.

2. Why is there such a mess in the world?

When Adam and Eve rebelled against God, sin entered the world. As their descendants, we have all been born with a sinful nature, separating us from fellowship with God. Our natural tendency is to live to please ourselves, instead of living for God (Genesis 3; Romans 3:23, 5:12).

God's character reflects His unchanging moral standard for the world, the standard which defines right and wrong behavior.

3. What hope do I have?

God's Son, Jesus Christ, came to earth to die on the cross for our sins. He was raised to life again, so that if we believe in Him, we can have a personal relationship with God (John 3:16; Romans 10:9-10; I Corinthians 15:3-4). We become His children and receive salvation, through Jesus Christ, as a gift of God's grace, not because of anything we have done (Ephesians 2:8-9).

4. What is my purpose in life?

My purpose on earth is to love God, to love others unconditionally, and to live life to the fullest (Matthew 22:36-40; John 10:10).

My goal is to imitate God in what I do, say, and think. As I live my life in Christ, I can, through the leading of the Holy Spirit, be a part of leading others into a relationship with Jesus Christ. I will also work for the renewal of our culture so that justice and righteousness will reign here on earth (Genesis 1:28).

5. What happens when I die?

Those who believe in Jesus Christ will live forever with Him in heaven (John 3:16, 14:2-3; Revelation 21:1-4).

The Framing Exercise

In this framing exercise, you will learn how to see others as God sees them; this is the heartbeat of biblical worldview. God has commanded us to love one another well including our family, friends and yes, our enemies. From a human perspective, it seems like an impossible task. However, when we understand who we are from God's perspective, we begin to understand that all things are possible. Loving those irregular people in our life, including ourselves, is not only possible but extremely important as we live out our life journeys.

The idea behind framing is to see all persons the way God sees them and realizing that we are all broken and in need of God's love and grace'. The amazing thing about God is that His love for us is unconditional. He loves all those whom He has created; he shows no favorites. Relying on your feelings and past experiences to define God will deceive you. God is very clear in the Scriptures in teaching all who read, exactly who he is. This framing exercise allows you to speak that truth into those who you want to impact. To interject your opinion or your bias or a short sermon is not for this exercise. To frame someone is to see them, and sometimes speak into them, how God sees them throughout the Scriptures through the work of the Holy Spirit.

Framing a Christian "I love you. I have loved you before the beginning of time. I put you together in your mother's womb. You are fearfully and wonderfully made.[1] You matter to me. I made you different than all the people that I have created from the beginning of time. The iris of your eye, your thumbprint and your DNA are unique to just you. I am a relational God who designed you in my image so that you can reason, make moral choices and have a relationship with me.[2] I designed you in love to receive my love and have the choice to love and obey me. Because you believe that I loved you so much that I sacrificed my only son to be crucified to pay the price for all your sins:[3] past, present and future, I have made you my child[4] and sent the Holy Spirit, to live in you forever.[5] The Spirit is not a little piece of me, but all of me. Through the work of the Holy Spirit in you, you now have access to all that you will ever need to live life to the full. You can experience love, joy, peace, patience, kindness, goodness, faithfulness, gentleness and self-control.[6] Through me, as you read my Word you will learn more about who I am, who you are and what I require of you. I do not want your performance as an attempt to earn my love, acceptance or acknowledgment. You already have it. As my child, I want you to be a light of hope and encouragement to the world.[7] I want you to love me and to love others by loving and serving them and by being ready and willing to tell them about me.[8] Yes, I designed you with a purpose to live life to the fullest extent and when you die, you will no longer experience suffering and death but will live with me in heaven forever." [9]

1	Psalms 139:13-16
2	Genesis 1:26
3	John 3:16
4	1 John 3:2
5	Ephesians 1:13
6	Galatians 5:22
7	Matthew 5:14-16
8	Luke 10:27
9	John 3:16

Lesson 1: What Is the Christian Worldview?

Small Group Objective:

The goal is to get to know your small group and to begin to develop a sense of community. The student needs to know that the small group is a safe place and one that encourages questions about life, God and anything in between. Each student needs to be given the opportunity to speak. Do not let one person dominate the discussion.

✓ Check Points:

☐ Bring 3 x 5 cards for your students to write down any questions they may have which aren't answered during the discussion.

☐ Prepare a brief personal testimony to share with your small group.

Small Group Discussion: (Do **not** feel that you must cover all questions. Make sure that you keep your group on topic. <u>Always end in prayer</u>!)

1. As the small group leader(s), introduce yourself. Share a <u>brief</u> testimony of how you came to have a personal relationship with Jesus Christ and why you wanted to lead <u>this</u> small group.

2. Pass around a sign up sheet for each student's name, address, email, phone, school, and where they are going after high school. Type them up and send the information to the person in charge of recording all students' names.

3. Have each student introduce him/herself and ask what school he/she goes to and what he/she likes to do outside of school.

4. What makes an effective small group?

   a. Be on time and be committed to come every time the class meets.

   b. No question is a stupid question; you can always pass if you are called on and you do not wish to answer.

   c. Be courteous and listen to others.

   d. Pray for each other even if you forget other student's names.

   e. Be bold and meet other students. It is good practice for next year.

5. Have the students turn to the devotionals in the back of their notes and show them how to use them this coming week by doing day one together.

(*Note*: When contacting them this next week, make sure to ask them, "What is it about the devotionals you like?" Tell them that this is what you will be asking. Once they do one, they will love it!!)

6. What do you hope to get out of your involvement with Anchorsaway?

7. Has someone ever challenged you in your faith? How did you respond?

8. What are some things that you want to study in Anchorsaway?

9. What questions do you want answered?

(*Note*: If your students respond to question 7 or 8, take note and share it with the Teacher so that they can be addressed.)

10. How would you define the Christian worldview?

11. How would you frame yourself?

12. Why is it important for you to know how God sees you?

13. Do most Christians live out who they really are? Why or why not?

14. When someone sees you, what worldview would they think that you embraced?

15. Ask for prayer requests and tell students that you will be faithful to pray for them.

16. Encourage students to record prayer requests in the prayer request section of their handbooks.

17. Spend the remaining time in prayer.

(*Note*: If the students have questions that you are unable to answer, simply thank them for the great question and tell them you don't know the answer, but will get back to them by the following week. Be sure to call or email your members in your small group each week. Talk about a question they raised or how their week is going. Send group questions to the large group leader so they can be answered at the beginning of the next week's lesson.)

★ After the Session

1. Contact each small group member during the week. Ask them about their devotional time, a question they have raised, or how their week is going.

Prayer Requests

Student Devotionals written by T.M. Moore

What is the Christian Worldview?

The daily readings are intended to supplement the material presented in the lessons, to establish the biblical basis for worldview thinking, and to help students develop the discipline of allowing the Word of God to dwell in them richly (Colossians 3:16).

Begin each reading in prayer, using the suggested words from one of the Psalms to get you started. Allow the Holy Spirit to lead your prayer along the trajectory indicated by the Psalms as you prepare to read and meditate in God's Word.

Next, read and meditate on the text, paying careful attention to key words, action words, and words that stand out as important for you personally. Let the questions provided guide your meditation as you reflect on the text you have read. (All Scripture references are from the English Standard Version, Crossway Books.)

In the journal section, complete a one-sentence thought that you can take with you into the day to help you further internalize the Word of God. Let the words provided get you started, but make the thought as personal to your own situation as you can.

Close your devotional time in prayer, beginning with the words provided and letting the Holy Spirit lead you on from there.

Day 1: Your Word is Truth

Pray: "...the rules of the LORD are true, and righteous altogether" (Psalm 19:9).

Read: John 17:14-17

Meditate: Who is the speaker?

                To "sanctify" means to "set apart for holy purposes." What would be some examples of "holy purposes" I might undertake today?

                How does the Word of God help me to be set apart for holy purposes? Can I fulfill such purposes apart from the Word of God?

                If God is going to be able to set me apart for holy purposes through His Word of truth, what will this require of me?

Journal: Today my friends will be able to tell that God has set me apart for holy purposes when…

Pray: *"My heart is steadfast, O God"* (Psalm 108:1).

Day 2: Let God Be True

Pray: *"The sum of your word is truth, and every one of your righteous rules endures forever"* (Psalm 119:160).

Read: Romans 3:3, 4

Meditate: What does it mean to be "unfaithful?" Is this somehow related to God's truth? How?

Does the unfaithfulness of people affect God's truth? How about when I am unfaithful to Him?

In their unfaithfulness, people may "judge" God (v. 4), concluding that His Word is not truth. What does it mean to say that God will be true and justified in what He says, even though people may lie about Him and His Word? Do I ever lie about God?

Journal: I want to be faithful to God's Word, so, today…

Pray: *"Make me to know your ways, O LORD; teach me your paths"* (Psalm 25:4).

Day 3: Choose This Day!

Pray: *"Then they cried to the LORD in their trouble…He sent out his word and healed them"* (Psalm 107:19, 20).

Read: Joshua 24:14, 15

Meditate: Joshua is calling the people of Israel to get serious about the Lord. Do people today serve other "gods" besides the Lord? What might be some examples of these "gods?"

Would Joshua encourage me to think that I could serve both God the Lord and any of these other "gods?" What would he say to me?

Can I say what Joshua did at the end of v. 24? What does it mean to "serve the LORD?" What is one way I can do that today?

Journal: Today I will have many opportunities to choose between the false "gods" of unbelieving worldviews and the God of truth; therefore...

Pray: *"You are my King, O God"* (Psalm 44:4).

Day 4: Who Loves Ya, Baby?

Pray: *"Oh give thanks to the LORD, for he is good, for his steadfast love endures forever!"* (Psalm 107:1).

Read: Romans 8:35-39

Meditate: According to Paul, what kinds of things are God's love for me stronger than? Are these things able to make God stop loving me?

Let me see if I've got this right: The God whose Word is true, even though everyone else is lying and serving false "gods," this God keeps loving me even through tribulation, distress, danger, and all the rest? If He holds so tightly to me, what does that suggest about how I need to respond? What does that require of me?

I'm going to say vv. 38 and 39 aloud. Now I'm going to say them again. Do I really believe this? Is there someone I can tell this to today?

Journal: Today I'll probably meet someone who is distressed or troubled or otherwise bummed out. I'm going to tell that person...

Pray: *"Let the redeemed of the LORD say so, whom he has redeemed from trouble"* (Psalm 107:2).

Day 5: Set Your Mind

Pray: *"Your people will offer themselves freely in the day of your power"* (Psalm 110:3).

Read: Colossians 3:1-3

Meditate: Have I been "raised with Christ?" What does that mean? For now? Forever?

I need to choose this day what to "set" my mind on. How would I explain to my friends what it means to "set" their minds "on things that are above?" What will try to distract me from that?

My life is hidden with Christ in God, and nothing can separate me from His love. How can I keep this thought in mind throughout the day ahead?

Journal: When I think of Jesus, seated at the right hand of God, and my life hidden with Him...

Pray: *"Your throne, O God, is forever and ever. The scepter of your kingdom is a scepter of righteousness; you have loved righteousness and hated wickedness"* (Psalm 45:6, 7).

Key Books:

Barna, George. Think like Jesus: Make the Right Decision Every Time. Nashville: Integrity, 2003.

Bertrand, J. Mark. (Re)Thinking Worldview. Wheaton, IL: Crossway Books, 2007

Boa, Kenneth. Faith Has Its Reason: Integrative Approaches to Defending the Christian Faith. Waynesboro, GA: Paternoster, 2006.

Colson, Charles W., and Nigel M. De S. Cameron. Human Dignity in the Biotech Century: A Christian Vision for Public Policy. Downers Grove, IL: InterVarsity, 2004.

Colson, Charles, and Nancy Pearcy. How Now Shall We Live? Wheaton, IL: Tyndale House Publishers, 1999.

Federer, William J. America's God and Country: Encyclopedia of Quotations. St. Louis, MO: Amerisearch, 2000.

Geisler, Norman L., and Ronald M. Brooks. Come, Let Us Reason: An Introduction to Logical Thinking. Grand Rapids, MI: Baker Book House, 1990.

Hemingway, Ernest. A Farewell to Arms. New York: Charles Scribner's Sons, 1929. Reprint, New York: Scribner's, 1995.

Keller, Timothy. The Reason for God: Belief in an Age of Skepticism. New York, NY: Riverhead Book, 2008.

Kinnaman, David. Good Faith: Being a Christian When Society Thinks You're Irrelevant and Extreme. Grand Rapids, MI: Baker., 2016.

Kinnaman, David, and Gabe Lyons. Unchristian: What a New Generation Really Thinks about Christianity-- and Why It Matters. Grand Rapids, MI: Baker, 2007.

Kreeft, Peter, and Ronald K. Tacelli. Handbook of Christian Apologetics: Hundreds of Answers to Crucial Questions. Downers Grove, IL: InterVarsity, 1994.

Mooreland, James Porter, and William Lane. Craig. Philosophical Foundations for a Chrisitan Worldview. Downers Grove, IL:InterVarsity, 2003

McDowell, Josh, and David H. Bellis. The Last Christian Generation. Holiday, FL: Green Key, 2006.

McDowell, Josh and Bob Hostetler. Beyond Belief to Conviction. Wheaton, IL: Tyndale House Publishers, 2002.

Moore, T. M. Culture Matters: A Call for Consensus on Christian Cultural Engagement. Grand Rapids, MI: Brazos, 2007.

Overman, Christian. God's Pleasure at Work: Bridging the Sacred-secular Divide. Bellevue, WA: Ablaze Publications, 2009.

Pearcy, Nancy. Total Truth. Wheaton, IL: Crossway Books, 2004.

Phillips, W. Gary., William E. Brown, and John Stonestreet. Making Sense of Your World: A Biblical World View. Salem, WI: Sheffield Pub., 2008.

Lesson 2: What Are the Five Major Worldviews?

"The way a man perceives God is the way he will live his life." – Author Unknown

A. What is a worldview?

1. It is the way in which one views the world.

2. An understanding of how the world works and one's purpose in the world

3. The basic set of beliefs by which one explains the world, interprets circumstances and lives his/her life

4. The foundation from which one lives, views life, thinks and responds to the world in which he/she lives

B. All people wrestle with the Five Life Questions:

1. From where did I come?

2. Why is there such a mess in the world?

3. What hope do I have?

4. What is my purpose in life?

5. What happens when I die?[1]

"I believe in Christianity as I believe that the sun has risen, not only because I see it, but because by it I see everything else."
– C.S. Lewis[2]

Naturalism

The naturalist/humanist does not believe in God, and therefore, makes no room for Him. Instead, man becomes the center of his own universe, seeking self-rule by pursuing those things which gratify his own self-interests.

A. Key Characteristics of Naturalism/Humanism

1. Man, not God, is at the center of all things.

2. Since there is no God, there are no moral absolutes; nothing is absolutely wrong.

3. Science allows us to study the material world, which holds the key to understanding life and ultimately provides mankind's salvation.

4. Man is believed to be inherently good, making it possible to achieve Utopia.

5. A person's value system is directly related to what he/she needs for personal satisfaction.

6. Reaching mankind's full potential holds the key to progress.

7. Humanists don't necessarily agree with the generally accepted answers to the real questions of life. They feel free to discover their own answers.

8. Knowledge does not come from faith in Christ, but is based on the human intellect and the ability to reason.

9. Naturalism emphasizes bringing out the best in people by promoting scientific inquiry, individual freedom, human reason, tolerance and self-determination.

10. Generally accepted standards for moral behavior are developed or discovered, and their value is tested by their consequences.

B. How does the Naturalism/Humanism worldview answer the "Five Life Questions?"

1. From where did I come?

The universe created itself. The universe (and everything in it) is the result of random, impersonal, undirected forces of nature. We did not come from a transcendent Creator God. Humanity is the result of purposeless evolutionary development over millions of years. In the beginning was the Big Bang.

2. Why is there such a mess in the world?

Man is inherently good, but people have not fully actualized their human potential. Without this self-actualization, these people do not have the ability to fully cooperate with others.

3. Is there any hope?

Humanity is the only hope for getting the world out of the mess it is in. The pursuit of knowledge and human progress will bring about the eventual elimination of all that is wrong with the world. This will ultimately make Utopia here on earth possible.

4. What is my purpose in life?

Mankind's purpose is to simply pursue mutual agreement and cooperation of basic human wants and needs. All people are to seek the knowledge necessary to fix what's wrong with the world.

5. What happens when I die?

All people will experience a physical death and nothing more beyond this life.

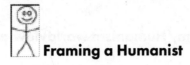

Framing a Humanist

"I realize that you don't know me, but I want to make sure you understand a few things about me that perhaps you haven't heard before. I love you.[1] There has not been a moment in time that I have not loved you. On your best and your worse day, I love you. I created you in my image with the purpose of you knowing, trusting and loving me.[2] You are not a mistake. You were not formed from random molecules through random chance. You are unique; I have created no one else like you.[3] Even the iris of your eye, thumbprint, and DNA are different from all others I have created. You were designed with the purpose of personally knowing and trusting in me. You are searching for meaning and purpose in a world that can not give those things to you. The things of this world will not fill the void that is within you. The love, peace, and joy that you are looking for can only be found in me.[4] I know your heart. It is broken just like the hearts of all humans who live on this earth. I am your only hope both now and for eternity. Only by believing that I died and rose again to pay the penalty of your sin, will you become free to be the person I created you to be. There is nothing you can do to earn it; it is a gift from me to you.[5] When you place your trust me, I will become your Savior, you will become my child, and my Spirit will live in you forever.[6] I will be your hope both now and for eternity and when you die, you will spend eternity with me in heaven. Until then, I want you to be a light to a broken world so that when others see you, they will see me. In this life, you will have troubles, but know that those struggles are designed to draw you and others closer to me. When you trust in me, you can know for sure that when you die, there will be no more pain and suffering. You will be with me forever in Heaven!"[7]

---

1 Romans 8:35-39
2 Ganesis 1:27
3 Psalm 139:13
4 Galatians 3:14
5 John 11:25-26
6 John 16:33
7 John 3:16

Postmodernism

Like Humanism, the postmodern man rejects God and His binding moral authority. Instead, he embraces a morality relative to his culture, and ultimately, a life without purpose. Postmodernism is a reactionary movement against Enlightenment principles, progress and the objective search for truth and morality.

A. Key Characteristics of Postmodernism

1. There is no belief in a transcendent God.

2. Postmodernism rejects the idea of a grand narrative (metanarrative), a single principle or story which attempts to explain all of human history. Postmodernists are skeptical and suspicious. They attempt to deconstruct everything in life.

3. There is no belief in objective truth. Any truth is determined solely by one's own culture. According to Nietzsche, "There are no facts, only interpretations..."[3]

4. There are no moral absolutes, only moral relativity. Each person decides his/her own standards by which to live.

5. Absolute tolerance is a primary virtue.

6. Subjective feelings direct one's life. Postmodernism looks for therapeutic (quick fixes) to the problems of life.

7. Postmodernism seeks the soul and spirit. It prefers the experiential to the rational. It values direct participation in all aspects of life, as opposed to representation. Images are more important than words, and community is valued over a person.

8. Postmodernism, in its purest form, leads to a life without hope. It reflects a pessimistic view that everything is meaningless (nihilism).

B. How does Postmodernism answer the Five Life Questions?

1. From where did I come?

The universe created itself. The universe (and everything in it) is the result of random, impersonal, undirected forces of nature. We did not come from a transcendent Creator God. Humanity is the result of purposeless evolutionary development over millions of years. In the beginning was the Big Bang.

2. Why is there such a mess in the world?

People who advocate universal truths are the source of all the problems in the world. Their belief in absolutes results in power struggles, such as the Inquisition or the Crusades, in which one individual or group attempts to assert power over another.

3. Is there any hope?

There is nothing we can put our trust in, since absolute truth is non-existent.

4. What is my purpose in life?

We must each continually question everything in our world, applying the postmodern practice of deconstruction. We must also be tolerant of everything.

5. What happens when I die?

The human body experiences physical death and nothing more beyond this life.

Framing a Postmodern

"I know that you don't believe in me at this point in your life, but I want you to hear the story of how much I love you. I have loved you since the beginning of time. On your good days and messy days, I love you. I created you in my image with love and purpose.[1] Your life is not a mistake. I have created no one else like you. Even the iris of your eye, thumbprint, and DNA are unique from all others I have created. You were designed with the purpose of knowing, trusting and loving me. I created you to enjoy an incredible life with me and with others. You don't have to rely on the culture around you to define who you are. There is an unshakable hope and absolute truth to be found in me alone. No one in this world can offer peace, unconditional love, and belonging that you've always desired. I love you so much that I died and rose again for the forgiveness of all your sins: past, present, and future.[2] When you believe that I am your God, your Savior, you will become my child,[3] and my Spirit will live in you forever.[4] When you die, you will spend eternity with me in heaven.[5] Never will I condemn or shame you.[6] I want you to know that you I have plans for you that will give you hope and a purpose for living. I know that the thought of living in a broken world can be depressing. I have come that you might have life and have it to all fullness.[7] When you trust me, I will give you the love, joy, and peace that will change the way you live and the way you think.[8] I have designed you to be a light in a broken world so that when others see you, they will see me. Through me, you will be able to give hope to others. Through you, others will put their trust in me. By being my child, your life will not be easy but take heart, know that those struggles are designed to draw you and others closer to me.[9] I want you to know that I will never leave you.[10] I love you now and forever."

---

1 Genesis 1:27
2 John 3:16
3 1 John 3:2
4 Ephesians 1:13
5 Romans 8:1
6 John 3:13
7 John 10:10
8 Galatians 5:22-23
9 John 16:33
10 Hebrews 13:5

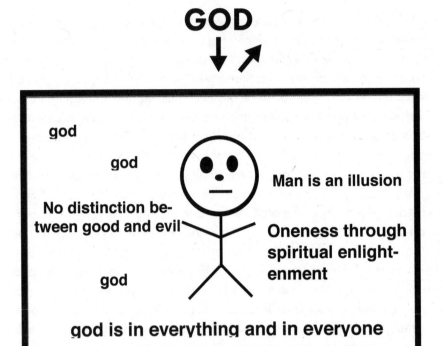

Pantheism

Pantheism asserts that God is part of creation, not separate from it. Everything is god. For the pantheist, man is one with ultimate reality, continually seeking spiritual enlightenment.

A. Key Characteristics of Pantheism

1. God is in everything and everyone.

2. The universe (and everything in it) is divine; therefore, everything is interconnected.

3. Only the spiritual dimension exists, but it is unknowable.

4. Man is one with ultimate reality.

5. Truth comes through a "oneness with the universe."

6. Man must seek this oneness through spiritual enlightenment, not rational thought.

7. There is no distinction between good and evil, only "enlightened" and "unenlightened."

B. How does Pantheism answer the Five Life Questions?

1. From where did I come?

The universe created itself. The universe (and everything in it) is the result of random, impersonal, undirected forces of nature. We did not come from a transcendent Creator God. Humanity is the result of purposeless evolutionary development over millions of years. In the beginning was the Big Bang.

2. Why is there such a mess in the world?

Science has been abused to harm nature and human beings.

3. Is there any hope?

The only hope of saving the earth is with better, more ethical science. The future is ours to make, or unmake.

4. What is my purpose in life?

Man's only purpose is to "connect more deeply and harmoniously with the universe, nature, and other humans, and to help others to do so." Through meditation we can learn to perceive our unity with the universe, understand it, and act upon it.

5. What happens when I die?

The body will die and go through many rebirths, or reincarnations, until it eventually becomes one with the universe. This oneness is called nirvana. Once it is reached, there is no more need to be reborn.

 **Framing a Pantheist.**

"I know that you don't believe in me but, I want to make sure you hear a few things about me that perhaps you haven't heard before. I love you.[1] There has not been a moment in time that I have not loved you. On your best and your worse day, I love you. I created you in my image with the purpose of you knowing, trusting and loving me.[2] You are not a mistake. You were not formed from being reincarnated but rather by my own hands. You are unique; I have created no one else like you. Even the iris of your eye, thumbprint, and DNA are different from all others I have created. You were designed with the purpose of personally knowing me.[3] I am God and I am the only one who can give you all that you have ever needed. The wisdom, love, peace, and joy that you are looking for can only be found in me.[4] The hope of becoming a god will not fill the void that is within you. I know your heart. It is broken just like the hearts of all humans who live on this earth. I am your only hope both now and for eternity. Only by believing that I died and rose again to pay the penalty of your sin, will you become free to be the person I created you to be.[5] There is nothing you can do to earn it; it is a gift from me to you.[6] When you place your trust me, I will become your Savior, you will become my child, and my Spirit will live in you forever.[7] I will be your hope both now and for eternity and when you die, you will not have to suffer another reincarnation but rather spend eternity with me in heaven.[8] Until then, I want you to be a light to a broken world so that when others see you, they will see me. In this life, you will have troubles, but know that those struggles are designed to draw you and others closer to me. I promise that I will never leave you or forsake you.[9] When you trust in me completely, know that you will be free to no longer trust in only yourself but can trust in me to be with you to love and protect you always. "

10

---

1 Psalm 86:5
2 Genesis 1:27
3 John 10:10
4 Galatians 5:22-23
5 Hosea 11:9
6 John 3:16
7 Ephesians 2:8-9
8 Galatians 3:14
9 Hebrews 13:5

GOD

Spiritism

The spiritist rejects the God of the Bible. Instead, his focus is on all who dwell in the spirit world as the reason for everything that happens in life. The goal is to please the spirits. Wicca is a big part of this movement.

A. Key Characteristics of Spiritism

1. The focus is on the spirit world, a world of good and bad spirits and an intelligent force, known as god.

2. All of life is interpreted through a spiritual lens because the spirits control everything that happens in the world.

3. The idea of "cause and effect" influences much of the spiritist philosophy.

4. Truth is found through the shaman, a medium who serves as the liaison between humans and the spirit world.

5. Contact with the spirit world brings one into communion with various spirits and god, the transcendent "creative intelligence" of the universe.

6. Moral values are determined by things which either honor or irritate the spirits.

7. Good works in life help ensure a person greater spiritual evolution through reincarnation.

8. Jesus Christ's good works make him a positive model to follow, but he is not viewed as God.

B. How does Spiritism answer the Five Life Questions?

1. From where did I come?

God, as "the Supreme Intelligence," is the primary cause of everything. He is not described as a being, "who," but as a thing. "It" created the universe and everything in it, including the spirits. The spirits have incarnated into the material world as human beings.

2. Why is there such a mess in the world?

The problems and "ugliness" in the world are the result of less advanced, imperfect spirits trying to incite the human beings in which they dwell, toward evil.

3. Is there any hope?

"Without charity, there is no salvation." One's salvation ultimately comes through an evolution from spiritual infancy to a state of spiritual perfection through reincarnation. The goal through charitable behavior is the moral and spiritual transformation of mankind.

4. What is my purpose in life?

Our purpose is to continually strive to do good in order to improve our position on our spiritual journey. Through reincarnation, one will progress more quickly toward spiritual perfection and ultimate happiness.

5. What happens when I die?

The spirit is continually reincarnated, and death merely means a change of wavelength for the deceased. A medium is said to be able to receive messages from these new frequencies which others cannot sense.

Framing a Spiritist

"I know that you don't know me, but I want to make sure you understand a few things about me that perhaps you haven't heard before. I love you. There has not been a moment in time that I have not loved you.[1] On your best and your worse day, I love you. I created you in my image for the purpose of you knowing, trusting and loving me.[2] You did not reincarnate as a spirit and become a human. You are unique; I have created no one else like you. Even the iris of your eye, thumbprint, and DNA are different from all others I have created. You were designed with the purpose of personally knowing me and living a full life here on earth.[3] The love, peace, and joy that you are looking for can only be found in me.[4] The things of this world will not fill the void that is within you. I alone am God, not man.[5] I know your heart. It is broken just like the hearts of all humans who live on this earth. I know that you think that your only hope is that of reincarnation and charitable behavior. I do not seek after your performance for your salvation. I alone am your only hope both now and for eternity. All I require is that you believe with your heart that I died and rose again to pay the penalty of your sin, then, and only then, will you be free to be the person I created you to be.[6] There is nothing you can do to earn it; it is a gift from me to you.[7] When you place your trust me, I will become your Savior, you will become my child and my Holy Spirit, not just another spirit, will live in you forever. I will be your hope both now and for eternity and when you die, you will spend eternity with me in heaven. Until that time comes,[8] I want you to get to know me through the Bible and other Christians who can answer your questions. In this life, you will have troubles, but know that I have overcome your troubles. I promise that I will never leave you or forsake you.[9] You can trust me completely to love and protect you always."

---

1 Psalm 86:5

2 Genesis 1:27

3 John 10:10

4 Galatians 5:22-23

5 Hosea 11:9

6 John 3:16

7 Ephesians 2:8-10

8 Galatians 3:14

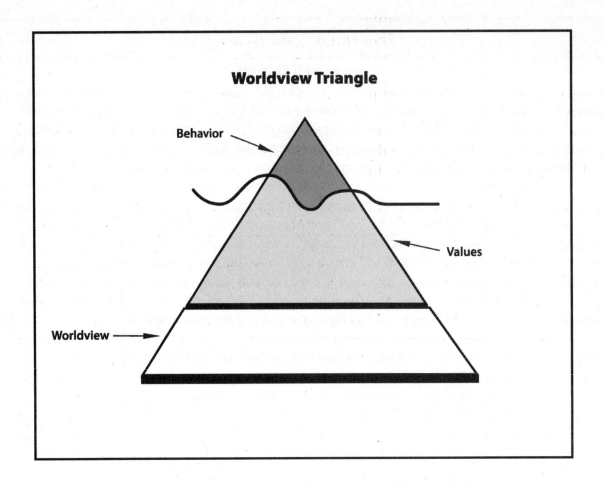

**Our behavior is shaped
by our values, which are ultimately
built upon the foundation of our worldview.**

Lesson 2: What Are the Five Major Worldviews? - Anchorsaway Worldview Handbook ©

It sometimes seems as if there are more philosophical and religious views than any normal person could ever know. Indeed, there are more than six thousand distinct religions in the world today. However, some people are surprised to find that the world's religions and philosophies tend to break down into a few major categories. These five worldviews include all the dominant outlooks in the world today. This chart is adapted from Christianity: The Faith That Makes Sense by Dennis McCallum.[4]

	REALITY	MAN	TRUTH	VALUES
Theism Christianity Neo-Christianity Judaism Islam (heresy)	An infinite, personal God exists. He created a finite, material world. Reality is both material and spiritual. The universe had a beginning and will have an end.	Humankind is the unique creation of God. People were created "in the image of God," which means that we are personal, eternal, spiritual, and biological.	Truth about God is known through revelation and the Bible. Truth about the material world is gained via revelation and the five senses in conjunction with rational thought.	Moral values are the objective expression of an absolute moral being.
Naturalism Atheism Agnosticism Existentialism	The material universe is all that exists. Reality is "one-dimensional." There is no such thing as a soul or a spirit. Everything can be explained on the basis of natural law.	Man is the chance product of a biological process of evolution. Man is entirely material. The human species will one day pass out of existence.	Truth is usually understood as scientific proof. Only that which can be observed with the five senses is accepted as real or true.	No objective values or morals exist. Morals are individual preferences or socially useful behaviors. Even social morals are subject to evolution and change.
Postmodernism	Reality must be interpreted through our language and cultural "paradigm." Therefore, reality is "socially constructed."	Humans are nodes in a cultural reality – they are a product of their social setting. The idea that people are autonomous and free is a myth.	Truths are mental constructs meaningful to people within their own cultural paradigm. They do not apply to other paradigms. Truth is relative to one's culture.	Values are part of our social paradigms, as well. Tolerances, freedom of expression, inclusion, and refusal to claim to have the answers are the only universal values.

	REALITY	MAN	TRUTH	VALUES
Pantheism Hinduism Taoism Buddhism Much New Age Consciousness	Only the spiritual dimension exists. All else is illusion, Maya. Spiritual reality, Brahman, is eternal, impersonal, and unknowable. It is possible to say that everything is a part of god, or that god is in everything and everyone.	Man is one with ultimate reality. Thus man is spiritual, eternal, and impersonal. Man's belief that he is an individual is illusion.	Truth is an experience of unity with "the oneness" of the universe. Truth is beyond all rational description. Rational thought as it is understood in the West cannot show us reality.	Because ultimate reality is impersonal, many pantheistic thinkers believe that there is no real distinction between good and evil. Instead, "unenlightened" behavior is that which fails to understand essential unity.
Spiritism and Polytheism Thousands of Religions (including Wicca and Witchcraft)	The world is populated by spirit beings who govern what goes on. Gods and demons are the real reason behind "natural" events. Material things are real, but they have spirits associated with them and, therefore, can be interpreted spiritually.	Man is a creation of the gods like the rest of the creatures on earth. Often, tribes or races have a special relationship with some gods who protect them and can punish them.	Truth about the natural world is discovered through the shaman figure who has visions telling him what the gods and demons are doing and how they feel.	Moral values take the form of taboos, which are things that irritate or anger various spirits. These taboos are different from the idea of "good and evil" because it is just as important to avoid irritating evil spirits as it is good ones.

Dennis McCallum. *Christianity: The Faith That Makes Sense.* rev. ed. Wheaton, IL: Tyndale House Publishers, 1997. 36-37.

Lesson 2: What Are the Five Major Worldviews?

Small Group Objective:

This week's discussion is designed to help students identify their own worldview. If they are not committed to the Christian worldview, this is a great opportunity for them to wrestle with truths, while exploring their own worldview.

Your goal is to help students develop a foundational understanding of the four major worldviews that are competing with Christianity in today's culture. It is especially important that they confidently know how each worldview answers the "Five Life Questions."

✓ **Check Points:**

☐ Bring 3 x 5 cards for your students to write down any questions they may have which aren't answered during the discussion.

☐ Enlist a student to share a brief personal testimony.

Discussion Questions:

1. Review prayer requests from the week before and ask how the students are doing.

2. Lead a time of discussion, asking the following questions:

(*Note*: Work through as many of the following questions as possible. The goal is not to get through all of them, but to encourage each student to participate in the discussion as part of the learning process.)

   a. What day of the devotional did you find most meaningful?

   b. How did last week's lesson impact your life? Did you share it with someone?

   c. Can worldviews change? Is that good or bad news?

   d. Frame someone who is role playing a Humanist, Postmodern, Pantheist, Spiritist.

   e. Have any of you ever been in a situation where people were expressing views that were not necessarily Christian? What were some of the things they were suggesting?

   f. How might we be able to engage someone who rejects the Bible and suggests that the universe, and everything in it, did not come from God?

   g. Are there any problems with the idea of moral relativism? If so, what are they?

    h.   Is reincarnation incompatible with Christianity? How might we constructively respond to someone who believes in reincarnation? (Hebrews 9:27 and Matthew 25:46).

    i.   What questions, if any, come to mind as a result of this week's lesson?

    j.   What is one way you can go out and apply what you have learned at Anchorsaway this week?

3. Ask for prayer requests and tell students that you will be faithful to pray for them during the week. Encourage students to record the prayer requests in the prayer request section of their handbooks, so they can pray for one another during the week. Begin the prayer time by sharing your own request. Spend the remaining   time in prayer.

★ After the Session

1. Contact each small group member during the week. Ask them about their devotional time, a question they have raised, or how their week is going.

Prayer Requests

Lesson 2: What Are the Five Major Worldviews? - Anchorsaway Worldview Handbook ©

Student Devotionals written by T.M. Moore

What Are The Five Major Worldviews?

Remember to let the prayers provided be a kind of "jump start" for your own prayers. In the meditation section, prayerfully consider how you might answer the questions posed. Then, as you journal, bring your meditation to focus in a concise and practical sentence that you can carry with you throughout the day.

Day 1: From Where Did We Come?

Pray: *"O Lord, you are God! You made us, and we are yours. We are your people, and the sheep of your pasture"* (Psalm 100:3, adapted).

Read: Genesis 1:26-28

Meditate: God said, "Let us make man..." With whom is God conversing here? What do you suppose each of the three persons of the Godhead – Father, Son, and Spirit – contributed to the creation of man and woman?

What is an "image?" What does "likeness" mean? Of what does God's image and likeness consist in me?

For what purposes did God create me? How should I pursue fulfilling those purposes? What does it mean to be "blessed" by God?

Journal: Today, if God's image and likeness were to be seen in me, it would look like...

Pray: *"Thank you, Lord, for making me a little lower than the heavenly beings, and for crowning me with glory and honor"* (Psalm 8:5, adapted).

Day 2: What Went Wrong?

Pray: *"You are not a God who delights in wickedness; evil may not dwell with you"* (Psalm 6:4).

Read: Romans 5:12-17

Meditate: Adam and Eve must have "died" when they first sinned against God? What did that
                     "death" look like? Do I experience any of that in my life?

                     What evidence do I see that, as Paul says, death has spread to all people? In the
                     world? Among my friends at school?

                     What has God done to rescue people out of the death-trap of sin? As one who has
                     been freed from that trap by God's grace, what is my responsibility to those who are yet
                     ensnared by it?

Journal: If I saw someone about to be hit by a car, I'd at least cry out, and maybe even run to
                     help. So, today, as I think about all the people I know who are ensnared by sin and
                     death...

Pray: *"Restore to me the joy of your salvation, and uphold me with a willing spirit. Then I will teach
                     transgressors your ways, and sinners will return to you"* (Psalm 51:12, 13).

Day 3: The Foundation of Hope

Pray: *"Preserve me, O God, for in you I take refuge. I say to the LORD, 'You are my Lord; I have no
                     good apart from you'"* (Psalm 16:1, 2).

Read: Ephesians 2:11-16

Meditate: Who are you without hope? What is that like? Do I know any people who seem to
                     have no hope in life?

                     How does Jesus' bringing me near to God give me hope? For what do I hope? What
                     does it mean that I have been "reconciled" to God?

                     I have hope because I am part of a community of people who have hope in Jesus. Am
                     I a "hope-giver?" Do others find their hope in God strengthened when they're around
                     me? How can I be more of a "hope-giver?"

Journal: Peter says that people should be able to see the hope that I have (1 Peter 3:15). That's what I want. Today, as I go among my friends, I'm trusting God to let them see in me...

Pray: *"You make known to me the path of life; in your presence there is fullness of joy; at your right hand are pleasures forevermore"* (Psalm 16:11).

Day 4: This One Thing

Pray: *"Whom have I in heaven but you? And there is nothing on earth that I desire besides you"* (Psalm 73:25).

Read: Philippians 3:12-16

Meditate: What is the "upward call of God in Christ Jesus?" Am I "pressing on" to realize that as my highest priority in life?

What kinds of things keep me from pressing on toward this? Are they really more valuable, more precious, more filled with meaning and joy than Jesus?

What is my responsibility to my friends, who are also "pressing on" toward Jesus?

Journal: Today, as I seek to "press on" toward knowing Jesus, I expect to encounter many obstacles and distractions. Therefore...

Pray: *"With my voice I cry out to the LORD; with my voice I plead for mercy to the LORD...When my spirit faints within me, you know my way!"* (Psalm 142:1, 3).

Day 5: Better Than Life Itself!

Pray: *"Surely goodness and mercy shall follow me all the days of my life, and I shall dwell in the house of the LORD forever"* (Psalm 23:6).

Read: Philippians 1:21-26

Meditate: In what sense could dying possibly be better than living? When believers depart this life, where do they go?

Why is it better for me, like Paul, to be alive at this time? Just for my own sake? How does God want to use me in the life of others?

Do my friends "have ample cause to glory in Christ Jesus" because of my being their friend? Is there anything I can do to make that more the case?

Journal: If this life is merely preparation for a better world to come, and, if in this life I'm mainly here for what I can mean to others, then, today...

Pray: *"Let not those who hope in you be put to shame through me, O Lord GOD of hosts"* (Psalm 69:6).

ENDNOTES

[1] Adapted from Charles Colson and Nancy Pearcy, How Now Shall We Live? (Wheaton, IL: Tyndale House Publishers, 1999) xi, xiii.

[2] <www.thinkexist.com>.

[3] Stan Wallace, "The Real Issue: Discerning and Defining the Essentials of Postmodernism," Leadership U, 24 March 2005.

[4] Dennis McCallum, Christianity: The Faith That Makes Sense (Wheaton, IL: Tyndale House Publishers, 1997) 36-37.

Recommended Reading

Key Books:

Beckwith, Francis, and Gregory Koukl. Relativism: Feet Firmly Planted in Mid-air. Grand Rapids, MI: Baker, 1998.

Colson, Charles and Nancy Pearcy. How Now Shall We Live? Wheaton, IL: Tyndale House Publishers, 1999.

Flynn, Brian. Running Against the Wind. Silverton, OR: Lighthouse Trails Publishing, 2005.

Geisler, Norman L., and Peter Bocchino. Unshakable Foundations. Minneapolis, MN: Bethany House, 2001.

Halverson, Dean. The Compact Guide to World Religions. Minneapolis, MN: Bethany House Publishers, 1996.

Jeremiah, David. Invasion of Other Gods: Protecting Your Family from the Seduction of the New Spirituality. London: Word Publishing, 1995.

Koukl, Gregory. Tactics: A Game Plan for Discussing Your Christian Convictions. Grand Rapids, MI: Zondervan, 2009.

McCallum, Dennis. Christianity: The Faith That Makes Sense. Wheaton, IL: Tyndale House Publishers, 1997.

McDowell, Josh, and Bob Hostetler. Beyond Belief to Conviction. Wheaton, IL: Tyndale House Publishers, 2002.

McFarland, Alex. The 10 Most Common Objections to Christianity. Ventura, CA: Regal, 2007.

McFarland, Alex. Worldviews Comparison: Compare 8 Popular Worldviews. Torrance, CA: Rose, 2008

Nash, Ronald H. Worldviews In Conflict. Grand Rapids, MI: Zondervan, 1992.

Ridenour, Fritz. So What's the Difference? Ventura, CA: Regal Books, 2001.

Sire, James W. The Universe Next Door: A Basic Worldview Catalog. Downers Grove, IL: InterVarsity Press, 1997.

"Spiritism." Columbia Encyclopedia, 6th ed. 2005. Encyclopedia.com. 24 March 2005 <www. encyclopedia.com/html/s1/spiritis.asp>.

Veith, Gene Edward. Postmodern Times: A Christian Guide to Contemporary Thought and Culture. Wheaton, IL: Crossway Books, 1994.

Lesson 3: Who Is God?

⚓ **Anchor of the Week: God is Who He says He is.**

I. Engaging the Skeptic

What is the difference between an agnostic and an atheist? (An agnostic will acknowledge the possibility of a God; an atheist denies that there is even the possibility of a God.)

C.S. Lewis's "Dot-in-the-circle" diagram.[1]

The circle represents all experience and all knowledge from all times here on earth. Ask an atheist and mark on the circle how much knowledge they have as compared to all knowledge, wisdom, and truth for all time. This is usually noted by a small dot in the circle.

Then ask, "Might there be some truth that is beyond your own personal experience?" The idea here is to have the atheist see that there are occurrences, perhaps even truths, that exist beyond his/her own personal experience. This opens the door to plant a seed of doubt in his/her mind that might cause the person to question his/her godless faith. Hopefully, as a result of this open dialogue, more discussions about the possibility of the existence of a personal God that loves them and has a plan of purpose for their life can take place.

II. The Attributes of God: Who Does God Say That He Is?

"Diversity in our culture has come to mean we all have diverse beliefs, therefore we are all equal." – Josh McDowell

A. Are all religions similar? Do they all worship the same God?

B. Misconceptions of God: "'Who Do People Say I Am?'" – Jesus (Mark 8:27)

For Us to Know the real God, He must define Himself - not man.

C. The Attributes of God: Who does God say He is?[2]

1. **The one true God** – The God of the Bible is the only true God. He is set apart from all other gods. Because of this, He is also a jealous God. He wants to protect His honor, and He wants His created children to have abundant life and not be deceived by false gods who bring chaos, restlessness and unbelief into the world.

   a. Scriptural support: Isaiah 45:5-6, Deuteronomy 4:39, Exodus 34:14

   b. Significance for us: God Almighty is the only true God. There is no other god that can compare to Him, because all other gods find their origin in man. For this reason, He expects us to worship and serve Him, by giving our allegiance to Him alone.

2. **Independent (self-existent; self-sufficient)** – Although God desires to have a relationship with mankind; He does not need us or anything else in creation in order to exist. He comes "from Himself" and is in need of nothing. He is infinite. That is, He was never created and never came into being. He has always been and always will be.

   a. Scriptural support: Exodus 3:14, Psalm 90:2, Acts 17:24-25

   b. Significance for us: If God were in need of anything, He would cease to be God. No one has ever contributed anything to God that did not already come from Him in the first place. He is the supreme Creator from whom all else has come.

3. **Immutable (unchangeable)** – God does not change. He is who He is.

   a. Scriptural support: Malachi 3:6, Hebrews 13:8, James 1:17

   b. Significance for us: God is unchanging in His being, His character, and His purposes. Therefore, we can rest assured that God will always remain the same. We can put our trust in that fact, knowing that all the promises He has made will be fulfilled, and all scriptural prophecies will come true.

4. **Omnipresent** – God is "all-present," which means He is not limited with respect to space. He does not have size or spatial dimensions. God exists everywhere at all times, and cannot be contained by any space.

   a. Scriptural support: Jeremiah 23:23-24, Psalm 139:7-10

   b. Significance for us: Contrary to the pantheist's belief that God is everything, Scripture is clear that God, the Creator, is separate from His creation while being always present at all times (Ecclesiastes 12:14; Hebrews 4:13).

5. **Omniscient** – God is "all-knowing." He knows everything that has happened, is happening, and ever will happen. That is, He knows everything that is actual and everything that is possible. There is no such thing as a random molecule to God!

   a. Scriptural support: Psalm 139:2-4, Hebrews 4:13, 1 John 3:20

b. Significance for us: There is nothing that escapes the knowledge of God. He is not limited in His understanding of anything that happens in the time line of humanity. Thus, God's omniscience gives foundational credibility to the prophecies in Scripture. This is why we can say with confidence that Satan will be defeated in the end. Also, this attribute helps us understand God's love for us.

6. **Omnipotent** – God is "all-powerful," which means He is not limited by anything. There is nothing more powerful than God; He possesses all power. Because of this, He is able to exercise sovereignty over His creation, and He has the freedom to act in accordance with His will.

   a. Scriptural support: Psalm 33:9, Jeremiah 32:17, Matthew 19:26

   b. Significance for us: As we come to understand this aspect of God's character, we can rest in the fact that nothing is too much for God; there is nothing He cannot handle. "'...but with God all things are possible'" (Matthew 19:26). If God is on our side, we will always be on the winning side (Romans 8:31). The key is that we rest in His power and strength and resist the temptation to try to live life in our own strength (Philippians 4:13).

7. **Personal** – God interacts with us personally, and we can respond to Him as persons. He is not merely a supreme Force, as the spiritist would claim. Nor is He a being who has removed Himself from our world, as the deists would say.
   a. Scriptural support: Genesis 5:24, Deuteronomy 4:7, James 2:23

   b. Significance for us: Although God is the Creator of the universe, He is not distant from us. In fact, He has promised us that He will never leave us, nor forsake us (Deuteronomy 31:6; Hebrews 13:5). He watches over us like a parent over a child, which is why we can refer to God as Abba Father. God created us, because He is a personal God who desperately wants to be in a relationship with us. He cares about the smallest details of our lives and wants to be intimately involved with us. He wants complete access to our hearts.

To A Beautiful Person

If God had a refrigerator, your picture would be on it. If He had a wallet, your photo would be in it. He sends you flowers every spring. He sends you a sunrise every morning. Whenever you want to talk, He listens. He can live anywhere in the universe, but He chose your heart. Face it friend, He is crazy about you! – Author Unknown

---

8. **All Wise** – God always knows what is best and chooses to fulfill His purposes in the best way (according to what He knows is best). He is able to accomplish His perfect ends by His perfect means.

   a. Scriptural support: Psalm 18:30, 1 Corinthians 1:20, 25, Isaiah 40:13

b. Significance for us: Because God knows exactly what is needed in any given situation, we can rest secure in the knowledge that He is working everything out for good (Romans 8:28). Sometimes, it is easy for us to get angry with God about life's circumstances, but we must remember that our knowledge is limited. Though we might not always understand why certain things (like suffering and evil) happen in our lives and our world, we can rest secure in the fact that God knows everything and has the wisdom to oversee it all. We need not worry or be afraid about what may come our way. We must persevere in trusting Him about unseen circumstances, remembering that His ways are not always our ways (Isaiah 55:8-9).

9. **Truthful** – Everything about God is true. His knowledge and words are true and in Him is the final, unwavering standard of truth.

   a. Scriptural support: Psalm 31:5, John 14:6, John 17:17, Titus 1:2

   b. Significance for us: We live in an age of absolute tolerance and moral relativism in which people are asking Pontius Pilate's age-old question, *"What is truth?"* (John 18:38) A belief in truth is essential if we are to coexist peacefully in our world. Our unwavering standard of truth is rooted in the character of God. Because He is the God of Truth, who cannot lie, we can always trust Him to do what He promises.

> God didn't promise days without pain, laughter without sorrow, sun without rain, but He did promise strength for the day, comfort for the tears, and light for the way. – Author Unknown

10. **Good** – God is generous, kind, benevolent, and full of goodwill toward mankind. All that God is and does is worthy of our approval, because He is the standard of what is considered good.

    a. Scriptural support: Psalm 25:8, Nahum 1:7, Romans 8:28

    b. Significance for us: God's goodness is manifest in all of His attributes. His goodness is seen in His faithfulness, love, justice, mercy, and the like. Without this quality of goodness, those other attributes of His character disappear. How could a God who is not good be a God of justice, mercy, or love? He cannot. God is indeed a good God who wants to bless us. In fact, He promises to bless those who live faithfully for Him. He has called us to follow His example and demonstrate goodness to those around us (Galatians 6:10; Luke 6:27, 33-35).

11. **Loving** – God gives of Himself for the welfare of others (humanity), for our benefit. He finds pleasure in us, His creation, and He wants what is best for us.

    a. Scriptural support: 1 John 4:8, John 3:16, Romans 5:8

    b. Significance for us: God's love is the cause behind all that is. More importantly, it is God's love that has given us the opportunity for salvation. He created us because He loves us and wants to be in a relationship with us. His willingness to send Jesus to die for our sins was His greatest loving act. It opened up the way for us to be in a restored relationship with Him. This supreme act of God's love toward us provides the motivation for our own love in the world. We love because He first loved us (1 John 4:19).

12. **Faithful** – God's faithfulness is connected to His truthfulness. God can always be depended on to do what He says, and He will fulfill His promises.

   a. Scriptural support: Numbers 23:19, Deuteronomy 7:9, 2 Timothy 2:13

   b. Significance for us: Because God is always faithful, He is a God in whom we can wholeheartedly put our trust. We know that if He has promised to do something, He will see it through. God is One on whom we can always depend, no matter what.

13. **Righteous (just)** – God always does what is right, for He is the absolute standard of right and wrong. Anything that conforms to His character is right, while that which does not, is wrong. He loves all that conforms to His good character, but He directs His wrath against everything that opposes His standard of righteousness. God takes justice very seriously.

   a. Scriptural support: Deuteronomy 32:4, Isaiah 5:15-16, 1 John 1:9

   b. Significance for us: God is a God of justice, and we can depend on Him to judge rightly in every situation. This is a source of comfort when we think about all of the perceived injustices in the world, remembering that in the end, God's justice will reign supreme. However, this should also be a sobering reminder that we, too, will ultimately be judged by Him to whom we must all give account (Romans 14:12; Hebrews 4:13).

14. **Holy** – God possesses an infinite, incomprehensible degree of purity. He can have nothing to do with sin. This is why His justice and wrath are necessary at times.

   a. Scriptural support: Leviticus 19:1-2, Isaiah 6:3, 1 John 1:5

   b. Significance for us: God's holiness is what separates Him from sinful humanity. This quality has, by definition, created the chasm that prevents our being able to have a personal relationship with Him. That is why it was necessary that Jesus die for our sins, to make us blameless again before a holy God. We then must strive to live holy lives, lives that are distinct and set apart from this dark world. Our holiness should emanate from His holiness (1 Peter 1:15-16).

15. **Merciful (graceful, patient)** – God's compassion and goodness toward us are demonstrated by His withholding the condemnation we deserve.

   a. Scriptural support: Exodus 34:6, Ephesians 2:8, James 5:11

   b. Significance for us: God is a God of justice, but He is also a God of mercy. It is for this reason that we have been given the opportunity for salvation. Without His mercy in sending Christ to die for us, we would be lost in our sin forever. God wants to meet us in our misery and distress. He wants to pour out His mercy upon us. We need only be willing to accept it.

16. **Peaceful (orderly)** – God is separate from all confusion and disorder. His Being and character are active in well-ordered and controlled ways.

a. Scriptural support: 1 Corinthians 14:33, 2 Thessalonians 3:16, Isaiah 55:12

b. Significance for us: Our world is filled with much disorder and chaos – wars rage and governments rise and fall. Even in our own lives, there is often confusion and difficulty. But God is a God of peace and order. He promises to give us His peace as we face all that life brings. This particular attribute is important in light of our society's increasing interest in Islam. The God of the Bible is a peace-seeking God, while Allah encourages His followers to engage in 'jihad,' holy war, against all other infidels. (See the Qurán: Sura 9:5, 111.)

17. **Perfect** – God is without flaw or defect. He possesses all excellent qualities and lacks nothing. In fact, He is complete and absolute in His own character.

a. Scriptural support: Deuteronomy 32:4, Psalm 18:30, Matthew 5:48

b. Significance for us: God alone is the one who knows Himself perfectly. Because He is God, He can be nothing less than perfect. What a sense of peace and trust this should give us! For we know that God will always act in a way that is perfect. He is not like the other flawed, limited gods who have been conjured up in the minds of man. On the contrary, in all of the attributes of His character, He is perfect.

D. God and the Christian Faith:

1. Religions reach for a god through a variety of ways, whereas Christianity is about God first reaching down to man.

2. Faith in God does not come from a feeling...feelings can get us into trouble if we rely solely on them. – Reference Hebrews 11:1 in the NASB: *"Now faith is the assurance of things hoped for, the conviction of things not seen."* Because of the evidence, we are able to convict Christ of being Christ or the Bible of being true. Our faith is not a blind hope.

3. Faith in God comes from knowing who God says He is, not simply from man's opinion.

4. We know what God says about Himself from reading the Bible

---

One thing God is not: He is not a better you.

Remember: Because God is God, He does not need us. He wants us. He wants to have a relationship with us and wants to let us share in His perfect plan for us as we live out our lives in this world. Are you ready to completely trust your God? He is waiting for you to take that step.

God is a relational God

1. God has chosen to spend time and attention on you. He is patient and available (2 Peter 3:9).

2. God is kind and gracious on your behalf. He has chosen to bring help and intervention into your life (Psalm 103:8).

3. God will work all things for your good, even the hard things. He desires to give you His support and encouragement. You can trust Him (Romans 8:28).

4. God is constantly building you up and affirming you. He values you as His child, because He created you, and because you are in Christ (John 1:10-13).

5. God has included you in His family. You belong to Him (Ephesians 1:4-5).

6. God desires intimate fellowship with you. You are valuable and priceless in His eyes (Revelation 3:20).

7. God loves you just the way you are. You do not have to try to earn His love. (Ephesians 2:8-9).

8. God accepts you, regardless of your performance. He knows you more than you know yourself (Psalm 103:8-10).

9. God forgives you for your sins and failures and does not hold them against you. You can be trusted to do right, to come to Him when you have done wrong, knowing He has chosen to forgive you (1 John 1:9).

10. God will treat you fairly, and when He disciplines you, it will be done in love and for your own good (Hebrews 12:3-8).

11. God is reliable and is with you always. He will stick by you and support you (Lamentations 3:22, 23; Hebrews 13:5-6).

Comparison of World Religions[3]

This chart is adapted from Kenneth Boa: Cults, World Religions and the Occult

Christian Doctrine	Hinduism	Buddhism	Islam	Judaism
Jesus Christ John 1:1-3, 14; 8:58; Col. 1:16-20	Without recognition of any kind given to Christ.	Without ecognition of any kind given to Christ.	Jesus Christ is nothing more than a prophet of god.	Rabbinic teaching holds that there must be two Messiahs: Son of Joseph, who would die, and Son of David, who would establish the kingdom on earth.
Tri-Unity Luke 3:21-22; 1 Peter 1:2; Matt. 28:19; John 15:26	God is an "it" in Philosophical Hinduism, and in Popular Hinduism there are great multitudes of gods. In a sense: man is god.	Without recognition of the Tri-Unity. Most Buddhist sects are polytheistic, pantheistic or atheistic.	There is only one god and that is Allah.	There is only one God and that is Yahweh.
Everyone has an eternal spirit. Matt. 25:46; Dan. 12:2; Eccl. 2:7; Rev. 20:11-15	Yes, and it continues through many incarnations.	Guatama, founder of Buddhism, claimed that men have no souls.	Yes	Yes
Born a Lost Soul Ps. 51:5; James 1:15; Romans 5:12-21; 1 Cor. 15:21-22	Without recognition of sin and moral guilt. Sin is an illusion.	Guatama claimed that men do not have souls.	No	Judaism rejects the doctrine of original sin, saying that sin is an act, not a state.
Salvation John 3:14-17; Acts 16:31; Rom. 3: 21-30; 10:4, 9-10; Gal. 2:16	Hinduism is a works system. Forgiveness of sin does not fit into the picture of karma (cause and effect). Each person has many lives in which to reach salvation.	Theravada Buddhism: salvation by self-effort. Mahayana Buddhism: salvation of one dependent on the grace of others.	After the resurrection, each man's deeds will be weighed to determine his destiny - heaven or hell.	Man does not need redemption. Repentance (turning back to God) is all that is needed when one fails to live according to the law.
Sacred Books (Authority) The Holy Bible	Sruti-revealed script. Smriti-tradition. These groups of books contain many contradictions.	Buddhist scriptures and sayings attributed to Guatama were written about four centuries after his death, and there is no way to be certain they are really his words.	Koran - most important, Tauret, Pentateuch of Moses, Zabur (Psalms of David), Injil (Evangel of Jesus)	The Torah, The Old Testament, The Talmud
Suggested approaches for presenting the Christian faith.	Address the Hindu argument that all religions are the same. Emphasize the unique claims of Jesus. No other religion offers a real solution to the problem of sin. Books of the Bible are harmonious; Hindu scriptures contradict one another. Man is born as a lost human headed for hell because he inherited the sin of Adam.	Give a positive and clear exposition of the claims of Christ and His victory over sin and death. Christ offers salvation; Buddhism does not. Each person must work out his own salvation. Adjust and accommodate for the manner in which Buddhism has become embedded in the culture. Make a strong case for the Bible - archaeology, history and prophecy.	Christians must focus on the problem of sin, contrasting what God of the Bible has done about it, with what Allah has not done. Ask questions to determine views. Muslims have no personal relationship with God. Focus on the true deity of Jesus Christ, the lost nature of man, and the salvation offered by Jesus. Point out the error of works righteousness.	Original Christians were all Jews. Note that a Jew does not have to give up his Jewishness to become a Christian. Christianity is not a Gentile religion. NT was written by Jews (except Luke) and Jesus was a Jew. Emphasize Isaiah 53 as prophetic of Jesus' coming.

Many times people are confused by the difference between a cult and the occult. This chart will make some of those distinctions a little more clear. There are over 5,000 cults in the U.S. While the specifics for each cult differ, the underlying concepts are the same. If you will learn the biblical concepts in each of these areas, you will be able to defend the Scriptures against these attacks. You will then be able to provide answers to hurting people in need of the true Savior.

Christianity	Mormonism	Jehovah's Witnesses	Scientology[5]	Wicca[6]
God	Once a man as we are now. He is now an exalted man. Literally our heavenly father. He and his many wives have sex to produce spirit babies that eventually become the human race.	One person god, called Jehovah. There is no other name for god. Jesus is not God, he is the first thing that Jehovah created.	Does not define god or supreme being, but rejects the biblical God. Everyone is a "thetan," an immortal spirit with unlimited powers over its own universe, but all are not aware of this.	The supreme being is called the goddess, sometimes the goddess and god, or goddess and horned god. The goddess can be a symbol, the impersonal force in everything, or a personal being.
Jesus Christ John 1:1-3, 14; 8:58 Colossians 1:16-20	Jesus Christ, spirit brother of Lucifer, received a body of flesh and bone and is now elevated to deity. He is referred to as our "elder brother," one of many gods.	Jesus is a god, not God the Son. He is represented as the first creation of Jehovah. Before his incarnation he was Michael, captain of Jehovah's hosts.	Jesus is rarely mentioned. Jesus was not Creator, nor was he an "operating thetan" (in control of supernatural powers, cleared from mental defects). Jesus did not die for our sins.	Jesus is either rejected altogether or sometimes considered a spiritual teacher who taught love and compassion.
Tri-Unity Luke 3:21-22; I Peter 1:2 Matthew 28:19 John 15:26	Mormon theology is henotheistic. It exalts one god (the father-god) above the other gods in the universe. The Holy Spirit is a spiritual impersonal "force."	The doctrine of the Tri-Unity is denied emphatically. The deity of the Holy Spirit is denied—he is likened to a radar beam.	The doctrine of the Tri-Unity is denied. The Holy Spirit is not part of their belief.	The doctrine of the Trui-Unity is denied. The Holy Spirit is not part of their belief. Some Wiccans may refer to "Spirit" as a kind of divine energy.
Everyone has an eternal spirit Matthew 25:46 Daniel 12:2 Ecclesiastes 12:7 Revelation 20:11-15	Yes	They argue for painless extinction, indicating man does not possess an immortal soul, just a combination of breath and flesh. That is, unless you become part of the Organization or the 144,000.	There are no particular human incarnations of god as the universal life force (Theta) is inherent in all. All humans are immortal spiritual beings (thetans), capable of realizing a nearly godlike state.	Values are part of our social paradigms, as well. Tolerance, freedom of expression, inclusion, and refusal to claim to have the answers are the only universal values.

	Christianity	Mormonism	Jehovah's Witnesses	Scientology[7]	Wicca[8]
Born a Lost Soul Psalm 51:5 James 1:15 Romans 5:12-21 I Corinthians 15: 21-22		Mormons deny the doctrine of original sin and teach that the fall of man was a good and necessary thing. There is no imputed sin nature.	Adam's sin imputed to mankind, as federal head of the race. However, a sin nature apparently not inherited by the race.	No sin and no need to repent. Hell is a myth. People who get clear of "engrams" become operating "thetans."	Definitely not.
Suggested Approaches For Presenting The Christian Faith		1. Confront with the "pillars" of Mormonism: god, works, salvation. 2. Compare beliefs with Bible. 3. The archaeology of the New World refutes the Book of Mormon.	1. Present a clear biblical case of Christ's and Holy Spirit's deity. 2. Present the case of the Tri-Unity. 3. Challenge them to look at the whole of Scripture.	1. Ask why they think the world is in such a mess? 2. Ask how they know for sure that what they believe is true. 3. Present the gospel and the gift of eternal life.	1. Wicca is an occultic "nature religion." Explain the origins of this belief. 2. Ask them how they know that there is no God who loves. 3. Share with them the gospel of eternal life.
Other Beliefs		No alcohol, tobacco, coffee or tea. Baptism on behalf of the dead. Two year missionary commitment encouraged. Extensive social network.	Known as the Watchtower Bible and Tract Society. Meet in Kingdom Halls. Do not observe holidays or birthdays. Forbidden to vote, salute flag, work in military.	Highly controversial. Publication of Dianetics. Organizations related: Narconan, Criminon, Way to Happiness Foundation, WISE, Applied Scholastics.	Wiccans practice divination and spell-casting, with most rituals performed in a circle. Many Wiccans are part of a coven. Extremely occultic.

Lesson 3: Who is God? - Anchorsaway Worldview Handbook ©

Small Group Discussion Guide

Lesson 3: Who Is God?

Small Group Objective:

The goal is to help the students begin to better understand the character of God, and realize that what we think about God determines how we will live our lives.

✓ Check Points:

☐ Bring 3 x 5 cards for your students to write down any questions they may have which aren't answered during the discussion.

☐ Enlist a student to share a brief personal testimony.

Discussion Questions:

1. Review prayer requests from the week before and ask how the students are doing.

2. Lead a time of discussion, asking the following questions:

(Note: Work through as many of the following questions as possible. The goal is not to get through all of them, but to encourage each student to participate in the discussion as part of the learning process.)

   a. What day of the devotional did you find most meaningful?

   b. How did last week's lesson impact your life? Did you share it with someone?

   c. Do you know people who have formulated their own opinions of God? What are some of the things they believe about God? What are some potential problems with adopting your own view of who God is?

   d. How has this lesson changed your own ideas of God?

   e. Can you frame God? How does he frame you?

   f. How can knowing the true God change your life?

   g. How can a true understanding of God help you begin to find peace about some difficult things in your life?

   h. Why do we so often go to friends first, before consulting with God?

   i. How can you use what you learned to share with others about who God is?

      • God defines Himself. (Refer to the chapter on "Who Is God?").

      • God is not who I think He is. Rather, He is who He says He is.

- Our feelings about God can get in the way, and cloud our understanding of who He really is. It is important to be vigilant concerning this critical issue.

3. Ask for prayer requests and tell students that you will be faithful to pray for them during the week. Encourage students to record the prayer requests in the prayer request section of their handbooks, so they can pray for one another during the week. Begin the prayer time by sharing your own request. Spend the remaining time in prayer.

★ After the Session

1. Contact each small group member during the week. Ask them about their devotional time, a question they have raised, or how their week is going.

Prayer Requests

Student Devotionals written by T.M. Moore

Who is God?

We might sum-up the biblical teaching about God by saying that He is triune, holy, almighty, wise, and good. Let these concepts guide your reading, meditations, and journaling for the week to come.

Day 1: One God, Three Persons

Pray: *"Your righteousness, O God, reaches the high heavens. You who have done great things, O God, who is like you?"* (Psalm 71:19).

Read: Genesis 1:1-3

Meditate: The Hebrew word, "God," is, when referring to the God of Israel, haelohim – literally, the God. This word, while translated, "God," whenever it refers to our God, always has the definite article in front of it – ha, "the." Even more surprising, this word is a plural noun! Does God mean to suggest something about Himself in choosing this word by which to be identified?

            Can I see any indication in the passage for today that God exists in more than one form, or person? Can I see God acting as the Conceiver of creation? Agent (by His Word) of creation? Power bringing life to creation? To which of the three persons of the Godhead might these "roles" apply?

            When, in Genesis 1:26-28, God says, "Let us make man in our image," with whom is He speaking?

Journal: Jesus also affirmed the Trinity in Matthew 28:18-20, but this is still a great mystery. God is Father, Son, and Holy Spirit, each equally God, yet each with a different "function" in fulfilling God's purposes. So, today, as I think about God being with me...

Pray: *"But you, O LORD, are a shield about me, my glory, and the lifter of my head. I cried aloud to the LORD, and he answered me"* (Psalm 3:3, 4).

Day 2: Holy, Holy, Holy

Pray: *"The LORD is great in Zion; he is exalted over all the peoples. Let them praise your great and awesome name! Holy is he! "* (Psalm 99:2, 3).

Read: Isaiah 6:1-6

Meditate: Why did the angels cry "Holy!" Three times? Is the earth really full of the glory of the holy God? Where might I look to see that glory?

How did Isaiah respond to the appearance of God in His holiness? Why was this appropriate? Is this the way I respond to God? Why or why not?

And yet, the holy God appeared to sinful Isaiah! What does it say about our thrice-holy God that He makes Himself known to sinful creatures such as me? Does he have some purpose in mind for me?

Journal: God is God, and I am not; He is holy, and I am not. And yet He comes to make Himself known to me. Surely, He must want me to...

Pray: *"O God, you are my God; earnestly I seek you; my soul thirsts for you; my flesh faints for you, as in a dry and weary land where there is no water"* (Psalm 63:1).

Day 3: Almighty, Over All Things!

Pray: *"Once God has spoken; twice I have heard this: that power belongs to God, and that to you, O Lord, belongs steadfast love"* (Psalm 62:11, 12).

Read: Jeremiah 32:16-26

Meditate: God commanded Jeremiah to buy a piece of property in a land shortly to be taken over by the Babylonians. What was God saying to Jeremiah about the future? Jeremiah noted that God had previously spoken, and what He had said had come to pass (v. 24). Was Jeremiah's buying that land a gesture to the people of Jerusalem about God's sovereign power?

"Nothing is too hard" for God. Does that mean He will do whatever I ask Him to? Why or why not? What will God do (v. 24 again)?

        Lesson 3: Who is God? - Anchorsaway Worldview Handbook ©

Jeremiah was facing tough circumstances, but God wanted him to focus on Him, and not on his situation. Does this speak to me in any way? As I go out each day, am I looking more to the sovereign, almighty God than I am to my circumstances?

Journal: What God has spoken, He will do. Today, as I prepare to take on the hard circumstances of my life, it is comforting to know that...

Pray: *"Oh, how abundant is your goodness, which you have stored up for those who fear you and worked for those who take refuge in you"* (Psalm 31:19).

Day 4: All-wise, Always

Pray: *"The fear of the LORD is the beginning of wisdom; all those who practice it have a good understanding. Let your praise endure forever! "* (Psalm 111:10, adapted).

Read: Job 28:12-28

Meditate: Where do my friends look for wisdom? Do they seem to be finding it?

How valuable is the wisdom God can give, as Job understood it? Do I regard God's wisdom as that valuable?

God alone has wisdom and understanding. How can I begin to get in on that? What will that require of me? From what must I turn away?

Journal: Today, I want to have more of God's wisdom with me in all I do, and so...

Pray: *"Blessed is everyone who fears the LORD, who walks in his ways"* (Psalm 128:1).

Day 5: Good and Upright

Pray: *"You are good and do good; teach me your statutes"* (Psalm 119:68).

Read: Psalm 25:8-15

Meditate: What does the good and upright God do? For whom?

                 If I follow the paths of the good and upright God, where will they lead me? How will others see that in me?

                 What can keep me from following the good and upright way of the Lord (v. 11)? What does it mean to have "my eyes ever toward the LORD?" How can I do that? How can I help others to do that?

Journal: Today, I'm going to work harder at keeping my eyes on the good and upright God, and at walking in the paths He chooses for me. Let's see, I'd better...

Pray: *"May integrity and uprightness preserve me, for I wait for you"* (Psalm 25:21).

Lesson 3: Who is God? - Anchorsaway Worldview Handbook ©

ENDNOTES

[1] C. S. Lewis, Mere Christianity (Glasgow: William Collins Sons Co. Ltd., 1974) 54.
[2] Much of the information in this section has been adapted from Wayne Grudem, Systematic Theology: An Introduction to Biblical Doctrine (Grand Rapids: Zondervan, 1994) 156-225.
[3] Adapted from Kenneth Boa, Cults: World Religions and the Occult (Wheaton, IL: Victor Books, 1990) 264-277.
[4] Boa, Kenneth, Cults, World Religions and the Occult, (Wheaton, IL: Victor Books, 1990)
[5] Rose Publishing, Christianity, Cults & Religions chart. Compares 17 religions and cults.
[6] Ibid.
[7] Ibid.
[8] Ibid.

Recommended Reading

Key Books:

Boa, Kenneth. Cults, World Religions and the Occult. Wheaton, IL: Victor Books, 1990.

Cahill, Mark. One Thing You Can't Do In Heaven. Bartlesville, OK: Genesis Publishing Group, 2004.

Copan, Paul, And William Lane. Craig Contending with Chrisitianity's Critics: Answering New Atheist & Other Ojectors. Nashville: B & H Academic, 2009.

Copan, Paul. That's Just Your Interpretation: Responding to Skeptics Who Challenge Your Faith. Grand Rapids, MI: Baker, 2001.

Craig, William Lane., and Chad V. Meister. God is Great, God is Good: Why Believing in God Is Reasonable and Responsible. Downers Grove, IL: IVP, 2009

Dobson, Dr. James. When God Doesn't Make Sense. Wheaton, IL: Tyndale House Publishers, 1993.

Feinberg, John, No One Like Him: The Doctrine of God (Foundations of Evangelical Theology). Wheaton, IL: Crossway Books, 2001.

Grudem, Wayne. Systematic Theology: An Introduction to Biblical Doctrine. Grand Rapids: Zondervan, 1994.

Keller, Timothy. The Reason for God: Belief in an Age of Skepticism. New York: Dutton, 2008.

Lutzer, Erwin W. Ten Lies About God (And How You Might Already Be Deceived). Nashville, TN: Word Publishing, 2000.

McFarland, Alex. The God You Thought You Knew: Exposing the 10 Biggest Myths about Christianity. N.p.: n.p., n.d.

Packer, J.I. Knowing God. Downers Grove, IL: InterVarsity Press, 1993.

Teresa, Mother. A Simple Path. New York: Ballantine Books, 1995.

Tozer, A. W. The Attributes of God. Camp Hill, PA: Christian Publications, Inc., 1998.

Tozer, A. W. The Knowledge of the Holy. New York: HarperCollins Publishers, 1961.

Tozer, A. W. The Pursuit of God. Camp Hill, PA: Christian Publications, Inc., 1998.

Lesson 4: Is the Bible Reliable?

 Anchor of the Week: The Bible Is Reliable.

I. Introduction

A. Introduction of the 4 Deadly Questions

These are effective questions to use when your ideas are being attacked and when you wish to point out another idea's shortcomings.

#1. What do you mean by that? The true weakness of an argument lies in the fuzzy definition of terms used. When someone makes a truth claim, ask this question.

#2. How do you know that is true? Surprisingly, most people believe things for which they have absolutely no evidence. Try this question out on someone with strong opinions and be ready for a fascinating discussion.

#3. Where do you get your information? When someone makes a radical claim, you should always ask detailed questions about how they know what they know. Before long you will get to the end of their knowledge and will be on even terms in the discussion.

#4. What happens if you are wrong? It is one thing to claim a belief and yet another to stake your life on it. The most important question that can be asked in life is, "Where do you go when you die, and what happens if you are wrong?"

B. Questions of the week:

1. Is the Bible authentic, and is it historically reliable?

2. Could man, without God, have written the Bible?

C. What does God say about scripture

1. 2 Timothy 3:16-17 "All scripture is God-breathed and is useful for teaching, rebuking, correcting and training in righteousness, so that the man of God may be thoroughly equipped for every good work.

2. 2 Peter 1:20-21 "Above all, you must understand that no prophecy of scripture came about by the prophet's own interpretation. For prophecy never had its origin in the man, but men spoke from God as they were carried along by the Holy Spirit."

D. THE UNIQUENESS OF THE BIBLE

The Bible is a unique book – not like any other. It contains 66 books (39 in the Old Testament, 27 in the New Testament).

1. The Bible was written over a span of 1,500 years (over 40 generations).

2. There were 40 different authors.

3. The authors came from all walks of life:

   - Moses (Genesis-Deuteronomy) – political leader, trained in Egyptian universities
   - Peter (1 Peter and 2 Peter) – fisherman
   - Amos (Amos) – herdsman
   - Joshua (Joshua) – military general
   - Daniel (Daniel) – prime minister
   - Solomon (Proverbs - Song of Songs) – king
   - Luke (Luke, Acts) – doctor
   - Matthew (Matthew) – tax collector

4. It was written in different places (wilderness, dungeon/prison, palace, island).

5. It was written in different modes (ranging from great joy to deep sorrow).

6. It was written on three continents (Asia, Europe, and Africa).

7. It was written in three languages (Hebrew, Aramaic, and Greek).

> ONE CONTINUOUS THEME: The Redemption of Man
> Central character of Bible: The Messiah, the Lord Jesus Christ

8. The Bible has been translated into more languages than any other book (over 1,200). It is the most widely circulated book in the world.

9. The Bible is the most widely read and influential book in history.

10. It has survived throughout the ages despite immeasurable opposition.

11. Its teachings and content are unique (contains prophecy, history, poetry, prose, parables, songs, essays...).

12. It is simple enough that a child can understand its basic message, yet so profound that it can be studied for a lifetime and still not be exhausted.

13. The Bible is not an account of man's efforts to find God, but rather, God's efforts to reveal Himself to man. It contains precisely the things God wants man to know in exactly the form that He wants us to know them.

> **The amazing uniqueness of the Bible does not make it true.**[1]

The standard used to prove the reliability of the Scripture are the following:

A. Bibliographical Test: Examines the original manuscripts of the Old and New Testaments to determine how they have been handed down to us.

1. Methods of Scribes

2. Comparison study. How does the Bible compare to other works of antiquity?

B. Internal Evidence Tests: Are there any discrepancies in the Bible itself?

1. Prophecy

2. Archaeology

C. External Evidence Test: What works of literature, apart from the Bible, confirm its accuracy?

1. Eusebius – Ecclesiastical History (III.39)

2. Flavius Josephus – The Antiquities of the Jews (18.3.3)

3. Cornelius Tacitus – Annals (15.44)

The word scribe means 'counter.' 1 Chronicles 2:55 mentions the clans of scribes who inhabited Jabez. Scribes followed strict disciplines regarding the Scriptures. With meticulous care and fidelity, they insisted on the following conditions when copying the Scriptures:

- The text was written on the skin of a clean animal.

- The scroll was prepared for use in synagogue only by a Jew.

- It was fastened together with strings from a clean animal.

- Each skin contained a specified number of columns, equal throughout the entire book.

- The length of each column extended no less than forty-eight lines and no more than sixty lines.

- The breadth of each column consisted of exactly thirty letters.

- Each scribe used a specially prepared recipe of black ink.

- An authentic copy of the text served as an example for each scribe to follow.

- The scribes were to copy nothing from memory.

- The space between every consonant could be no more than the width of a thread.

- The breadth between every section must be the same as that of nine consonants.

- Between every book was the width of three lines.

- The Pentateuch must terminate exactly with a line.

- Copyists were required to sit in full Jewish dress.

- There was an absolute reverence for the Scripture and the name of God, such that a fresh quill was used each time the sacred name of God was penned. Also, scribes even refused to acknowledge the presence of a king when writing God's name.

- The scribes must produce a master copy.[2]

The Massoretes edited and standardized the Hebrew text, adding the vowel points to insure proper pronunciation. They went even further in their disciplines:

- They meticulously copied the text only one letter at a time (t-t; h-h; e-e; etc...).

- They counted the number of times each letter of the alphabet occurred in each book.

- They calculated the middle word.

- If more than three mistakes existed in a manuscript, it was destroyed.[3]

Bibliographical Test: The Manuscript Comparison

F.F. Bruce in *The New Testament Documents* vividly pictures the comparison between the New Testament and the ancient historical writings.

As Bruce also comments in *The Books and Parchments*, "There is no body of ancient literature in the world which enjoys such a wealth of good textual attestation as the New Testament."

Author	When Written	Earliest Copy	Time Span	No. of copies
Caesar	100-44 BC	AD 900	1,000 Yrs.	10
Plato	427-347 BC	AD 900	1,200 Yrs.	7
Sophocles	496-406 BC	AD 1000	1,400 Yrs.	193
Aristotle	384-322 BC	AD 1100	1,400 Yrs.	49

Historian J. Harold Greenlee rightfully concludes, "Since scholars accept as generally trustworthy the writings of the ancient classics even though the earliest MSS (handwritten copies of the Scriptures) written so long after the original writings and the number of extant MSS is in many instances so small, it is clear that the reliability of the text of the New Testament is likewise assured."

Bruce Metzger observes: "In the entire range of ancient Greek and Latin literature, the Iliad ranks next to the New Testament in possessing the greatest amount of manuscript testimony."

Work	When Written	Earliest Copy	Time span	No. of copies
Homer (Iliad)	900 BC	400 BC	500 yrs.	643
New Testament	40-100 AD	125 AD	25 yrs.	Over 24,000[4]

As Floyd McElveen has observed in *God's Word, Final, Infallible and Forever*,

"Even if someone deliberately or by accident amended or corrupted a manuscript, it would be corrected by the many other manuscripts available. To sum up; unless we want to throw a blanket over all of history and say that there is nothing knowable about the past, no history that can be trusted, no Grecian or Roman history, no Aristotle or Plato or Socrates, we had better not make any claims against the historicity and accuracy of the New Testament. The New Testament documents are far more numerous, older, demonstrably more accurate historically, and have been examined by a far greater battery of scholars, both friend and foe, than all the other ancient manuscripts put together. They have met the test impeccably!"[5]

The most common objection to prophecy is: The prophecies were written at, or after, the time of Jesus, and therefore, fulfill themselves. How do we respond to this challenge?[6]

ANSWER: If you are not satisfied with 450 BC as the historic date for the completion of the Old Testament, then take into consideration the following: the Septuagint, the Greek translation of the Hebrew scriptures, was initiated in the reign of Ptolemy Philadelphus (285—246 BC). Clearly, if you have a Greek translation initiated in 250 BC, then you had to have the Hebrew text from which it was written. This will suffice to indicate that there was at least a 250 year gap between the prophecies being written down and their fulfillment in the person of Christ.

1. BORN AT BETHLEHEM
- Prophecy: *"But as for you, Bethlehem Ephrathah, too little to be among the clans of Judah, from you One will go forth for Me to be ruler in Israel. His goings forth are from long ago, from the days of eternity"* (Micah 5:2, NAS). **750 BC**

- Fulfillment: *"Jesus was born in Bethlehem of Judea"* (Matthew 2:1; John 7:42).

2. PRECEDED BY MESSENGER
- Prophecy: *"A voice is calling, 'Clear the way for the Lord in the wilderness; Make smooth in the desert a highway for our God'"* (Isaiah 40:3; Malachi 3:1, NAS). **433 BC**

- Fulfillment: John the Baptist came, preaching in the wilderness of Judea, saying, *"Repent, for the kingdom of heaven is at hand"* (Matthew 3:1-3, 11:9-10; Luke 1:17; John 1:23, NAS).

3. HE WAS TO ENTER JERUSALEM ON A DONKEY
- Prophecy: *"Rejoice greatly, O Daughter of Zion! Shout in triumph, O daughter of Jerusalem! Behold, your king is coming to you; He is just and endowed with salvation, humble, and mounted on a donkey, even on a colt, the foal of a donkey"* (Zechariah 9:9, NAS). **520 BC**

- Fulfillment: *"And they brought it to Jesus, and they threw their garments on the colt, and put Jesus on it. And as He was going, they were spreading their garments in the road"* (Matthew 21:6-11; Luke 19:35-36, NAS).

4. BETRAYED BY A FRIEND
- Prophecy: *"Even my close friend in whom I trusted, who ate my bread has lifted up his heel against me"* (Psalm 41:9, 55:12-14, NAS). **300 BC**

- Fulfillment: *"Judas Iscariot was the one who betrayed Him"* (Matthew 10:4, 26:49-50, NAS).

5. SOLD FOR 30 PIECES OF SILVER
- Prophecy: *"And I said to them, 'If it is good in your sight, give me my wages; but if not, never mind!' So they weighed out thirty shekels of silver as my wages"* (Zechariah 11:12). **520 BC**

- Fulfillment: Judas Iscariot asked the price of betrayal, and *"they weighed out to him thirty pieces of silver"* (Matthew 26:15, 27:3, NAS).

6. MONEY TO BE THROWN IN GOD'S HOUSE

- Prophecy: *"So I took the thirty shekels of silver and threw them to the potter in the house of the Lord"* (Zechariah 11:13b, NAS). **520 BC**

- Fulfillment: *"And he threw the pieces of silver into the sanctuary and departed"* (Matthew 27:5a, NAS). *"And they counseled together and with the money bought the potter's field as a burial place for strangers"* (Matthew 27:7, NAS).

7. DUMB BEFORE ACCUSERS

- Prophecy: *"He was oppressed and He was afflicted, yet He did not open His mouth"* (Isaiah 53:7, NAS). **700 BC**

- Fulfillment: *"And while He was being accused by the chief priests and elders, He made no answer"* (Matthew 27:12, NAS).

8. HANDS AND FEET PIERCED

- Prophecy: *"They have pierced my hands and my feet"* (Psalm 22:16; Isaiah 53:5, NAS). **520 BC**

- Fulfillment: *"And when they came to the place called the Skull, there they crucified Him"* (Luke 23:33, NAS).

The Mathematical Probabilities of Jesus Fulfilling Prophecy:

Peter Stoner has said in *Science Speaks* that by using the modern science of probability in reference to the eight prophecies listed above:

"...we find that the chance that any man might have lived down to the present time and fulfilled all eight prophecies is 1 in 10^{17} (or 1 in 100,000,000,000,000,000).

Let us try to visualize this chance...Suppose we take 10^{17} silver dollars and lay them on the face of Texas. They will cover all of the state two feet deep. Now mark one of these silver dollars and stir the whole mass thoroughly, all over the state. Blindfold a man and tell him that he can travel as far as he wishes, but he must pick up one silver dollar and say that this is the right one. What chance would he have of getting the right one? Just the same chance that the prophets would have had of writing these eight prophecies and having them all come true in any one man, from their day to the present time, providing they wrote them in their own wisdom." [7]

When Stoner considers forty-eight prophecies, he says, *"We find the chance that any one man fulfilled all forty-eight prophecies to be 1 in 10^{157}."*[8]

What is one possible explanation for the staggering accuracy of the Old Testament prophecies? (1 Peter 1:20-21) He was chosen before the creation of the world, but was revealed in these last times for your sake. Through him you believe in God, who raised him from the dead and glorified him, and so your faith and hope are in God.

Probabilities of one man (Jesus) fulfilling 48 Old Testament prophecies:[9]

1. Scientific threshold for the impossible is 1 in 10^{50}

2. 8 prophecies: 1 in 10^{17}

   a. Concept Model: State of Texas covered with silver dollars, 2 feet deep. (Refer to the previous illustration from Peter Stoner.)

   b. If evolution were true that the earth is 10 billion years old, there would be only 10^{17} seconds in the history of the universe.

3. 16 prophecies: 1 in 10^{45}

   a. Concept Model: A ball of silver dollars: radius 30 times the distance of the Earth to the Sun. (This follows the same idea as the state of Texas concept model. Refer to Peter Stoner's illustration.)

4. 48 prophecies: 1 in 10^{157}

   a. **Concept Model: None, bigger than we can grasp**

Supplemental Observations:

1. Total Atoms in the Universe: 10^{66}

2. Total Particles: 10^{80}

3. Seconds in 10 billion years: 10^{17}

Conclusion:

For anyone to fulfill forty-eight biblical prophecies is scientifically absurd, and yet, the Bible reveals that Jesus did just that!

Anyone who rejects Jesus Christ as the Son of God is rejecting a fact proven more absolutely than any other fact in the world!

Internal Evidence: Messianic Prophecies:

Old Testament References and New Testament Fulfillment
(List Is Not All-Inclusive)

Topic:	Old Testament:	New Testament:
Messiah to be of the seed of the woman	Genesis 3:15	Galatians 4:4
Messiah to be of the seed of Abraham	Genesis 12:3, 18:18	Matthew 1:2; Luke 3:34; Acts 3:25; Galations 3:16
Messiah to be of the tribe of Judah	Genesis 49:10	Matthew 1:2; Luke 3:33
Messiah to be of the seed of Jacob	Numbers 24:17, 19	Matthew 1:2; Luke 3:34
Messiah to be of the seed of David	Psalm 132:11; Isaiah 11:10; Jeremiah 23:5-6; 33:15-16	Matthew 1:6; Luke 1:32-33; Acts 2:30; Romans 1:3
Messiah to be the Son of God	Psalm 2:7; Proverbs 30:4	Matthew 3:17; Luke 1:32
Messiah to be raised from the dead	Psalm 16:10	Acts 13:35-37
The crucifixion experience	Psalm 22, Psalm 69:21	Matthew 27:34-50; John 19:28-30
Messiah to be betrayed by a friend	Psalm 41:9	John 13:18, 21
Messiah ascends to heaven	Psalm 68:18	Luke 24:51; Acts 1:9
Homage and tribute paid to Messiah by great kings	Psalm 72:10-11	Matthew 2:1-11
Messiah to be a priest like Melchizedek	Psalm 110:4	Hebrews 5:5-6
Messiah to be at the right hand of God	Psalm 110:1	Matthew 26:64; Hebrews 1:3
Messiah, the stone which the builders rejected, became the head cornerstone	Psalm 118:22-23; Isaiah 8:14-15, 28:16	Matthew 21:42-43; Acts 4:11; Romans 9:32-33; 1 Peter 2:6-8; Eph. 2:20
Messiah to be born of a virgin	Isaiah 7:14	Matthew 1:18-25; Luke 1:26
Galilee to be the first area of Messiah's ministry	Isaiah 9:1-8	Matthew 4:12-16
Messiah will be meek and mild	Isaiah 42:2-3, 53:7	Matthew 12:18-20, 26:62-63
Messiah will minister to the Gentiles	Isaiah 42:1, 49:1, 8	Matthew 12:21

Topic:	Old Testament:	New Testament:
Messiah will be smitten	Isaiah 50:6	Matthew 26:67, 27:26, 30
The Gospel according to Isaiah: (The suffering Messiah brings salvation.)	Isaiah 52:13-53:12	The Four Gospels
The New and Everlasting Covenant	Isaiah 55:3-4; Jeremiah 31:31-33	Matthew 26:28; Mark 14:24; Luke 22:20; Hebrews 8:6-13
Messiah, the Right Arm of God	Isaiah 53:1, 59:16	John 12:38
Messiah as Intercessor	Isaiah 59:16	Hebrews 9:15
Two-fold mission of the Messiah	Isaiah 61:1-11	Luke 4:16-21
Messiah will perform miracles	Isaiah 35:5-6	Matthew 11:3-6; John 11:47
Messiah is called "The Lord"	Jeremiah 23:5-6	Acts 2:36
Time of Messiah's coming	Daniel 9:24-26	Galations 4:4; Ephesians 1:10
Bethlehem, the Messiah's birthplace	Micah 5:2	Matthew 2:1; Luke 2:4-6
Messiah will enter the Temple with authority	Malachi 3:1	Matthew 21:12
Messiah will enter Jerusalem on a donkey	Zechariah 9:9	Matthew 21:1-10
Messiah will be pierced	Zechariah 12:10; Psalm 22:16	John 19:34, 37
Messiah to be forsaken by His disciples	Zechariah 13:7	Matthew 26:31, 56
Coming of the Holy Spirit in the days of the Messiah	Joel 2:28	Acts 2:16-18
Opposition to the nations	Psalm 2:2	Revelation 19:19
Messiah's final victory over death	Isaiah 25:8	1 Corinthians 15:54; Revelation 7:17, 21:4
The glorious Messiah	Isaiah 63:1	Revelation 19:11-16
Messiah as King	Psalm 2:6-9	Revelation 19:15-16
Submission of nations to Messiah	Isaiah 2:4; Micah 4:1-4	Revelation 12:5
Gentiles shall seek Messiah of Israel	Isaiah 11:10	Romans 11:12

Lesson 4: Is the Bible Reliable? - Anchorsaway Worldview Handbook ©

In what ways have the discoveries of archaeology verified the reliability of the Bible? Over the years there have been many criticisms leveled against the Bible concerning its historical reliability. These criticisms are usually based on a lack of evidence from outside sources to confirm the biblical record. Since the Bible is a religious book, many scholars take the position that it is biased and cannot be trusted, unless we have corroborating evidence from extra-biblical sources. In other words, the Bible is guilty until proven innocent, and a lack of outside evidence places the biblical account in doubt.

This standard is far different from that applied to other ancient documents, even though many, if not most, have a religious element. They are considered to be accurate, unless there is evidence to show that they are not. Although it is not possible to verify every incident in the Bible, the discoveries of archaeology since the mid-1800's have demonstrated the reliability and plausibility of the Bible narrative. Here are some examples:

Clay tablets from Ebla: The discovery of the Ebla archive in northern Syria in the 1970's has shown the biblical writings concerning the Patriarchs to be viable. Documents written on clay tablets from around 2300 B.C. demonstrate that personal and place names in the Patriarchal accounts are genuine. The name "Canaan" was in use in Ebla, a name critics once said was not used at that time and was used incorrectly in the early chapters of the Bible. The word "tehom" ("the deep") in Genesis 1:2 was said to be a late word demonstrating the late writing of the creation story. "Tehom" was part of the vocabulary at Ebla, in use some 800 years before Moses. Ancient customs reflected in the stories of the Patriarchs have also been found in clay tablets from Nuzi and Mari.

The Hittites and Solomon: The Hittites were once thought to be a biblical legend, until their capital and records were discovered at Bogazkoy, Turkey. Many thought the biblical references to Solomon's wealth were greatly exaggerated. Recovered records from the past show that wealth in antiquity was concentrated with the king and Solomon's prosperity was entirely feasible.

King Sargon: It was once claimed there was no Assyrian king named Sargon as recorded in Isaiah 20:1, because his name was not known in any other record. Then, Sargon's palace was discovered in Khorsabad, Iraq. The very event mentioned in Isaiah 20, his capture of Ashdod, was recorded on the palace walls. What is more, fragments of a stela memorializing the victory were found at Ashdod, itself.

King Belshazzar: Another king who was in doubt was Belshazzar, king of Babylon, named in Daniel 5. The last king of Babylon was Nabonidus, according to recorded history. Tablets were found showing that Belshazzar was Nabonidus' son, who served as co-regent in Babylon. Thus, Belshazzar could offer to make Daniel "third highest ruler in the kingdom" (Daniel 5:16) for reading the handwriting on the wall, the highest available position. Here we see the "eye-witness" nature of the biblical record, as is so often brought out by the discoveries of archaeology.[10]

External Evidence Test: Historical Writers

There are a number of extra-biblical, historical works of literature that confirm the reliability of Scripture. The following are but a few:

Eusebius of Caesarea (AD 263 – 339) – His Ecclesiastical History preserved the writings of Papias, bishop of Hieropolis (AD 130). Papias, a friend of the Apostle John wrote:

> "The Elder (Apostle John) used to say this also: 'Mark, having been the interpreter of Peter, wrote down accurately all that he (Peter) mentioned, whether sayings or doings of Christ, not, however, in order. For he was neither a hearer nor companion of the Lord; but afterwards, as I said, he accompanied Peter, who adapted his teachings as necessity required, not as though he were making compilation of the sayings of the Lord. So then Mark made no mistake, writing down in this way some things as he (Peter) mentioned them; for he paid attention to this one thing, not to omit anything that he had heard, nor to include any false statement among them.'"[11]

Flavius Josephus (AD 37-100?) – was a Jewish historian who wrote one of the most comprehensive histories of the Jewish people, primarily for the benefit of the non-Jewish world. In The Antiquities of the Jews, he wrote:

> "Now there was about this time Jesus, a wise man, if it be lawful to call him a man, for he was a doer of wonderful works – a teacher of such men as receive truth with pleasure. He drew over to him both many of the Jews, and many of the Gentiles. He was [the] Christ; and when Pilate, at the suggestion of the principal men amongst us, had condemned him to the cross, those that loved him at the first did not forsake him, for he appeared to them alive again the third day, as the divine prophets had foretold these and ten thousand other wonderful things concerning him; and the tribe of Christians, so named from him, are not extinct to this day."[12] (18.3.3.)

Cornelius Tacitus (AD 56-117?) – a Roman aristocrat and historian who wrote a detailed history of the Roman empire under Nero. In his classical work, The Annals, he wrote the following excerpts about Christianity:

> "...Nero fastened the guilt and inflicted the most exquisite tortures on a class hated for their abominations, called Christians by the populace. Christus [Christ], from whom the name had its origin, suffered the extreme penalty during the reign of Tiberius at the hands of one of our procurators, Pontius Pilatus...."[13] (15.44)

III. Conclusion

Perhaps the best way to summarize the Bible is to say that God invites each one of us to read, study, and learn from the Truth Giver and then, through the Holy Spirit, believe and live out the truths that are found within its covers. He encourages us to give this Book the highest authority in our personal lives, and to use it as our instruction manual for living life to its full and for bringing Christ into our culture.

The Old Testament collection was written over many centuries. Scholars observe that there were oral traditions as well as written accounts. Stories were told over and over, detail by detail, when the covenant people gathered around their campfires. And the stories were preserved on parchment or animal skins, so the account of God's dealing with his people would never be forgotten. The parchments were rolled up into scrolls. Over the centuries, more scrolls were written and added to the collection. Some were recognized as having special importance and came to be regarded as sacred text or Holy Scripture.

Of course, none of the original scroll writings have been preserved. Scrolls would wear out and were given an honored burial. But before they wore out, copies would be made, and then copies of copies.

Inasmuch as the books were written over at least a thousand-year period, there was an ongoing process to gather the collection. The early books of the law were stored in the ark of the tabernacle (Deuteronomy 31:26). The nation re-consecrated its devotion to the sacred writings at different times (II Kings 23:1-3; Nehemiah 8:1ff).

By the time of Jesus it seems that there was general agreement on what constituted the recognized collection of sacred scrolls for the Jewish people. They are summed up in Jesus' reference to the three main sections of the Hebrew Scriptures, when He noted that "Everything must be fulfilled that is written about me in the Law of Moses, the Prophets and the Psalms" (Luke 24:44).

A major tragedy in the life of the Jewish nation occurred in 70 AD when the Jewish temple, the center of Jewish religious life, was destroyed by the Romans under Titus Livy. It is commonly thought that at a gathering of rabbis in the city of Jamnia in 90 AD there was a re-affirmation and confirmation of what fully and finally constituted the Hebrew Scriptures.

The Jewish historian Josephus, writing in the early 90's AD in his Against Apion, observed: "For we have not countless books among us, disagreeing and contradicting one another but only twenty-two books, which contain the records of all the past times; which are justly believed to be divine...and how firmly we have given credit to these books of our nation is evident by what we do; for during so many ages as have already passed, no one hath been so bold as either to add anything to them, to take anything from them, or to make any change in them, but it has become natural to all Jews, immediately and from their very birth, to esteem these books to contain divine doctrines, and to persist in them, and if occasion be, willingly to die for them." [14]

It is helpful to note that the New Testament, as we know it today, came long after the first Jewish Christians lived. The early church used the Old Testament exclusively in the years following the resurrection of Jesus. When the church spread outside of Jerusalem, letters were sent to the different churches to encourage, to admonish and to teach the truth of Jesus and His teachings.

When people forgot what was taught by Jesus or exactly what happened to Jesus, letters were written by those who had been close to Jesus or, as in Paul's case, had a personal encounter with Jesus. "Long before councils were ever convened, Christians, especially local church elders, were constantly collecting, evaluating and deciding which of the many writings of their day carried the authority of the Apostles (Cf. Colossians 4:16; 2 Peter 3:15, 16). The question asked of any writing to be read in the churches was: To what extent is this book (epistle, narrative, apocalypse, or gospel) an authentic and pure representation of the life and teachings of Jesus and His Apostles? Thus, the New Testament was determined to be true by how it was used and not by a meeting, a council or men."[15]

The early Christians knew that Jesus fulfilled the prophecy of the coming Messiah and they also knew that Jesus Christ died, was buried and raised on the third day. They were part of the 500 who witnessed the resurrected Christ. It is no wonder then, that the very words of Christ were seen as words of truth of God. They wanted to make sure that they were not perverted or changed in any way, so the writings gained credibility. Remember that oral communication was more important in that day than written communications. The oral accounts matched with the written accounts and the books continued to gain credibility.

Times came when there were many falsified writings of Paul, Luke, Peter and Mark. From the perverted writings, there were heretical or unauthentic writings that began to be circulated to the various churches. The books were then scrutinized by the early church fathers, and in the end, the 27 books of the New Testament were found to be completely authentic and reliable.

The tests used for inclusion in the canon were:
- Is it authoritative? Did it come from the hand of God?
- Is it prophetic? Was it written by a man of God?
- Is it authentic? "If in doubt, throw it out."
- Is it dynamic? Did it come from the life-transforming power of God?
- Was it received, collected, read and used? Was it accepted by the people of God?[16]

Those books that were not included (the books of the Apocrypha and Pseudepigrapha) were rejected because:
- "They abound in historical and geographical inaccuracies and anachronisms.
- They teach doctrines which are false and foster practices which are at variance with inspired Scripture.
- They resort to literary types and display an artificiality of subject matter and styling out of keeping with inspired Scripture.
- They lack the distinctive elements which give genuine Scripture their divine character, such as prophetic power and poetic and religious feeling."[17]

An easy way to remember why we can trust the Bible is to use the acronym **M.A.P. S.**

M - Stands for manuscript evidence. We have studied about the original manuscripts of the Old and New Testaments. We have compared them to other works of antiquity. We have also seen external manuscripts and writers that support biblical history and existing biblical manuscripts.

A - Stands for archaeology. We have seen how numerous archaeological finds have provided evidence to support biblical history, names and places.

P - Stands for prophecy. We have seen how Jesus Christ has fulfilled over forty-eight pure prophecies. The likelihood of one person fulfilling all of those prophecies is statistically impossible.

S - Stands for science. As we look at the field of science we can see that the world is filled with things that are irreducibly complex. When we realize that we are part of a universe that is full of design, we must look for a designer. The Bible tells us who that designer is. It also provides evidence that can be verified in the physical world that the God of the Bible is the designer of our universe.

Lesson 4: Is the Bible Reliable?

Small Group Objective:

The goal is to help the students understand the completeness of God's revelation of His Word. From the uniqueness of the Bible, itself, to the proofs for the reliability, this much we know – the Bible can be trusted because it was written by God, Himself. No man, without the inspiration of the Holy Spirit, could have written with such accuracy, insight and foresight. Only with God are such things possible!

✓ **Check Points:**

☐ Bring 3 x 5 cards for your students to write down any questions they may have which aren't answered during the discussion.

☐ Enlist a student to share a brief personal testimony.

Discussion Questions:

1. Review prayer requests from the week before and ask how the students are doing.

2. Lead a time of discussion, asking the following questions:

(Note: Work through as many of the following questions as possible. The goal is not to get through all of them, but to encourage each student to participate in the discussion as part of the learning process.)

 a. What day of the devotional did you find most meaningful?

 b. How did last week's lesson impact your life? Did you share it?

 c. Is the Bible authentic, and is it historically reliable?

 d. Could man, without God, have written the Bible? Why or why not?

 e. What have you learned about the character of God by the way he inspired the Bible to be written?

 f. Role play with students the way that a discussion can always lead back to the reliability of the Bible. Point out the importance of knowing where the listener is coming from so that the comments about the Bible can be directed to their individual interest, i.e. mathematics (prophecy), literature (comparison of great books), history (biblical references from extra-biblical works of antiquity)...

 g. How much faith does it take to know that the Bible was written by God and is true? Do we see God using favortism in choosing those to write the Scripture? Frame a fisherman.

 h. What proof of Scripture was most meaningful to you?

i. Have a student make a claim that the Bible is truth, using the 4 Deadly Questions.

j. How does the Bible reflect God's character?

k. When you hear from a professor that there is no truth, what might your response be, using the Four Deadly Questions?

l. When you have moments of doubt, what are some of the truths you should remember about God and the Bible?

m. Why do you think God gave us several ways to prove the Bible was written by Him?

n. How can someone's life be changed when they realize that the Bible is the truth?

o. What questions, if any, come to mind as a result of this week's lesson?

3. Ask for prayer requests and tell students that you will be faithful to pray for them during the week. Encourage students to record the prayer requests in the prayer request section of their handbooks, so they can pray for one another during the week. Begin the prayer time by sharing your own request. Spend the remaining time in prayer.

★ After the Session

1. Contact each small group member during the week. Ask them about their devotional time, a question they have raised, or how their week is going.

Prayer Requests

Student Devotionals written by T.M. Moore

Is the Bible Reliable?

Be sure to set aside the time you will need each day for the following devotionals. The combination of prayer, reading, meditation, and journaling will help you to let the Word of Christ dwell in you richly (Colossians 3:16). Take your time and do a thorough job in each section. Remember to let the beginning and ending prayers be a "starter" for you, and use them for a more extended time of talking with God about the subject of the day's reading.

Day 1: Inspired by God

Pray: *"Teach me, O LORD, the way of your statutes; and I will keep it to the end"* (Psalm 119:33).

Read: 2 Timothy 3:14-17

Meditate: What does it mean to "continue in what you have learned?" How would I explain this to someone else?

            The Scriptures are able to make people wise unto salvation. What are the implications of this for me? For the work of evangelism? Why is this so (v. 16; Romans 1:16, 17)?

            What is the difference between teaching, reproof, correction, and training in righteousness? Is the Word of God doing this in me? How do I know?

Journal: I have many priorities in my life, many things to do. But if God has spoken in His Word in such a way that I might be made "competent, equipped for every good work," then...

Pray: *"My soul longs for your salvation; I hope in your Word"* (Psalm 119:81).

Day 2: Better Than Visions

Pray: *"I am your servant; give me understanding, that I may know your testimonies"* (Psalm 119:135).

Read: 2 Peter 1:16-21

Meditate: What did Peter see (vv. 16, 17; cf. Matthew 17:1-8)? How would I have felt if I'd seen that?

But does my faith ultimately depend on such "mountaintop experiences?" What does Peter say is "more sure" than this? Why (v. 21)?

How can I guard against imposing my own interpretation on God's Word? Why should I do this?

Journal: Peter says I need to "pay attention" to the Word, "as to a lamp shining in a dark place." I'll be going into some "dark places" today; therefore, if I want to find the way of light and truth, I'll need to...

Pray: *"Let my cry come before you, O LORD; give me understanding according to your word"* (Psalm 119:169).

Day 3: One Constant Theme

Pray: *"You are near, O LORD, and all your commandments are true"* (Psalm 119:151).

Read: John 5:36-39

Meditate: What is that "testimony" Jesus had which He said is greater than that of John the Baptist? Why is this more reliable than the testimony of John?

Jesus said that, if we would hear the Father speaking to us, we must have His Word abiding in us? What does that mean? Is this true of me? How do I know? What should I be doing to make this true?

Jesus said that the Word of God – referring to the Old Testament – testified of Him? How is this so? What did we see about this in the lesson for this week? Do I feel confident that I could show how the Scriptures speak about Jesus throughout?

Journal: Wait a minute: If Jesus is the theme of all the Scriptures, then, whenever I'm reading or studying the Bible...

Pray: *"I will meditate on your precepts and fix my eyes on your ways. I will delight in your statutes; I will not forget your word"* (Psalm 119:15, 16).

Day 4: To Study, Do, and Teach

Pray: *"My lips will pour forth praise, for you teach me your statutes"* (Psalm 119:171).

Read: Ezra 7:7-10

Meditate: What three things was Ezra committed to with respect to the Word (Law) of God? What did each of these require of him? Is this true of me, also?

            What was the result of Ezra's diligence in the Word of God (v. 9)? What does that mean? How would I know if this was true of me?

            How much time do I spend studying the Word of God each week? How faithful am I in living out what I study? To whom might I teach the things God is showing me in His Word?

Journal: I want to be like Ezra! I want the "good hand of the Lord" to be on me every day. Therefore, I need to...

Pray: *"I find delight in your commandments, which I love"* (Psalm 119:47).

Day 5: When the Word Doesn't Seem to Speak

Pray: *"I will run in the way of your commandments when you enlarge my heart"* (Psalm 119:32).

Read: Isaiah 55:8-11

Meditate: Sometimes reading and studying the Bible doesn't seem to say much to me. Why might this be, according to this passage?

But, even if I don't always understand what I'm reading, or don't seem to be "getting anything" out of my time in the Word, what does this passage promise? Do I believe this? If so, how should that affect my time in the Word?

God has His own purposes for me, and, when He is speaking to me from His Word, I can believe He is working those purposes out in my life. How can I learn more about God's purposes for me? Is it reasonable to expect that I should always understand what I read in the Bible? Is it reasonable to expect that I should keep on reading, anyway? Why?

Journal: God's purposes and ways are perfect, even though they can sometimes be hard to understand, or may seem to be slow in coming. Nevertheless, if I want to know His purposes for me...

Pray: *"In your steadfast love give me life, that I may keep the testimonies of your mouth"* (Psalm 119:88).

ENDNOTES

[1] Josh McDowell, Evidence That Demands a Verdict vol. 1 (1979; Nashville, TN: Thomas Nelson Publishers, 1999) 15-24. (information adapted from)

[2] The information in this section was adapted from page 14 of "Discovering the Bible: A simple introduction to the Bible, what it is, how we got it, and how to use it," the publication accompanying the video series, Discovering the Bible prod. Gateway Films, Worchester, PA. video series. Christian History Institute, 1996.

[3] Some of this information on the Massoretes also comes from McDowell, Evidence That Demands a Verdict, 54-55.

[4] Josh McDowell, 43. McDowell points out, "There are now more than 5,300 known Greek manuscripts of the New Testament. Add over 10,000 Latin Vulgate and at least 9,300 other early versions and we have more than 24,000 manuscript copies of portions of the New Testament in existence."

[5] Floyd McElveen, God's Word, Final, Infallible and Forever (Grand Rapids: Gospel Truth Ministries, 1985) 19.

[6] Josh McDowell, 144-167.

[7] Peter Stoner, Science Speaks (Chicago: Moody Press, 1958), ed. < http://sciencespeaks.dstoner.net/Christ_of_Prophecy.html#c9 >, chap. 3.

[9] Chuck Missler, "Footprints of the Messiah" audiocassette, Koinonia House, 1991.

[10] Bryant C. Wood, "In what ways have the discoveries of archeology verified the reliability of the Bible?", 1995, Associates of Biblical Research 30 March 2005 <http://www.christiananswers.net/q-abr/abr-a008.html>.

[11] Eusebius, Ecclesiastical History III.39 found in McDowell, Evidence That Demands a Verdict 63.

[12] Flavius Josephus, The Works of Josephus, trans. William Whiston (Peabody, MA: Hendrickson Publishers, Inc., 1987) 480.

[13] Cornelius Tacitus, The Annals. Robert Maynard Hutchins, Great Books of the Western World 15 (Chicago: Encyclopedia Britannica, 1952) 168.

[14] "Discovering the Bible," 13.

[15] Josh McDowell, A Ready Defense (Nashville: Thomas Nelson Publishers, 1993) 38.

[16] Josh McDowell, 39.

[17] Josh McDowell, 40.

Recommended Reading

Key Books:

Blomberg, Craig. *The Historical Reliability of the Gospels.* Leicester, England: InterVarsity, 1987.

Bruce, F.F. The New Testament Documents: Are The Reliable? Grand Rapids: Eerdmans, 1960.

Boa, Ken and Larry Moody. I'm Glad You Asked. Colorado Springs, CO: Victor Books/SP Publications, 1994.

Copan, Paul. *That's Just Your Interpretation: Responding to Skeptics Who Challenge Your Faith.* Grand Rapids, MI: Baker 2001.

"Discovering the Bible: A simple introduction to the Bible, what it is, how we got it, and how to use it." Discovering the Bible. Prod. Gateway Films, Worchester, PA. Video series. Christian History Institute, 1996..

Habermas, Gary R., and Mike Licona. The Case for the Ressurection of Jesus . Grand Rapids, MI: Kregel Publications, 2004.

Josephus, Flavius. The Works of Josephus. Trans. William Whiston. Peabody, MA: Hendrickson Publishers, 1987.

Kennedy, D. James. Why I Believe. Nashville, TN: Thomas Nelson Publishers, 1999.

McDowell, Josh. Evidence That Demands a Verdict. Vol. 1. 1979. Nashville, TN: Thomas Nelson Publishers, 1999.

McDowell, Josh and Dave Sterrett. *Is the Bible True-- Really?: A Dialogue on skepticism, Evidence, and the Truth.* Chicago: Moody, 2011.

McDowell, Josh, and Bill Wilson. A Ready Defense: The Best of Josh McDowell. Nashville, TN: Thomas Nelson Publishers, 1993.

McElveen, Floyd. God's Word, Final, Infallible and Forever. Grand Rapids: Gospel Truth Ministries, 1985.

McRay, John. Archaeology & The New Testament. Grand Rapids, MI: Baker Book House, 2003.

Mears, Henrietta C. What the Bible Is All About. Ventura, CA: Regal Books, 1998.

Missler, Chuck. "Footprints of the Messiah." Audiocassette. Koinonia House, 1991.

Sheler, Jeffery L. *Is the Bible True?: How Modern Debates and Discoveries Affirm the Essence of the Scriptures.* San Francisco, CA: Harper, San Francisco, 1999.

Stoner, Peter. Science Speaks. Chicago: Moody Press, 1958. Ed. Donald W. Stoner. 2002. 30 March 2005 <http://www.geocities.com/stonerdon/science_speaks.html#c2>.

Strobel, Lee, The Case for Christ, Grand Rapids, MI 49530, Zondervan, 1998.

Tacitus, Cornelius. The Annals. Ed. Robert Maynard Hutchins. Great Books of the Western World 15. Chicago: Encyclopedia Britannica, Inc., 1952.

Walvoord, John F. Every Prophecy of the Bible. Colorado Springs, CO: Chariot Victor Publishing, 1999.

Wilkins, Michael J., and James Porter Moreland. *Jesus under Fire: Modern Scholarship Reinvents the Historical Jesus.* Grand Rapids, MI: Zondervan, 1995

Yancey, Philip. A Guided Tour of the Bible. Grand Rapids: Zondervan, 1989.

Lesson 5: Was Jesus Christ Resurrected? Why Does It Matter?

The intellect is not the enemy of faith!   – Don Beirle[1]

A. What does Scripture say about the resurrection?

1. 1 Corinthians 15:1-8 *"Now, brothers, I want to remind you of the gospel I preached to you, which you received and on which you have taken your stand. By this gospel you are saved, if you hold firmly to the word I preached to you. Otherwise, you have believed in vain. For what I received I passed on to you as of first importance: that Christ died for our sins according to the Scriptures, that he was buried, that he was raised on the third day according to the Scriptures, and that he appeared to Peter, and then to the Twelve. After that, he appeared to more than five hundred of the brothers at the same time, most of whom are still living, though some have fallen asleep. Then he appeared to James, then to all the apostles, and last of all he appeared to me also, as to one abnormally born."*

2. 1 Corinthians 15:12-19 *"But if it is preached that Christ has been raised from the dead, how can some of you say that there is no resurrection of the dead? If there is no resurrection of the dead, then not even Christ has been raised. And if Christ has not been raised, our preaching is useless and so is your faith. More than that, we are then found to be false witnesses about God, for we have testified about God that he raised Christ from the dead. But he did not raise him if in fact the dead are not raised. For if the dead are not raised, then Christ has not been raised either. And if Christ has not been raised, your faith is futile; you are still in your sins. Then those also who have fallen asleep in Christ are lost. If only for this life we have hope in Christ, we are to be pitied more than all men."*

B. Through the death and resurrection of Jesus Christ, we see:

1. Christ's love.

2. Christ's deity.

3. Christ's desire to have a relationship with us.

4. Christ's conquering death, which gives those who believe hope of eternal Life.

1. **Jesus foretold that He would die and be raised again.**

   a. Mark 8:31-32

   b. Mark 10:33-34

2. **Jesus said that He was God. Jews saw it as blasphemy and wanted to get rid of Christ.**

   a. John 10:31-33

3. **Jesus prays in the garden before His death. (Thursday)**

   a. Mark 14:32-36

   b. John 17:20-26

4. **The arrest: another proof of the deity of Christ (Thursday)**

   a. John 18:2-13

   b. Luke 22:49-51

5. **Accusations against Christ (Friday) (six trials - three Roman and three Jewish)**

   a. Luke 23:13-15

6. **The custom of whipping**

   a. Matthew 27:26-31

   b. After the verdict of crucifixion had been pronounced by the court, it was customary to tie the accused to a post at the tribunal. The criminal was stripped of his clothes, and severely whipped by the lictors, or scourgers.

The Death and Burial of Jesus Christ

1. **The cross**

   a. John 19:31-34

   b. A man condemned to be crucified had to carry his own crossbar from prison to the place of his execution. A long piece of wood used for barring doors, known as a patibulum, was commonly used for this purpose. The patibulum weighed approximately 110 pounds and was strapped to the victim's shoulders.

   c. When the authorities wanted to hasten death or terminate the torture, the victim's legs were broken below the knees with a club. This prevented him from pushing himself upward to relieve the tension on the pectoral or chest muscles. Either rapid suffocation or coronary insufficiency followed. In the case of Christ, the legs of the two thieves crucified with Him were broken, but Christ's were not, because the executioners observed He already was dead.

2. The burial (Friday PM)

a. Mark 15:42-45

b. The body of Christ was placed in a new tomb hewn out of a solid rock, in a private burial area. Jewish tombs usually had an entrance 4½ to 5 feet high. Most tombs, or sepulchers, of this period had a forecourt that led into the burial chamber. A rectangular pit in the center of the burial chamber enabled one to stand upright.

3. Jewish burial customs

a. John 19:39-40

b. Aromatic spices composed of fragments of fragrant wood pounded into a dust, known as aloes, were mixed with a gummy substance known as myrrh. Starting at the feet, they would wrap the body with the linen cloth. Between the folds were placed the spices, mixed with the gummy substance.

4. The very large stone

a. Matthew 27:59-60

b. The size of stone needed to roll against a 4½ to 5 foot doorway would have to have had a minimum weight of 1½ to 2 tons.

5. Roman security guard and the seal

a. Matthew 27:62-66

b. This seal could only be placed on the stone in the presence of the Roman guards who were left in charge. After the guard inspected the tomb and rolled the stone in place, a cord was stretched across the rock.

c. A Roman guard unit was a 4-to-16-man security force.

Numerous religious fears and political motives caused both the Jews and the Roman governor, Pontius Pilate, to kill Jesus Christ.

To make sure He remained dead and buried, six important security precautions were taken:

1. Christ was put to death by crucifixion, one of the most effective, cruel and hideous methods of execution ever devised.

2. The body of Christ was buried in a solid rock tomb.

3. Christ's body was wrapped with more than 100 pounds of spices according to precise, Jewish burial customs.

4. The stone rolled in front of the tomb entrance weighed about two tons.

5. The tomb was sealed shut with the official authority and signet of Rome.

6. A Roman security guard, one of the most effective fighting units devised, was positioned to guard the tomb.

Jesus' disciples returned to the city of Jerusalem to preach. If their teaching was false, their message would have been easily disproved. The resurrection account would not have been believed for a moment, in Jerusalem, if the tomb had not been empty.

1. **The stone was removed uphill. (Sunday)**

   a. John 20:1

   b. The verb for "taken away" in the Greek manuscript is "airo," which means "to pick something up and carry it away."[2]

2. **The Roman guards go AWOL.**

   a. Matthew 28:11-15

   b. If the soldiers were sleeping, how could they say the disciples stole the body?

3. **Grave clothes tell a tale.**

   a. John 20:3-9

   b. A glance at these grave clothes proved the reality, and indicated the nature, of the resurrection. They had been neither touched, nor folded, nor manipulated by any human being. They were like a discarded chrysalis, or cocoon, from which the butterfly has emerged.

4. **The women saw Him first.**

   a. Luke 24:9-11

   b. According to Jewish principles of legal evidence, women were invalid. They did not have a right to give testimony in a court of law. Therefore, if the resurrection accounts had been manufactured, women would never have been included in the story, at least, not as first witnesses.

5. **Christ's appearances were confirmed by eyewitnesses.**

   a. 1 Corinthians 15:3-8

   b. Concerning the first-hand accounts of other eyewitnesses, Paul says in effect, "If you do not believe me, you can ask them."

   c. When the disciples of Jesus proclaimed the resurrection, they did so as eyewitnesses, and they did so while people were still alive who had contact with the events about which they spoke. In 56 AD, Paul wrote that over 500 people had seen the risen Jesus and that most of them were still alive (1 Corinthians 15:6). As Thomas Hale points out, "If Jesus had, in fact, not risen from the dead, Paul could not have written these words; there were too many people still around who would have called him a liar!"[3]

d. It passes the bounds of credibility that the early Christians could have manufactured such a tale, and then preached it among those who might easily have refuted it, simply by producing the body of Jesus.

e. Acts 1:3-4

IN SUMMARY

The dramatic fact of the resurrection changed the course of history. Two thousand years later, man is still not the same. Critics who wish to deny the resurrection of Jesus Christ must adequately explain away seven historical facts:

1. The feared power of Rome was ignored by the breaking of the Roman seal at the tomb.

2. Both the Jews and the Romans admitted that the tomb was empty.

3. A two-ton stone was somehow moved from the tomb entrance while a Roman guard stood watch.

4. A highly disciplined Roman military guard fled their watch and had to be bribed by the authorities to lie about what actually happened.

5. The undisturbed grave clothes no longer contained a body.

6. Christ subsequently appeared to as many as 500 witnesses at one time in a variety of situations.

7. Because of the low Jewish view of the reliability of women, manufacturers of a resurrection story would never have selected them to be the first witnesses to the fact.

Attempted Explanations

---

1. Unknown Tomb Theory

a. This theory argues that the executioners probably cast the body into an unknown burial pit.

b. What is the error in this explanation?

2. The Wrong Tomb Theory

a. This explanation is similar to the first theory. It advocates that when the women returned on Sunday morning to honor Christ, they went to the wrong tomb.

b. What is the error in this explanation?

c. If the women had gone to the wrong tomb, who else would have had to go to the wrong tomb? (Even if the women, the disciples, the Romans and the Jews all went to the wrong tomb, one thing is sure: Joseph of Arimathea would not have gone to the wrong tomb, because he owned it.)

3. Stolen by Disciples

  a. This explanation was promoted by the chief priests and religious leaders and has been circulated to this day (Matthew 28:11-15).

  b. What is the error in this explanation?

4. Authorities Stole the Body

  a. This theory alleges that the Roman or Jewish authorities took the body and put it in safekeeping, so there could be no deception by anyone suggesting that Jesus was resurrected from the dead.

  b. What is the error in this explanation?

5. The Resuscitation Theory (Swoon Theory)

  a. This theory suggests that Jesus didn't really die on the cross. They don't deny that He was nailed to the cross and suffered from shock, pain and loss of blood, but instead of dying, they claim that He merely fainted (swooned) from exhaustion. The disciples, mistaking Him for dead, then buried Him alive. The cold sepulcher in which He was placed revived Him. His disciples were so ignorant; they couldn't believe mere resuscitation revived Him, so they insisted it was a resurrection from the dead.

  b. This theory would have to say that Jesus:

  • went through six trials - three Roman and three Jewish.

  • was beaten almost beyond description with the Roman flagrum.

  • was so weak He could not carry his own patibulum (wooden cross bar).

  • had spikes driven through His hands and feet as He was crucified.

  • had a sword thrust in His side by the Romans.

  • had his executioners confirm his death - they must have been mistaken.

  • had 100-plus pounds of spices and a gummy substance encased around His body. (He must have breathed through it all.)

  • was put into a cold, damp tomb.

  • had a large stone lodged against the entrance of His tomb.

  • had a Roman guard stationed there, and a seal was placed across the entrance.

  c. What is the error in this explanation?

1. **Changed lives of disciples**

   a. As Dr. D. James Kennedy reminds us, "In the history of psychology it has never been known that a person was willing to give up life for what he or she knew to be a lie." The gruesome deaths of the disciples are further evidence of the truth of the resurrection.

2. **The Church began**

   a. Within a few weeks after Jesus' resurrection, Peter preached at Pentecost, and the Christian church was born, with 3,000 new converts added on that first day (Acts 2:41).

3. **Celebration of Easter instead of Passover**

   a. In the Old Testament, the Jewish people celebrated Passover every year to commemorate their escape from Egypt. At that time, God required that they sacrifice the blood of an animal and put the blood on the door frames of their homes. When the destroyer of the Lord passed through the land, he did not kill the firstborn of the Israelite families who had blood on their door frames, but instead, "passed over" them (Exodus 11-12).

   b. When Jesus went to the cross, He became the sacrificial lamb for all of humanity. Therefore, sacrifices were no longer needed. That is why we now celebrate Easter, instead of the Passover, because the debt has been paid (Hebrews 7:27, 10:1-18).

4. **Historical evidence supporting the resurrection of Jesus Christ**

   a. Professor Thomas Arnold, author of the three-volume History of Rome and an appointee to the chair of modern history at Oxford University, writes,

   "The evidence for our Lord's life and death and resurrection may be, and often has been, shown to be satisfactory; it is good according to the common rules for distinguishing good evidence from bad. Thousands and tens of thousands of persons have gone through it piece by piece, as carefully as every judge summing up on a most important case. I have myself done it many times over, not to persuade others, but to satisfy myself. I have been used for many years to study the histories of other times, and to examine and weigh the evidence of those who have written about them. I know of no one fact in the history of mankind which is proved by better and fuller evidence of every sort, to the understanding of a fair inquirer, than the great sign which God had given us that Christ died and rose again from the dead."[4]

   b. Likewise, author Dr. D. James Kennedy in his book, *Why I Believe*, writes:

   "The evidence for the resurrection of Jesus Christ has been examined more carefully than the evidence for any other fact in history. It has been weighed and considered by the greatest of scholars, among them Simon Greenleaf, the Royal professor of law at Harvard from 1833 to 1848 who helped bring Harvard Law School to preeminence, and who has been called the greatest authority on legal evidences in the history of the world. When Greenleaf turned his mind upon the resurrection of Christ and focused upon it the light of all the laws of evidence, he concluded that the resurrection of Christ was a reality, that it was a historical event, and that anyone who examined the evidence for it honestly would be convinced this was the case."[5]

5. Impact on you and me

a. What happened on the cross reflects all of the attributes and character of God. Know and understand the cross and then you will know God.

b. Lloyd John Ogilvie captures this idea in the March 18 devotional reading from *God's Best for My Life:*

"Love means the cross. God's mercy was expressed in the cross. He did not condemn the world, but came in forgiving love. Becoming a Christian means a deathlike surrender of our life to Christ. We die to our own rights, control of our life, and plans for our future. We will to be willing to receive, do, go, stay, speak, and serve as He wills. Christ then comes to live within us to express His loving mercy for others through us.

"The cross becomes the basis of our relationships. Our time, energy, resources, and skill are put at Christ's disposal for others. We forgive because we have been forgiven. People do not need to measure up any more than we had to measure up in order for God to love us. We take on the troubles, frustrations, and problems of others as Christ took the cross. Because we have died, we have nothing to lose and everything to give."[6]

c. Paul Little, in his classic book, *Know Why You Believe*, says,

"Either Jesus did or did not rise from the dead. If he did, it was the most sensational event in all of history and gives us conclusive answers to the most profound questions of our existence:

- From where have we come?
- Why are we here?
- What is our future destiny?

"If Christ rose, we know with certainty that God exists, what he is like and that he cares for each of us individually. The universe, then, takes on meaning and purpose and we can experience the living God in contemporary life."[7]

d. In *Six Hours One Friday*, Max Lucado writes,

"Those six hours were no normal six hours. They were the most critical hours in history. For during those six hours on that Friday, God embedded in the earth three anchor points sturdy enough to withstand any hurricane.

"Anchor point #1 – My life is not futile...there is truth. Someone is in control and I have a purpose.

"Anchor point #2 – My failures are not fatal...The one who has the right to condemn you provided the way to acquit you. You make mistakes. God doesn't. And he made you.

"Anchor point #3 – My death is not final...He only went into the tomb to prove he could come out. And on the way out, he took the stone with him and turned it into an anchor point. He dropped it deep into the uncharted waters of death."

6. Knowing what Jesus did for you, how would you frame Him?

e. And in *He Chose the Nails,* Lucado pens this poem:[9]

> The diadem of pain
>
> which sliced your gentle face,
>
> three spikes piercing flesh and wood
>
> to hold you in your place.
>
> The need for blood I understand.
>
> Your sacrifice I embrace.
>
> But the bitter sponge, the cutting spear,
>
> and the spit upon your face?
>
> Did it have to be a cross?
>
> Did not a kinder death exist
>
> than six hours hanging between life and death,
>
> all spurred by a betrayer's kiss?
>
> "Oh, Father," you pose,
>
> heart-stilled at what could be,
>
> "I'm sorry to ask, but I long to know,
>
> did you do this for me?"
>
> ...Pause and listen.
>
> Perchance you will hear Him whisper:
>
> "I did it just for you."
>
> Max Lucado

Conclusion

If Christ did not rise from the dead, then Christ is at best, as C.S. Lewis says, a liar or lunatic. After studying the historical accounts of the death and resurrection of Jesus Christ, there is absolutely no possibility that Christ was left in a tomb. Because of the overwhelming proof, we know that He lives and provides the hope for all believers, that when our bodies die we, like Christ, will live again. Praise be to God! What an awesome God we worship!

There was little question with the disciples that Jesus Christ died and rose again. These external writings help us all as Christians be bold in our defending and sharing of our faith in the death and resurrection of our Lord!

Josephus – renowned Jewish historian:

> "Now there was about this time Jesus, a wise man, if it be lawful to call him a man; for he was a doer of wonderful works, a teacher of such men as receive the truth with pleasure. He drew over to him many Jews, and also many of the Greeks. This man was the Christ. And when Pilate had condemned him to the cross, upon his impeachment by the principal man among us, those who had loved him from the first did not forsake him, for he appeared to them alive on the third day, the divine prophets having spoken these and thousands of other wonderful things about him. And even now, the race of Christians, so named from him, has not died out."[10]

Cornelius Tacitus – born Circa AD 52-55. Senator under the reign of Vespasian. Later held the office of consul and in the years 112-13 was proconsul, or governor, of Asia. Considered the most reliable of historians, he writes in The Annals:

> "...Nero fastened the guilt and inflicted the most exquisite tortures on a class hated for their abominations, called Christians by the populace. Christus, from whom the name had its origin, suffered the extreme penalty during the reign of Tiberius at the hands of one of our procurators, Pontius Pilatus, and a most mischievous superstition, thus checked for the moment, again broke out not only in Judaea, the first source of the evil, but even in Rome, where all things hideous and shameful from every part of the world find their centre and become popular. Accordingly, an arrest was first made of all who pleaded guilty; then, upon their information, an immense multitude was convicted, not so much of the crime of firing the city, as of hatred against mankind. Mockery of every sort was added to their deaths. Covered with the skins of beasts, they were torn by dogs and perished, or were nailed to crosses, or were doomed to the flames and burnt, to serve as a nightly illumination, when daylight had expired."[11]

Lucian of Samosata – writing circa AD 170. A Greek satirist, Lucian wrote of the early Christians and of "their lawgiver" in The Death of the Peregrine:

> "The Christians, you know, worship a man to this day - the distinguished personage who introduced their novel rites, and was crucified on that account...you see, these misguided creatures start with the general conviction that they are immortal for all time, which explains the contempt of death and voluntary self-devotion which are so common among them; and then it was impressed on them by their original lawgiver that they are all brothers, from the moment that they are converted, and deny the gods of Greece, and worship the crucified sage, and live after his laws. All this they take quite on faith, with the result that they despise all worldly goods alike, regarding them merely as common property."[12]

Lesson 5: Was Jesus Christ Resurrected? Why Does It Matter? - Anchorsaway Worldview Handbook ©

Lesson 5: Was Jesus Christ Resurrected?
Why Does It Matter?

Small Group Objective:

The goal is to reinforce with the students that the resurrection of Jesus Christ is scripturally and historically true. The questions are designed to emphasize this, so that they will not only be able to answer those who ask why they believe in the resurrection, but, also, to help them understand its significance for their own life. The resurrection of Christ is the central event of the Christian faith, and, hopefully, the students will develop a greater appreciation for Christ and what He accomplished for us through His death and resurrection.

✓ Check Points:

☐ Bring 3 x 5 cards for your students to write down any questions they may have which aren't answered during the discussion.

☐ Enlist a student to share a brief personal testimony.

Discussion Questions:

1. Review prayer requests from the week before and ask how the students are doing.

2. Lead a time of discussion, asking the following questions:

(Note: Work through as many of the following questions as possible. The goal is not to get through all of them, but to encourage each student to participate in the discussion as part of the learning process.)

   a. What day of the devotional did you find most meaningful?

   b. How did last week's lesson impact your life? Did you share it?

   c. Are there any answers to prayer this week? Does this prove that Jesus lives?

   d. Why is the resurrection so critical to the Christian?

   e. What does the resurrection show about : the character of God, His love, His deity, and his desire to have a relationship with us?

   f. Use the Four Deadly Questions to explore the claim that Jesus showed His deity through the death and resurrection.

g. Jesus paid the penalty of sin, which is death, when He died on the cross for each of us. Does this mean that there are no consequences to sin? Why/why not?

h. What do you think it means to die to yourself?

i. What hope do I have because of the resurrection of Christ?

j. How might my life be different this week because of the resurrection of Christ?

k. If you were to write a thank you note to Jesus what might it say?

l. What questions, if any, come to mind as a result of this week's lesson?

3. Ask for prayer requests and tell students that you will be faithful to pray for them during the week. Encourage students to record the prayer requests in the prayer request section of their handbooks, so they can pray for one another during the week. Begin the prayer time by sharing your own request. Spend the remaining time in prayer.

★ **After the Session**

1. Contact each small group member during the week. Ask them about their devotional time, a question they have raised, or how their week is going.

<u>**Prayer Requests**</u>

Student Devotionals written by T.M. Moore

Was Jesus Christ Resurrected? Why Does It Matter?

The resurrection of Jesus is a central doctrine of the Christian life. We need to understand that this important event is not only recorded in the New Testament, but was predicted in the Old, as well. Let your prayers during these devotionals dwell on the power of God revealed in the resurrection of Jesus, and on the implications of that power for your life now and in the days to come. Remember that the prayers provided are just to get you started. Take time to let them lead you in whatever direction, to whatever prayers the Spirit of God may suggest. Don't be in a hurry.

Day 1: Isaiah and the Resurrection of Jesus

Pray:
"'As for me, I have set my King on Zion, my holy hill.' I will tell of the decree: The LORD said to me, 'You are my Son; today I have begotten you'" (Psalm 2:7).

Read:
Isaiah 53:1-10

Meditate:
Which part of this passage seems to indicate that the suffering Servant would once again live after He had suffered for our sins?

After that, after the Servant comes to life again, what does God promise will happen?

Is this happening in my life? In what ways? How do others see this evidence of the risen Christ at work in me?

Journal:
I want the will of the Lord, in the power of Jesus' resurrected life, to prosper in me today. Therefore, I will need to...

Pray:
"Then my tongue shall tell of your righteousness and of your praise all the day long" (Psalm 35:28).

Day 2: Job's Hope for Resurrection

Pray: *"For with the LORD there is steadfast love, and with him is plentiful redemption"*
(Psalm 130:7).

Read: Job 14:1-14; Job 19:23-27

Meditate: Do people I know think about what will happen to them after they die? Who? Whom can I ask about this today?

In the second reading, what did Job say he knew? Did Job believe that he would see his living Redeemer after he had died? How did he express this?

Do I really expect to see the risen Christ after I have died? Why do I believe this? What will it be like to see Him face-to-face?

Journal: Jesus is risen from the dead; He is alive today. One day I am going to see Him as He is, face-to-face. Knowing this day is coming, not only for me, but for my friends, as well...

Pray: *"As for me, I shall behold your face in righteousness; when I awake, I shall be satisfied with your likeness"* (Psalm 17:15).

Day 3: Because He Lives

Pray: *"You make known to me the path of life; in your presence there is fullness of joy; at your right hand are pleasures forevermore"* (Psalm 16:11).

Read: Psalm 16; Acts 2:22-28

Meditate: How did Peter, in Acts 2, interpret David's ecstatic vision in Psalm 16?

How did knowing that God's Holy One would not "see corruption" affect David (Psalm 16:9, 10)? How did it affect Peter and the other disciples in Acts 2? Does it affect me in this way? Why or why not?

If I could keep a vision of the resurrected Jesus always before my mind throughout the day, how might that affect the way others see me?

Journal: Jesus Christ is alive! How happy and excited this makes me! What a wondrous promise it holds out for me after I have died! I want everyone I know to know that...

Pray: *"The LORD is my chosen portion and my cup; you hold my lot. The lines have fallen for me in pleasant places; indeed, I have a beautiful inheritance"* (Psalm 16:6).

Day 4: What John Saw on the Isle of Patmos

Pray: *"You are the most handsome of the sons of men; grace is poured upon your lips; therefore God has blessed you forever"* (Psalm 45:2).

Read: Revelation 1:9-20

Meditate: How would I feel if I had seen what John saw?

                Do I ever think of the risen Christ like this? Should I? If I did, if I could envision Jesus like this more consistently, how might it affect me?

                What about this vision of Jesus is most striking to me? What does this mean to suggest to me about the risen Christ? What is the significance of this for my life?

Journal: The risen, powerful, "most handsome" Jesus has His hand on me today. Therefore, I expect...

Pray: *"Your throne, O God, is forever and ever. The scepter of your kingdom is a scepter of uprightness; you have loved righteousness and hated wickedness"* (Psalm 45:6).

Day 5: A Little Chat with Jesus

Pray: *"For with you is the fountain of life; in your light do we see light"* (Psalm 36:9).

Read: Luke 24:13-25

Meditate: Jesus took these two disciples on a "whirlwind tour" of the Old Testament. What was the central theme of His teaching? Have I seen something of that from the Old Testament this week?

                      What did it take for these two disciples to "see" the resurrected Jesus (v. 31)? How does that happen (John 6:63)? What does this suggest about how my unsaved friends can come to "see" Jesus?

                      I can see two responses that these friends made to their little chat with Jesus (vv. 32-34). What were they? Is this the way I respond to Him? Why or why not?

Journal: I want my heart to "burn" with love for the resurrected Jesus, and I want to tell everyone I know about Him. Today is as good a day as any to begin. So...

Pray: *"I lift my eyes to the hill. From where does my help come? My help comes from the LORD, who made heaven and earth"* (Psalm 131:1, 2).

ENDNOTES

1. Adapted from Don Bierle, Surprised by Faith (Lynnwood, WA: Emerald Books, 1992) 8.
2. W. E. Vine, An Expository Dictionary of New Testament Words (Nashville, TN: Thomas Nelson Publishers, 1996) 616.
3. Thomas Hale, The Applied New Testament Commentary (Colorado Springs, CO: Victor Books, 1996) 682.
4. Josh McDowell, Evidence That Demands a Verdict vol. 1 (1979; Nashville: Thomas Nelson Publishers, 1999) 190-191.
5. D. James Kennedy, Why I Believe (Nashville, TN: W Publishing Group, 1999) 135.
6. Lloyd John Ogilvie, God's Best for My Life (Eugene, OR: Harvest House Publishers, 1981) 18.
7. Paul E. Little, Know Why You Believe 5th ed. (Colorado Springs, CO: Victor Books, 2003) 37.
8. Max Lucado, 25.
9. Max Lucado, He Chose the Nails (Nashville, TN: Word Publishing, 2000) 8-9.
10. Josh McDowell, 187.
11. Cornelius Tacitus, The Annals, ed. Robert Maynard Hutchins, Great Books of the Western World 15 (Chicago: Encyclopedia Britannica, 1952) 168.
12. Matthew J. Slick, "Non biblical accounts of New Testament events and/or people," Christian Apologetics and Research Ministry 31 March 2005 <http://www.carm.org/bible/extrabiblical_accounts.htm>.

Recommended Reading

Key Books:

Boa, Ken, and Larry Moody. I'm Glad You Asked. Colorado Springs, CO: Victor Books/SP Publications, 1994.

Carson, D. A. Scandalous: The Cross and Resurrection of Jesus. Wheaton, IL: Crossway, 2010.

Carson, D. A. Jesus the Son of God: A Christological Title Often Overlooked, Sometimes Misunderstood, and Currently Disputed. Wheaton, IL: Crossway, 2012

Davis, C. Truman. "A Physician Analyzes Crucifixion." Arizona Medicine. March 1965. Arizona Medical Association 31 March 2005. <http://www.restoredword.org/a_physician_analyzes_ the_crucifi.htm>.

Habermas, Gary R., and Gary R. Habermas. The Historical Jesus: Ancient Evidence for the Life of Christ. Joplin, MO: College Pub., 1996.

Hanegraff, Hank. Resurrection. Nashville, TN: W Publishing Group, 2000.

Kennedy, D. James. Why I Believe. Nashville, TN: W Publishing Group, 1999.

Little, Paul. Know Why You Believe. 5th ed. Colorado Springs, CO: Victor Books, 2003.

Lucado, Max. He Chose the Nails. Nashville, TN: Word Publishing, 2000.

Lucado, Max. Six Hours One Friday: Anchoring to the Cross. Portland: Multnomah, 1989.

McDowell, Josh. Evidence That Demands a Verdict. Vol. 1. 1979. Nashville, TN: Thomas Nelson Publishers, 1999.

Ogilvie, Lloyd John. God's Best for My Life. Eugene, OR: Harvest House Publishers, 1981.

Wilkins, Michael J., and James Porter Moreland Jesus under Fire: Modern Scholarship Reinvents the

Lesson 5: Was Jesus Christ Resurrected? Why Does It Matter? - Anchorsaway Worldview Handbook ©

Lesson 6: Is Jesus Christ God? What Is the Trinity?

⚓ **Anchor of the Week: Jesus is God.**

I. What is the Trinity? Trinity means, "tri-unity" or "three-in-oneness." [1]

A Brief Definition of the Trinity by Dr. James White

I know that one of the most oft-repeated questions I have dealt with is, "How does one explain, or even understand, the doctrine of the Trinity?" Indeed, few topics are made such a football by various groups that, normally, claim to be the "only" real religion, and who prey upon Christians as "convert fodder." Be that as it may, when the Christian is confronted with this difficult issue of the Trinity, how might it best be explained?

For me, simplifying the doctrine to its most basic elements has been very important and very useful. When we reduce the discussion to the three clear Biblical teachings that underline the Trinity, we can move our discussion from the abstract to the concrete Biblical data, and can help those involved in false religions to recognize which of the Biblical teachings it is denying.

We must first remember that very few have a good idea of what the Trinity is in the first place. Hence, accuracy in definition will be very important. <u>The doctrine of the Trinity is simply that there is one eternal being of God – indivisible and infinite. This one being of God is shared by three co-equal, co-eternal persons: the Father, the Son, and the Spirit.</u>

It is necessary here to distinguish between the terms "being" and "person." It would be a contradiction to say there are three beings within one being, or three persons within one person. So what is the difference? We clearly recognize the difference between being and person every day. We recognize what something is, yet we also recognize individuals within a classification. For example, we speak of the "being" of man – human being. A rock has "being" – the being of a rock, as does a cat, a dog, etc. Yet, we also know there are personal attributes, as well. That is, we recognize both "what" and "who" when we talk about a person.

<u>The Bible tells us there are three classifications of personal beings – God, man, and angels. What is personality? The ability to have emotion, will, and being able to express oneself.</u> Rocks cannot speak. Cats cannot think of themselves over others and work for the common good of "cat kind." Thus, we are saying that there is one eternal, infinite being of God shared fully and completely by three persons, Father, Son and Spirit. One what, three who's.

NOTE: We are *not* saying that the Father is the Son, or the Son the Spirit, or the Spirit the Father. It is very common for people to misunderstand the doctrine as to mean that we are saying Jesus is the Father. The doctrine of the Trinity does not in any way say this!

The three Biblical doctrines that flow directly into the river that is the Trinity are as follows:

1. There is one and only one God, eternal, immutable.

2. There are three eternal Persons described in Scripture – the Father, the Son, and the Spirit. These Persons are never identified as one in the same – that is, they are clearly differentiated as Persons.

3. The Father, the Son, and the Spirit are identified as being fully deity – that is, the Bible teaches the Deity of Christ and the Deity of the Holy Spirit.

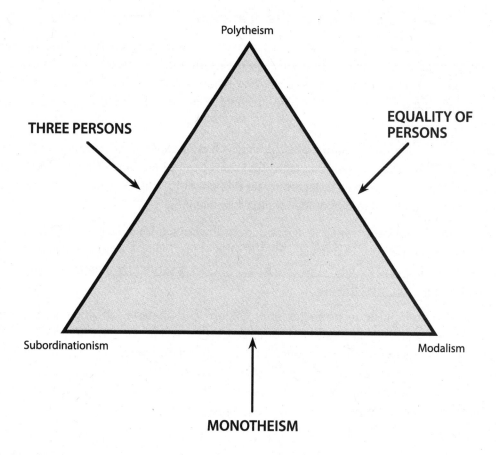

One can represent this as follows: The three sides of the triangle represent the three biblical doctrines, as labeled. When one denies any of these three teachings, the other two sides point to the result. Hence, if one denies that there are Three Persons, one is left with the two sides of Full Equality and Oneness, resulting in the "Oneness" teaching of the United Pentecostal Church and others. If one denies Full Equality, one is left with Three Persons and One God, resulting in "subordinationism" as seen in Jehovah's Witnesses, the Way International, etc. (though to be perfectly accurate, the Witnesses deny all three of the sides in some way – they deny Full Equality)

(i.e. Jesus is Michael the Archangel), Three Persons (the Holy Spirit is an impersonal, active "force" like electricity) and One God (they say Jesus is "a god" – a lesser divinity than Yahweh; hence they are in reality not monotheists but henotheists). And, if one denies One God, one is left with polytheism, the belief in many gods, as seen clearly in the Mormon Church, the most polytheistic religion I have encountered.[2]

II. Where do we see the Trinity in Scripture?

A. Creation:

1. Genesis 1:1-2 *"In the beginning God created the heavens and the earth. Now the earth was formless and empty, darkness was over the surface of the deep, and the Spirit of God was hovering over the waters"* (See also John 1:1-3, 17:5).

2. John 1:1-3 *"In the beginning was the Word, and the Word was with God, and the Word was God. He was with God in the beginning. Through him all things were made; without him nothing was made that has been made."*

B. Christ's birth:

1. Luke 1:30-35 *"But the angel said to her, 'Do not be afraid, Mary, you have found favor with God. You will be with child and give birth to a son, and you are to give him the name Jesus. He will be great and will be called the Son of the Most High. The Lord God will give him the throne of his father David....'*

   "'How will this be,' Mary asked the angel, 'since I am a virgin?'

   "The angel answered, 'The Holy Spirit will come upon you, and the power of the Most High will overshadow you. So the holy one to be born will be called the Son of God.'"

2. (See mention of God in v. 30, Jesus in v. 31, and the Holy Spirit in v. 35.)

C. Christ's baptism:

1. Matthew 3:16-17 *"As soon as Jesus was baptized, he went up out of the water. At that moment heaven was opened, and he saw the Spirit of God descending like a dove and lighting on him. And a voice from heaven said, 'This is my Son, whom I love; with him I am well pleased'"* (See also Mark 1:10-11; Luke 3:21-22).

D. The Great Commission:

1. Matthew 28:19 *"'Therefore go and make disciples of all nations, baptizing them in the name of the Father and of the Son and of the Holy Spirit....'"*

E. Other scriptural references to the Trinity:

1. 2 Corinthians 13:14 *"May the grace of the Lord Jesus Christ, and the love of God, and the fellowship of the Holy Spirit be with you all."*

2. Ephesians 1:17 *"I keep asking that the God of our Lord Jesus Christ, the glorious Father, may give you the Spirit of wisdom and revelation, so that you may know him better"* (See also John 14:26; 1 Corinthians 12:4-6; Ephesians 4:4-6; 1 Peter 1:2; Jude 20-21).

III. What is the significance of the Trinity for us?

A. One of the foundational beliefs of Christianity, which sets it apart from all other religious cults and belief systems, is the conviction that Jesus is truly God. In no way does Jesus play a supporting role to the Father, and the Holy Spirit. He is fully God, just as they are, and equal member of the Trinity.

IV. Who is the Holy Spirit?

A. The Holy Spirit is not an "it." He is God (Matt. 28:1; 2 Cor. 3:16-18; Eph. 4:4-6).

B. Because Christ paid the penalty for our sin, we have restored relationship with God. God wants to be in a personal relationship with each of us on a moment-by-moment basis, which is why He has given us Himself, the Holy Spirit, to dwell in us. This is the new Covenant.

C. The primary function of the Holy Spirit is the person of the Trinity who is actively present with us in the world.

D. The Holy Spirit: (Not an inclusive list)

1. gives life (John 6:63)

2. empowers (1 Samuel 16:13; Matthew 3:16; Acts 1:8)

3. protects (Ephesians 6:17)

4. cleanses us (1 John 1:9)

5. convicts the world of sin (John 16:8-11)

6. guides (Matthew 4:1; Luke 4:1)

7. scriptural support (Luke 24:49; John 14:26; Romans 8:9b)

V. Common questions/challenges regarding the Deity of Christ

A. Do Other Religions Believe That Jesus Christ is God?

1. Answer: The major issue that separates Christianity from all other religions and cults is this: All other religions deny that Jesus is truly God.

B. Is Jesus Christ God?

1. Jesus Christ is unique:

a. He founded His religion on Himself, not on some random teaching or dream as other religions do.

b. He is the only perfect person who ever lived (Hebrews 4:15).

    c. He never needed to:

        i. Confess a sin (Hebrews 4:15)

        ii. Repent of anything (Hebrews 7:27)

        iii. Apologize to anyone for anything

    d. Other people proclaimed His divinity (Isaiah 7:14, 9:6; Matthew 16:16; John 1:29, 20:28).

    e. He claimed to be God (Luke 8:38-39; John 8:53-58 tied to Exodus 3:14; John 10:22-33).

    f. He was the Messiah, the God man (Matthew 16:13-17, 22:41-46).

    g. He is the I AM (John 8:53-58 tied to Exodus 3:14).

    h. He has authority to forgive us for our sins (Luke 5:17-26).

    i. He has authority over death (Luke 7:11-16).

    j. He offers eternal life freely (John 5:21; 10:27-28; 11:25-26).

2. Christ possesses the attributes of God. The following is a brief comparison between Christ and some of the attributes of God.

    a. **Omnipresence:**

        i. God: Psalm 139:7-10; Proverbs 15:3

        ii. Jesus: Matthew 18:20; Ephesians 4:10

    b. **Omniscience:**

        i. God: 1 Kings 8:39; Psalm 147:5

        ii. Jesus: Matthew 9:4; John 2:24-25

    c. **Omnipotence:**

        i. God: Psalm 62:11; Revelation 19:6

        ii. Jesus: Matthew 28:18; Hebrews 1:3

    d. **Eternal:**

        i. God: Psalm 102:26, 27; Deuteronomy 33:27

        ii. Jesus: Micah 5:2; John 8:58

    e. **Immutability:**

        i. God: Malachi 3:6; James 1:17

        ii. Jesus: Hebrews 1:10-13, 13:8

    f. **Sinless (perfection):**

        i. God: Exodus. 15:11; 1 Samuel 2:2

        ii. Jesus: John 8:46; 2 Corinthians 5:21; Hebrews 4:15

     g. **Holiness:**

        i. God: Leviticus 19:1-2; Psalm 99:9

        ii. Jesus: Luke 1:35; Acts 3:14

     h. **Love:**

        i. God: Deuteronomy 7:9; 1 John 4:8

        ii. Jesus: John 15:9; Ephesians 3:18

3. Jesus is Yahweh (God). Let's look at the biblical names of God. Does Jesus possess those same names?

    a. The references to Jesus are the same as those for God the Father.

    b. See "Jesus is Yahweh" chart.

C. If God is who He says He is, then why do we need Jesus? (Isn't God enough by Himself?)

1. Through Jesus we can know God.

    a. Matthew 11:27 "'All things have been committed to me by my Father. No one knows the Son except the Father, and no one knows the Father except the Son and those to whom the Son chooses to reveal him.'"

    b. John 1:1-2, 14 "In the beginning was the Word, and the Word was with God, and the Word was God...The Word became flesh and made his dwelling among us."

    c. John 8:19 *"Then they asked him, 'Where is your father?' 'You do not know me or my Father,' Jesus replied. 'If you knew me, you would know my Father also.'"*

    d. John 10:30 "'I and the Father are one.'"

    e. John 14:9-11a *"Jesus answered: 'Don't you know me, Philip, even after I have been among you such a long time? Anyone who has seen me has seen the Father. How can you say, 'Show us the Father'? Don't you believe that I am in the Father and that the Father is in me? The words I say to you are not just my own. Rather, it is the Father, living in me, who is doing his work. Believe me when I say that I am in the Father and the Father is in me....'"*

    f. John 15:23 *"'He who hates me hates my Father as well.'"*

2. Only Jesus Christ is the mediator between sinful humanity (us) and a holy God. Without Jesus, we have no means of salvation.

    a. Luke 2:11 *"'Today in the town of David a Savior has been born to you; he is Christ the Lord.'"*

    b. John 10:28 *"'I give them eternal life, and they shall never perish....'"*

    c. 1 Timothy 2:5-6a *"For there is one God and one mediator between God and men, the man Christ Jesus, who gave himself as a ransom for all men...."*

d. Hebrews 7:25-27 *"Therefore he is able to save completely those who come to God through him, because he always lives to intercede for them. Such a high priest meets our need – one who is holy, blameless, pure, set apart from sinners, exalted above the heavens. Unlike the other high priests, he does not need to offer sacrifices day after day, first for his own sins, and then for the sins of the people. He sacrificed for their sins once for all when he offered himself."*

e. John 14:6 *"Jesus answered, 'I am the way and the truth and the life. No one comes to the Father except through me.'"*

f. 1 John 5:11-12 *"And this is the testimony: God has given us eternal life, and this life is in his Son. He who has the Son has life; he who does not have the Son of God does not have life."*

This chart is adapted from Kenneth Boa, Cults: World Religions and the Occult [3]

Christian Doctrine	Hinduism	Buddhism	Islam	Judaism
Jesus Christ John 1:1-3, 14; 8:58; Col. 1:16-20	No recognition of any kind given to Christ.	No recognition of any kind given to Christ.	Jesus Christ is nothing more than a prophet of God.	Rabbinic teaching holds that there must be two Messiahs: Son of Joseph, who would die: and Son of David, who would establish the kingdom on earth.
Tri-Unity Luke 3:21-22; 1 Peter 1:2; Matt. 28:19; John 15:26	God is an IT in Philosophical Hinduism, and in Popular Hinduism there are great multitudes of gods. In a sense: man is god.	No recognition of the Tri-Unity. Most Buddhist sects are polytheistic, pantheistic or atheistic.	There is only one god and that is Allah.	There is only one God and that is Yahweh.
Everyone has an eternal spirit Matt. 25:46; Dan. 12:2; Eccl. 2:7; Rev. 20:11-15	Yes and it continues through many incarnations.	Guatama, founder of Buddhism, claimed that men have no souls.	Yes	Yes
Born a Lost Soul Ps. 51:5; James 1:15; Romans 5:12-21; 1 Cor. 15:21-22	No recognition of sin and moral guilt. Sin is an illusion.	Guatama claimed that men do not have souls.	No	Judaism rejects the doctrine of original sin, saying that sin is an act, not a state.
Salvation John 3:14-17; Acts 16:31; Rom. 3: 21-30; 10:4, 9-10; Gal. 2:16	Hinduism is a works system. Forgiveness of sin does not fit into the picture of karma (cause and effect). Each person has many lives in which to reach salvation.	Theravada Buddhism: salvation by self-effort. Mahayana Buddhism: salvation of one dependent on the grace of others.	After the resurrection, each man's deeds will be weighed to determine his destiny - heaven or hell.	Man does not need redemption. Repentance (turning back to God) is all that is needed when one fails to live according to the law.
Sacred Books (Authority) The Holy Bible	Sruti-revealed script. Smriti-tradition. These groups of books contain many contradictions.	Buddhist scriptures and sayings attributed to Guatama were written about four centuries after his death and there is no way to be certain they are really his words.	Koran - most important, Tauret, Pentateuch of Moses, Zabur (Psalms of David), Injil (Evangel of Jesus)	The Torah, The Old Testament, The Talmud
Suggested approaches for presenting the Christian faith	Address the Hindu argument that all religions are the same. Emphasize the unique claims of Jesus. No other religion offers a real solution to the problem of sin. Books of the Bible are harmonious; Hindu scriptures contradict one another. Man is born as a lost human headed for hell because he inherited the sin of Adam.	Give a positive and clear exposition of the claims of Christ and His victory over sin and death. Christ offers salvation; Buddhism does not. Each person must work out his own salvation. Adjust and accommodate for the manner in which Buddhism has become embedded in the culture. Make a strong case for the Bible - archaeology, history and prophecy.	Christians must focus on the problem of sin, contrasting what God of the Bible has done about it, with what Allah has not done. Ask questions to determine views. Muslims have no personal relationship with God. Focus on the true deity of Jesus Christ, the lost nature of man, and the salvation offered by Jesus. Point out the error of works righteousness.	Original Christians were all Jews. Note that a Jew does not have to give up his Jewishness to become a Christian. Christianity is not a Gentile religion. NT was written by Jews (except Luke) and Jesus was a Jew. Emphasize Isaiah 53 as prophetic of Jesus' coming.

Is Jesus a liar, lunatic or God?

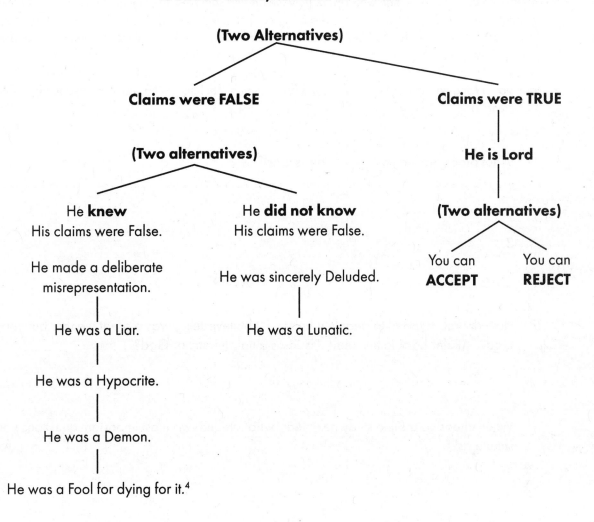

(Two Alternatives)

Claims were FALSE   **Claims were TRUE**

(Two alternatives)   **He is Lord**

He knew   **He did not know**   **(Two alternatives)**
His claims were False.   His claims were False.

He made a deliberate   He was sincerely Deluded.   You can   You can
misrepresentation.   **ACCEPT**   **REJECT**

He was a Liar.   He was a Lunatic.

He was a Hypocrite.

He was a Demon.

He was a Fool for dying for it.[4]

Some speak of Jesus as a great man. To some He was the founder of a new religion. Others consider him a prophet. But Jesus himself claimed that He was God. If this claim were not true, He could not be called even a good man, but would be an imposter and a liar.

The Chrisitan writer, C.S. Lewis, explains the significance of Christ's claims to diety:

"...Among these Jews there suddenly turns up a man who goes about talking as if He was God. He claims to forgive sins. He says He has always existed. He says He is coming to judge the world at the end of time. Now let us get this clear. Among Pantheists, like the Indians, anyone might say that he was a part of God, or one with God: there would be nothing very odd about it. But this man, since He was a Jew, could not mean that kind of God. God in their language, meant the Being outside the world Who had made it and was infinitely different from anything else. And when you have grasped that, you will see that what this man said was, quite simply, the most shocking thing that has ever been uttered by human lips..."

"I am trying here to prevent anyone saying the really foolish thing that people often say about Him: 'I'm ready to accept Jesus as a great moral teacher, but I don't accept His claim to be God.' That is the one thing we must not say. A man who was merely a man and said the sort of things Jesus said, would not be a great moral teacher. He would either be a lunatic – on a level with the man who says he is a poached egg – or else he should be the Devil of Hell. You must make your choice. Either this man was, and is, the Son of God: or else a madman or something worse. You can shut Him up for a fool, you can spit at Him and kill Him as a demon; or you can fall at His feet and call Him Lord and God. But let us not come with any patronizing nonsense about His being a great human teacher. He has not left that open to us. He did not intend to."[5]

D. What proofs do we have that Jesus is God?

   1.

   2.

   3.

   4.

E. How do you respond to people who say, "I believe Jesus was a great teacher but not God?" (Refer back to the chart, "Is Jesus a liar, lunatic or God?")

F. When choosing a Bible study next year, what are the two most important questions you should ask?

   1.

   2.

What Do Jesus and God Have in Common?

Many people like to pick and choose which parts of the Bible they will believe. Since we can trust the Bible as truth, we can also trust what the Bible says about the relationship between Jesus and God. In John 10:30, Jesus says, "'I and the Father are one.'" In the next passage from John, you can substitute Jesus every time you see "the Word." Take a look at what John had to say about Jesus:

"In the beginning was the Word, and the Word was with God, and the Word was God. He was with God in the beginning. Through him all things were made; without him nothing was made that has been made. In him was life, and that life was the light of men . . . The Word became flesh and made his dwelling among us. We have seen his glory, the glory of the One and Only, who came from the Father, full of grace and truth."
(John 1:1-4, 14)

First is the fact that Jesus as God of the universe came to earth to redeem us. He wants to have a relationship with us; He is not distant. Secondly, it means that Jesus Christ has all the attributes of God the Father; He too is perfect, holy, sinless, loving, just. Yet, He also became fully man (Romans 8:3). Thirdly, this means that we can believe that He is the Messiah, the Savior sent to save us from our sins. Jesus accomplished this by living a pure, sinless life; being crucified; and doing what no human could possibly do – conquering death by rising from the dead.

The coming of the "Messiah" has been prophesied throughout all of the Old Testament. The foreshadowing of His coming is even evident in Genesis, when Satan is told: *"He (Jesus) will crush your head, and you will strike His heel"* (Genesis 3:15b).

John 3:16-17 is one of the most well-known passages in the Bible, and it shows the relationship between God the Father and God the Son: *"For God so loved the world that he gave his one and only Son, that whoever believes in him shall not perish but have eternal life. For God did not send his Son into the world to condemn the world, but to save the world through him."*

Jesus is part of the Trinity of God. We know this because the entire Trinity is seen at Jesus' baptism. *"As soon as Jesus was baptized, he saw the Spirit of God descending like a dove and lighting on him. And a voice from heaven said, 'This is my Son, whom I love; with him I am well pleased'"* (Matthew 3:16-17).

Hebrews 13:8 *"Jesus Christ is the same yesterday and today and forever."*[6]

"'I and the Father are one.'" John 10:30

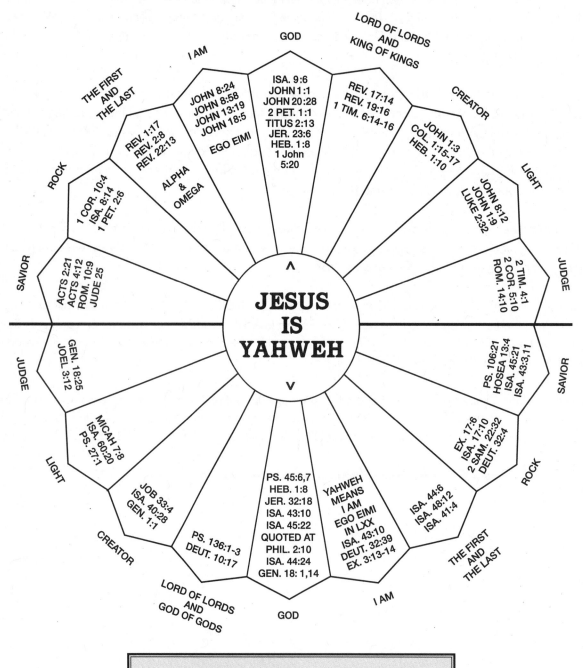

GOD

LORD OF LORDS AND KING OF KINGS

I AM

THE FIRST AND THE LAST

CREATOR

ROCK

REV. 1:17
REV. 2:8
REV. 22:13

JOHN 8:24
JOHN 8:58
JOHN 13:19
JOHN 18:5

EGO EIMI

ISA. 9:6
JOHN 1:1
JOHN 20:28
2 PET. 1:1
TITUS 2:13
JER. 23:6
HEB. 1:8
1 John 5:20

REV. 17:14
REV. 19:16
1 TIM. 6:14-16

JOHN 1:3
COL. 1:15-17
HEB. 1:10

LIGHT

1 COR. 10:4
ISA. 8:14
1 PET. 2:6

ALPHA & OMEGA

JOHN 8:12
JOHN 1:9
LUKE 2:32

SAVIOR

ACTS 2:21
ACTS 4:12
ROM. 10:9
JUDE 25

JUDGE

2 TIM. 4:1
2 COR. 5:10
ROM. 14:10

JESUS IS YAHWEH

SAVIOR

JUDGE

GEN. 18:25
JOEL 3:12

PS. 106:21
HOSEA 13:4
ISA. 45:21
ISA. 43:3,11

ROCK

MICAH 7:8
ISA. 60:20
PS. 27:1

EX. 17:6
ISA. 17:10
2 SAM. 22:32
DEUT. 32:4

LIGHT

JOB 33:4
ISA. 40:28
GEN. 1:1

ISA. 44:6
ISA. 48:12
ISA. 41:4

THE FIRST AND THE LAST

CREATOR

PS. 136:1-3
DEUT. 10:17

PS. 45:6,7
HEB. 1:8
JER. 32:18
ISA. 43:10
ISA. 45:22
QUOTED AT
PHIL. 2:10
ISA. 44:24
GEN. 18: 1,14

YAHWEH MEANS I AM EGO EIMI IN LXX
ISA. 43:10
DEUT. 32:39
EX. 3:13-14

I AM

LORD OF LORDS AND GOD OF GODS

GOD

"To us there is one God."

1 Corinthians 8:6

Lesson 6: Is Jesus Christ God? What Is the Trinity? - Anchorsaway Worldview Handbook ©

Prayer Requests

Lesson 6: Is Jesus Christ God? What Is the Trinity?

Small Group Objective:

The question, "Is Jesus Christ God?", is one that should be on the lips of all believers as they are inquiring about a church's doctrine, whether or not to attend a certain Bible study, or finding out where a friend is coming from spiritually. Students need to understand the gravity of the issue of the deity of Christ. If Jesus Christ is a good man or a great prophet, but not God, then He is not the Christ of Scripture. The goal is to help the students begin to better understand the implications of Christ's deity for our lives, the concept of the Trinity, and our purpose within the Christian worldview.

✓ **Check Points**

☐ Bring 3 x 5 cards for your students to write down any questions they may have which aren't answered during the discussion.

☐ Enlist a student to share a brief personal testimony.

Discussion Questions:

1. Review prayer requests from the week before and ask how the students are doing.

2. Lead a time of discussion, asking the following questions:

(Note: Work through as many of the following questions as possible. The goal is not to get through all of them, but to encourage each student to participate in the discussion as part of the learning process.)

    a. What day of the devotional did you find most meaningful?

    b. How did last week's lesson impact your life? Did you share it?

    c. Did your understanding of Jesus change at all as a result of this week's lesson? If so, in what way(s)? In light of that, how would you frame Jesus?

    d. Why is it so important to know that Jesus is God? (This is what separates Christianity from all other religions.)

    e. What if Jesus is not God? (Then Jesus is either a liar or a lunatic and should not be worshiped. He would not be able to change lives.)

    f. If God is who He says He is, then why do we need Jesus? Isn't God enough by Himself? (Through Jesus we can know God, because He is our only means of salvation. – John 14:6)

g. What do you say to people who believe, "Because I'm a good person, that's enough."?

h. Can you now answer the common question of why "good" people can go to hell? (There are no "good" people, because we all have sinned and violated God's holy standard – Romans 3:23. Therefore, only belief in Christ and obedience to His commands will ensure that any of us is able to go to heaven.)

i. How can we be sure that Jesus is God? (Scripture, personal testimonies from people whose lives have been changed by Christ, and the resurrection – a topic that will be studied another week.)

(*Note*: Have students take time to read through the "Jesus is Yahweh" chart and respond to it.)

j. Though you may believe in God and Jesus, what does it mean to you personally?

k. How has your life changed since you came to know Jesus?

l. What are some ways that God has answered prayer for you in the past week? If God did not answer your prayer specifically, do you have peace that He is working on it?

3. Ask for prayer requests and tell students that you will be faithful to pray for them during the week. Encourage students to record the prayer requests in the prayer request section of their handbooks, so they can pray for one another during the week. Begin the prayer time by sharing your own request. Spend the remaining time in prayer.

★ **After the Session**

1. Contact small group members during the week. Ask them about their devotional time, a question they have raised, or how their week is going.

Student Devotionals written by T.M. Moore

Is Jesus Christ God? What Is The Trinity?

Our readings for the next five days will allow us to look more closely at the Biblical teaching concerning the deity of Christ. Take time to meditate deeply on the questions provided, allowing the teaching of the text to saturate your mind and penetrate your heart.

Remember that the prayers provided are just to get you started. Let the Spirit lead you through His Words into a fuller time of prayer using your own.

Day 1: The Old Testament on the Deity of Christ

Pray: *"The Lord is at your right hand; he will shatter kings on the day of his wrath"* (Psalm 110:5).

Read: Daniel 7:9-22

Meditate: Jesus often referred to Himself as the "Son of Man." Was He consciously thinking of this passage? Trying to identify with the Son of Man pictured here? Why would He want to do that?

What does the Ancient of Days do for the Son of Man here (vv. 13, 14)? What does the Son of Man do with this (v. 18)? Have I received this? How do I know?

What happens to those who receive this precious gift (vv. 21, 22)? What does that look like? Do I ever experience anything like this? How should I prepare for it?

Journal: Jesus, the Son of Man, has given me the Kingdom He received from His Father. Wow! Since this is true, I need to...

Pray: *"All your works shall give thanks to you, O LORD, and all your saints shall bless you! They shall speak of the glory of your kingdom"* (Psalm 145:10, 11).

Day 2: Even His Enemies Understood

Pray: *"Surely the wrath of man shall praise you; the remnant of wrath you will put on like a belt"* (Psalm 76:10).

Read: John 10:22-42

Meditate: Why did the religious leaders want to stone Jesus (vv. 31-33)? Why do people seem to get so upset over Jesus' claim to be God?

Jesus said He and the Father are one – in what sense? How did His enemies understand what He was saying?

Jesus, who claimed to be God, said no one could snatch us out of the Father's hand? Is this something I ever worry about? Why? How can knowing that Jesus is God help to relieve my concern about this?

Journal: They didn't like Jesus when He said He was God, but they sure seem to have understood Him well. I want people to understand that, too, so...

Pray: *"We give thanks to you, O God; we give thanks, for your name is near. We recount your wondrous deeds"* (Psalm 75:1).

Day 3: The Testimony of the Apostles

Pray: *"God my King is from old, working salvation in the midst of the earth"* (Psalm 74:12).

Read: Hebrews 1:1-4

Meditate: What is a radiance? What is God's glory? In what ways did Jesus radiate the glory of God while He was on earth? Have I ever experienced that radiating of God's glory from Jesus?

Jesus is the "exact imprint" of God's nature. What should looking carefully at Jesus tell me about God?

Jesus accomplished three things while on earth. They are in vv. 1, 3a, and 3c. What are they? Plus, He has three other works to His credit: can I see them (vv. 1 [the end], 3b, and 3 [the end])? Do I benefit from these works today? How?

Journal: Hmm...if Jesus were to "radiate" God's glory and speak His words and express God's "imprint" in me today...

Pray: *"But for me it is good to be near God; I have made the LORD my God my refuge, that I may tell of all your works"* (Psalm 73:28).

Day 4: Unmistakably God!

Pray: *"Whom have I in heaven but you? And there is nothing on earth that I desire besides you"* (Psalm 73:25).

Read: John 20:24-29

Meditate: Why did Thomas doubt the words of the apostles? Do I ever feel like that? Why? Do I know people like Thomas today?

How did Jesus resolve Thomas' doubts? What was it that finally convinced Thomas to confess Jesus as God? Should we expect such opportunities today? Why or why not?

Whom did Jesus promise to bless (v. 28)? On what basis? So how should I be seeking to bring the blessing of Jesus as God to my friends?

Journal: I can't reason people into believing in Jesus, and He's not going to show Himself in a vision to them; yet they need to believe in His Word, and the testimony of His disciples, and so...

Pray: *"May all who seek you rejoice and be glad in you! May those who love your salvation say evermore, 'God is great!'"* (Psalm 70:4).

Day 5: If Jesus is God, I'm Not!

Pray: *"Know that the LORD, he is God!"* (Psalm 100:3).

Read: Acts 9:1-18

Meditate: What happened to Saul? How would I have felt if that had happened to me? Would I have been embarrassed? Afraid?

Saul was a pretty self-confident young man before this episode on the Road to Damascus. How did Jesus "bring him down a notch or two?" Does Jesus still do this? How? Have I ever experienced this? Of what did this serve to remind Saul?

Do I know anyone like Saul – cocky, headstrong, angry, and dead-set against the Lord? What is my attitude toward that person? Am I like Ananias or something else? How might God use me in that person's life?

Journal: Jesus is God and I'm not. I think I know what's best for me, but, really...

Pray: *"O you who love the LORD, hate evil! He preserves the lives of his saints"* (Psalm 98:10).

ENDNOTES

[1] Wayne Grudem, Systematic Theology: An Introduction to Biblical Doctrine (Grand Rapids: Zondervan, 1994) 226. Grudem's definition of the Trinity is similar to James White's explanation. He summarizes the Bible's teachings about the Trinity through the following three statements: 1. God is three persons. 2. Each person is fully God. 3. There is one God., 231.

[2] James White, "A Brief Definition of the Trinity," <u>Alpha and Omega Ministries</u>

[3] Kenneth Boa, Cults: World Religions and the Occult rev. ed. (Wheaton, IL: Victor Books, 1990)

[4] Josh McDowell, Evidence That Demands a Verdict vol. 1 (1979; Nashville, TN: Thomas Nelson Publishers, 1999) 104.

[5] C. S. Lewis, Mere Christianity (1952; San Francisco: HarperCollins, 2001) 51-52.

Recommended Reading

Key Books:

Boa, Kenneth. Cults, World Religions and the Occult. Rev. ed. Wheaton, IL: Victor Books, 1990.

Fox, Richard Wightman. Jesus In America. San Francisco: HarperCollins, 2004.

Graham, Franklin. It's Who You Know. Nashville: Thomas Nelson Publishers, 2002.

Graham, Franklin. The Name. Nashville: Thomas Nelson Publishers, 2002.

Grudem, Wayne. Systematic Theology: An Introduction to Biblical Doctrine. Grand Rapids: Zondervan, 1994.

Kennedy, D. James, and Jerry Newcombe. What If Jesus Had Never Been Born? Nashville: Thomas Nelson Publishers, 1994.

Lewis, C. S. Mere Christianity. 1952. San Francisco: HarperCollins, 2001.

McDowell, Josh. Evidence That Demands a Verdict. Vol. 1. 1979. Nashville, TN: Thomas Nelson Publishers, 1999.

McDowell, Josh. More Than a Carpenter. Wheaton, IL: Tyndale House Publishers, 1987.

Miller, Calvin. The Book of Jesus. New York: Simon & Schuster, 1996.

Sanders, Fred. The Deep Things of God: How the Trinity Changes Everything. Wheaton, IL: Crossway, 2010.

Strobel, Lee. The Case for Christ. Grand Rapids, MI: Zondervan, 1998.

White, James R. The Forgotten Trinity. Minneapolis, MN: Bethany House, 1998

Yancey, Philip. The Jesus I Never Knew. Grand Rapids, MI: Zondervan, 1995.

Zacharias, Ravi. Jesus Among Other Gods. Nashville: Word Publishing, 2000.

Lesson 7: What Is a Christian? Am I One?

⚓ **Anchor of the Week: The Christian believes in Christ and follows Him.**

I. Christianity and the Four People Groups

A. There are those who are...

1. Saved by faith through Christ and know it.

2. Saved by faith through Christ and do not know it.

3. Not saved by faith through Christ and know it.

4. Not saved by faith through Christ and do not know it. (They think that they are Christians but are not.)

B. What is **Neo-Christianity?**

II. What is a Christian?

A. A person does not become a Christian just by coming forward to an altar or saying a prayer.

B. Becoming a Christian, a follower of Christ, is a gift from God by way of the cross to all who choose to believe that Jesus Christ is God and the only Savior of the world.

1. John 3:16 *"'For God so loved the world that he gave his one and only Son, that whoever believes in him shall not perish but have eternal life.'"*

   a. The Greek word for believe, pisteuo, means "to be persuaded of." Therefore, to believe in Jesus is "to place confidence in, to trust" in Him.[1]

   b. This sense of the word signifies reliance upon, not mere credence.

2. Ephesians 2:8-9 *"For it is by grace you have been saved, through faith – and this not from yourselves, it is the gift of God – not by works, so that no one can boast."*

3. Romans 10:9-10 *"That if you confess with your mouth, 'Jesus is Lord,' and believe in your heart that God raised him from the dead, you will be saved. For it is with your heart that you believe and are justified, and it is with your mouth that you confess and are saved."*

C. What is faith? *"Now faith is being sure of what we hope for and certain of what we do not see."* Hebrews 11:1 – Reference Hebrews 11:1 in the NASB: *"Now faith is the assurance of things hoped for, the <u>conviction</u> of things not seen."* Because of the evidence, we are able to <u>convict</u> Christ of being Christ and the Bible of being true. Our faith is not a blind faith.

1. Faith must have an object. How do we live by faith? We do it every day all day (i.e. sitting on chairs, driving a car, using an alarm clock, ordering a Coke® at McDonald's®...)! God wants us to live by faith in Him. To believe in Him by trusting Him completely requires faith, no matter how much we know about God.

2. <u>Our salvation comes when we, through faith, accept God's gift of grace.</u>(Ephesians 2:8).

D. Responding to God's gift of grace: "Lord I thank you for loving me and for drawing me to you. I know now that you died for all of my sins and the greater one being denying your Son Jesus as my Savior. Thank you for forgiving me of my sins, as I put my trust completely in You and You alone. Because I believe and I trust you with all of my life thank you for giving to me the gift of the Holy Spirit who now lives in me forever."

E. Is the state of being saved one of fact or emotion? True Christianity is NOT an act or a job. It is NOT an emotional experience in and of itself. In fact, many genuine conversions take place without an emotional experience, per se.

F. Do I have to have a point in life when I went through a conversion experience from being a non-Christian to a Christian? Not all Christians can remember a specific moment in time when they first believed in Christ as their Savior. For many people, God has blessed them with the privilege of growing up in a strong Christian home and as a result many have "grown" into a relationship with Christ. Regardless of a person's background, the important thing is that we each take ownership of <u>our</u> faith and seek to make Christ our Savior and Lord.

III. Who am I as a believer in Jesus Christ?

A. Totally and completely loved – There is nothing you can do to make Him love you more than He does right now.

1. Romans 8:38-39 *"For I am convinced that neither death nor life, neither angels nor demons, neither the present, nor the future, nor any powers, neither height nor depth, nor anything else in all creation, will be able to separate us from the love of God that is in Christ Jesus our Lord."*

2. We are beyond condemnation, because we have been set free from the chains of our sinful nature: Romans 8:1-2 *"Therefore, there is now no condemnation for those who are in Christ Jesus, because through Christ Jesus the law of the Spirit of life set me free from the law of sin and death."*

B. Forgiven – Though we are not perfect, we are forgiven (I John 1:8-9).

1. How many of us would mentally agree with this principle, but in reality, we struggle to really accept that we have been forgiven? How can we know for sure that we are forgiven? What does Scripture say about this?

   a. John 19:30 *"...Jesus said, 'It is finished.' With that, he bowed his head and gave up his spirit."*

   b. What was finished? He died for <u>all</u> the sins of the world. Jesus paid the ultimate price of judgment for sin, death.

2. How many of us think that after we have confessed a sin, it will come back to haunt us, especially a really bad one? Scripture paints a different picture:

   a. 1 John 1:9 *"If we confess our sins, he is faithful and just and will forgive us our sins and purify us from all unrighteousness."*

   b. Psalm 103:11-12 *"For as high as the heavens are above the earth, so great is his love for those who fear him; as far as the east is from the west, so far has he removed our transgressions from us."*

   c. Psalm 32:1-2 *"Blessed is he whose transgressions are forgiven, whose sins are covered. Blessed is the man whose sin the Lord does not count against him and in whose spirit is no deceit."*

   d. 1 John 2:12 *"I write to you, dear children, because your sins have been forgiven on account of his name."*

C. Righteous (positional)

1. How many of you are as righteous and acceptable in the sight of God as your minister or pastor? How many are as righteous as Billy Graham? How many are as righteous as Jesus Christ? None of us is righteous in and of ourselves. But, because Jesus paid the price, we are considered righteous before God.

   a. 2 Corinthians 5:21 *"God made him who had no sin to be sin for us, so that in him we might become the righteousness of God."*

   b. Romans 5:19 *"For just as through the disobedience of the one man the many were made sinners, so also through the obedience of the one man the many will be made righteous."*

2. Not only are you forgiven, but you are also considered righteous by God's standard. This is hard to believe. It means that even though we are not perfect and we will still sin, the sins we commit are already forgiven through the shedding of Christ's blood on the cross, if we are willing to confess our sins to Him (Ephesians 1:7).

The saving blood of Jesus

The Believer

D. Can we be saved as a believer and still at times live separate from God?

1. We can be a right person who has taken a wrong turn.

    a. Scripture talks about such a person in the story of Lot (Genesis 19).

    b. 2 Peter 2:6-9 *"...if he (God) condemned the cities of Sodom and Gomorrah by burning them to ashes, and made them an example of what is going to happen to the ungodly; and if he rescued Lot, a righteous man, <u>who was distressed by the filthy</u> <u>lives</u> of lawless men (for that righteous man, living among them day after day, was tormented in his righteous soul by the lawless deeds he saw and heard) – if this is so, then the Lord knows how <u>to rescue godly</u> <u>men from trials</u> and to hold the unrighteous for the day of judgment, while continuing their punishment."* (Emphasis added)

2. There are consequences for those who choose to walk through life without God in the lead.

3. God is in the business of rescuing those who want to stop living the way they are today! For those of you who have chosen that path, there is good news: **God is in the business of rescuing us.**

    a. When our battle with temptation seems hopeless, God promises to give us an escape route. 1 Corinthians 10:12-13 *"So, if you think you are standing firm, be careful that you don't fall! No temptation has seized you except what is common to man. And God is faithful; he will not let you be tempted beyond what you can bear. But when you are tempted, he will provide also a way out so that you can stand up under it."*

    b. God wants everyone to be saved. 2 Peter 3:9b *"He is patient with you, not wanting anyone to perish, but everyone to come to repentance."*

    c. God chooses to save us, not because of how good we are, but because of how merciful He is and how much He loves us. Titus 3:4-5 *"But when the kindness and love of God our Savior appeared, he saved us, not because of righteous things we had done, but because of his mercy. He saved us through the washing of rebirth and renewal by the Holy Spirit...."*

IV. What should be our response to what Christ did for us all?

A. Our lives should be characterized by love and obedience.

1. The Two Greatest Commandments: Matthew 22:37-40 – *"Jesus replied, 'Love the Lord your God with all your heart and with all your soul and with all your mind.' This is the first and greatest commandment. And the second is like it: 'Love your neighbor as yourself.' All the Law and the Prophets hang on these two commandments."*

2. Our obedience to God demonstrates our love for Him (John 14:15).

3. Our love for others comes from God's love for us (1 John 4:11, 19).

4. Our love bears witness before others of our relationship with God (John 13:34-35).

B. The more we know God the more we will want others to know Him, too.

1. The Great Commission: Matthew 28:19-20 *"'Therefore go and make disciples of all nations, baptizing them in the name of the Father and of the Son and of the Holy Spirit, and teaching them to obey everything I have commanded you. And surely I am with you always, to the very end of the age.'"*

2. Look at the example of Andrew: John 1:40-42a *"Andrew, Simon Peter's brother, was one of the two who heard what John (the Baptist) had said and who had followed Jesus. The first thing Andrew did was to find his brother Simon and tell him, 'We have found the Messiah' (that is, the Christ). And he brought him to Jesus."*

C. How do different types of Chrisitans respond to what Christ did?

1. Believer

2. Evangelical

3. Revolutionary

Getting Right with God

When we decide to devote ourselves to Jesus Christ, He sets us free. Sometimes it is difficult to give ourselves to Him completely, or to boldly share Him with others. Here are some things for you to contemplate this week as you are on your journey of learning.

- In C.S. Lewis' book, *The Screwtape Letters*, Screwtape (Satan) writes instructions to his demon nephew, Wormwood, on how to keep a Christian from growing. He explains to Wormwood the doctrine of surrender: *"When He [God] talks of their losing their selves, He means only abandoning the clamor of self-will; once they have done that, He really gives them back all their personality, and boasts (I am afraid, sincerely) that when they are wholly His they will be more themselves than ever."*

- *"But in your hearts set apart Christ as Lord. Always be prepared to give an answer to everyone who asks you to give the reason for the hope that you have. But do this with gentleness and respect"* (1 Peter 3:15).

- These two texts illustrate the importance of realizing that God does not withhold anything good from you; He loves you completely. The more you give to Him, the more you become the person He has made you to be.

- *"So then, just as you received Christ Jesus as Lord, continue to live in him, rooted and built up in him, strengthened in the faith as you were taught, and overflowing with thankfulness. See to it that no one takes you captive through hollow and deceptive philosophy, which depends on human tradition and basic principles of this world rather than on Christ"* (Colossians 2:6-8).

- *"Be wise in the way you act toward outsiders; make the most of every opportunity. Let your conversation be always full of grace, seasoned with salt, so that you may know how to answer everyone"* (Colossians 4:5-6).

To learn how to share Christ with someone go to page 392.

Neil Anderson's Victory Over the Darkness[2] provides reminders of who you are when you put your faith in Christ Jesus. Use it for personal study or meditation and celebrate all that you are in Christ.

- I am the salt of the earth (Matthew 5:13).
- I am the light of the world (Matthew 5:14).
- I am a child of God (John 1:12).
- I am part of the true vine, a channel of Christ's life (John 15:1, 5).
- I am Christ's friend (John 15:15).
- I am chosen and appointed by Christ to bear His fruit (John 15:16).
- I am a slave of righteousness (Romans 6:18).
- I am enslaved to God (Romans 6:22).
- I am a son of God; God is spiritually my Father (Romans 8:14, 15; Galatians 3:26; 4:6).
- I am a joint heir with Christ, sharing His inheritance with Him (Romans 8:17).
- I am a temple, a dwelling place, of God. His Spirit and His life dwell in me (1 Corinthians 3:16; 6:19).
- I am united to the Lord and am one spirit with Him (1 Corinthians 6:17).
- I am a member of Christ's Body (1 Corinthians 12:27; Ephesians 5:30).
- I am a new creation (2 Corinthians 5:17).
- I am reconciled to God and am a minister of reconciliation (2 Corinthians 5:18, 19).
- I am a son of God and one in Christ (Galatians 3:26, 28).
- I am an heir of God since I am a son of God (Galatians 4:6, 7).
- I am a saint (Ephesians 1:1; 1 Corinthians 1:2; Philippians 1:1; Colossians 1:2).
- I am God's workmanship, His handiwork, born anew in Christ to do His work (Ephesians 2:10).
- I am a fellow citizen with the rest of God's family (Ephesians 2:19).
- I am a prisoner of Christ (Ephesians 3:1; 4:1).
- I am righteous and holy (Ephesians 4:24).
- I am a citizen of heaven, seated in heaven right now (Philippians 3:20; Ephesians 2:6).
- I am hidden with Christ in God (Colossians 3:3).
- I am an expression of the life of Christ because He is my life (Colossians 3:4).
- I am chosen of God, holy and dearly loved (Colossians 3:12; 1 Thessalonians 1:4).
- I am a son of light and not of darkness (1 Thessalonians 5:5).
- I am a holy partaker of a heavenly calling (Hebrews 3:1).
- I am a partaker of Christ; I share in His life (Hebrews 3:14).
- I am one of God's living stones, being built up in Christ as a spiritual house (1 Peter 2:5).
- I am a member of a chosen race, a royal priesthood, a holy nation, a people for God's own possession (1 Peter 2:9, 10).
- I am an alien and stranger to this world in which I temporarily live (1 Peter 2:11).
- I am an enemy of the devil (1 Peter 5:8).
- I am a child of God and I will resemble Christ when He returns (1 John 3:1, 2).
- I am born of God, and the evil one—the devil—cannot touch me (1 John 5:18).
- I am NOT the great "I am" (Exodus 3:14; John 3:28, 8:58), but by the grace of God, I am what I am (1 Corinthians 15:10).

A Conversation with God

by Steve Znachko

God, why Jesus? Because of sin.

Why did you introduce sin? I didn't, you did.

You allowed it ... why? To Love there must be free will not to love.

Why not just forgive sin ... why require sacrifice? Your question gives the answer, you do not understand how serious sin is ... you talk of it as if it is a cold that is a hindrance, but sin is a plague that destroys.

Sin cannot be **wished** away ... Sin must be **washed** away ... washed away by blood.

Is there any other way to Heaven? Yes, perfection. "... be perfect as I am perfect."

I can do that ... just give me the rules and I will obey them. That was the reason for the Law ... the entire Old Testament proves what I always knew ... you cannot do it on your own.

But certainly there are some people that live better lives than others ... do they make it? I don't grade on a curve.

If you did, there would be more people in Heaven. If I did, there would be no people in Heaven ... remember, the standard is perfection.

Why your Son? Because it was the only way.

No other way? If there was any other way, don't you think I would have spared my Son ... I heard his cries in the garden, I heard his pleas on the cross ... if there were any other way, don't you think I would have spared him?

Is the payment Jesus made open to everyone or just to those you really like? My Son died for the sins of the whole world, and I love every one of you.

What must we do to have Jesus pay for our sins? Believe.

That doesn't seem to be asking too much. It would not seem to be.

So why is it painted as such a mean thing and intolerant thing? Two reasons, really, the arrogance of people and the deception of your enemy. Remember, there is one who wants nothing more than to keep you from the gift that I gave.

So we all have sinned? Yes.

The payment for sin is death? Yes.

It was either our flesh and blood or Jesus' flesh and blood? Yes.

And you gave Jesus? Yes.

You really do love us, don't you? More than you know.

How much? This much. (Stretch out arms in the form of the cross.)[3]

The Privilege of Adoption

Children of royalty, crippled by the fall, permanently marred by sin; Living parenthetical lives in the chronicles of earth, only to be remembered by the king; Driven not by our beauty but by his promise, he calls us to Himself and invites us to take a permanent place at his table. Though we often limp more than we walk, we take our place next to the other sinners-made-saints and we share in God's glory.

May I share a partial list of what awaits you at his table?

- You are beyond condemnation (Romans 8:1).
- You are delivered from the law (Romans 7:6).
- You are near God (Ephesians 2:13).
- You are delivered from the power of evil (Colossians 1:13).
- You are a member of his kingdom (Colossians 1:13).
- You are justified (Romans 5:1).
- You are perfect (Hebrews 10:14).
- You have been adopted (Romans 8:15).
- You have access to God at any moment (Ephesians 2:18).
- You are a part of his priesthood (1 Peter 2:5).
- You will never be abandoned (Hebrews 13:5).
- You have an imperishable inheritance (1 Peter 1:4).
- You are a partner with Christ in life (Colossians 3:4) and privilege (Ephesians 2:6), suffering (2 Timothy 2:12), and service (1 Corinthians 1:9).
- You are a member of his body (1 Corinthians 12:13),
- You are a branch in the vine (John 15:5),
- You are a stone in the building (Ephesians 2:19-22),
- You are a bride for the groom (Ephesians 5:25-27),
- You are a priest in the new generation (1 Peter 2:9),
- You are a dwelling place of the Spirit (1 Corinthians 6:19).

John 10:29 – "'My Father, who has given them to me, is greater than all; no one can snatch them out of my Father's hand.'"

Hebrews 13:5 – "Keep your lives free from the love of money and be content with what you have, because God has said, 'Never will I leave you; never will I forsake you.'"

1 Samuel 12:22 – "For the sake of his great name the Lord will not reject his people, because the Lord was pleased to make you his own."

Psalm 37:28 – "For the Lord loves the just and will not forsake his faithful ones. They will be protected forever, but the offspring of the wicked will be cut off...."

I John 5:12-13 – "He who has the Son has life; he who does not have the Son of God does not have life. I write these things to you who believe in the name of the Son of God so that you may know that you have eternal life."

Small Group Discussion Guide

Lesson 7: What Is a Christian? Am I One?

Small Group Objective:

The goal is to help the students begin to better understand God's love for them, and the implications of their Christian faith on their daily lives.

✓ **Check Points**

☐ Bring 3 x 5 cards for your students to write down any questions they may have which aren't answered during the discussion.

☐ Enlist a student to share a brief personal testimony.

Discussion Questions:

1. Review prayer requests from the week before and ask how the students are doing.

2. Lead a time of discussion, asking the following questions:

(Note: Work through as many of the following questions as possible. The goal is not to get through all of them, but to encourage each student to participate in the discussion as part of the learning process.)

 a. What day of the devotional did you find most meaningful?

 b. How did last week's lesson impact your life? Did you share it?

 c. What is one way that you saw God apply last week's lesson to your life this week?

 d. Did your understanding of Christianity change at all as a result of this week's lesson? If so, in what way(s)?

 e. What do you love most about God?

 f. What have you been especially grateful for, regarding the result of Christ's death and resurrection? (Forgiveness, the opportunity for salvation, eternal life...)

 g. How should one's life reflect the fact that Christ lives?

 h. Is living for someone other than ourselves difficult? Why/why not?

 i. Why is it important that your faith become your own, and not merely a religious activity? Is yours your own?

 j. In our Christian life, how do we keep from being legalistic? (Pray and walk with God, not by rules.)

 k. What can I do to keep close to Christ?

l. What questions, if any, come to mind as a result of this week's lesson?

m. Frame a Christian.

(*Note*: As a final exercise, have each student refer to the Personal Reflection in their Student Worldview Handbook and follow the instructions. The purpose of this exercise is to personalize the reality of how Jesus views each of us.)

3. Ask for prayer requests and tell students that you will be faithful to pray for them during the week. Encourage students to record the prayer requests in the prayer request section of their handbooks, so they can pray for one another during the week. Begin the prayer time by sharing your own request. Spend the remaining time in prayer.

★ After the Session

1. Contact small group members during the week. Ask them about their devotional time, a question they have raised, or how their week is going.

Prayer Requests

Student Devotionals written by T.M. Moore

What is a Christian? Am I One?

This will be a good week to check-up on the state of our walk with the Lord as Christians. Remember, the opening and closing prayers are provided to get you started in prayer. Let the Spirit lead you as you fellowship more deeply and more personally with the Lord.

Day 1: Seeing Grace in Us

Pray: *"You have said, 'Seek my face.' My heart says to you, 'Your face, LORD, do I seek'"* (Psalm 27:8).

Read: Acts 11:19-26

Meditate: Luke says that Barnabas "saw the grace of God" in the believers in Antioch. I wonder what that looked like?

What were those believers doing in Antioch as a response to hearing the Gospel .... (vv. 19-21)? Are my friends and I doing this?

The believers were first called "Christians" in Antioch (v. 26). I wonder how the people of Antioch meant that term? Do the people I know think of me as a Christian? Why or why not?

Journal: I want people to think of me as a Christian, but I need to work on this somewhat. So, today...

Pray: *"Teach me your way, O LORD, and lead me on a level path"* (Psalm 27:11).

Day 2: What Christians Do

Pray: *"Behold, how good and pleasant it is when brothers dwell in unity"* (Psalm 133:1).

Read: Acts 2:42-47

Meditate: What kinds of things did those first Christians do? How can I see that love for God and love for one another was at work there?

           What kinds of feelings did those Christians express? Do I share those feelings? About God? About my fellow Christians?

           What happened as a result of these Christians living the way they did? How were they blessed? How was the city of Jerusalem affected?

Journal: Christians share an identity together, an identity that can change a whole community. Today, I want to help promote that identity, so...

Pray: *"For there the LORD has commanded the blessing, life forevermore"* (Psalm 133:3).

Day 3: Fishers of Men

Pray: *"Let the redeemed of the LORD say so, whom he has redeemed from trouble and gathered in from the lands..."* (Psalm 107:2, 3).

Read: Matthew 4:18-22

Meditate: What did it mean for those first disciples to "follow" Jesus? What did they give up to do so?

           What did Jesus promise would happen if they followed Him (v. 19)? Is that happening with me?

           What is involved in this matter of "fishing for men?" Am I equipped to do this? Do I really want to do this?

Journal: If I am a follower of Jesus, then I should be fishing for men. Hmm...that must mean that...

Pray: *"Whoever is wise, let him attend to these things..."* (Psalm 107:43).

Day 4: Pursuing Holiness

Pray: *"My soul makes its boast in the LORD; let the humble hear and be glad"* (Psalm 34:2).

Read: 2 Corinthians 6:14-7:1

Meditate: Am I yoked with unbelief in any unhealthy ways? Is this a good thing? Can I expect that others will be able to see that I'm a Christian if I stay yoked to unbelief?

What promises has God made to me as one of the followers of Christ (vv. 16, 18)? What does He expect me to do as a result (v. 17)?

How should having these promises motivate me (7:1)? What should I be doing? How will I be able to tell when this is happening?

Journal: I need to be "bringing holiness to completion" in my life. That sounds like a tall order. But I have the promises of God! So, today...

Pray: *"This poor man cried, and the LORD heard him, and saved him out of all his troubles"* (Psalm 34:6).

Day 5: A Community of Hope

Pray: *"I believe that I shall look upon the goodness of the LORD in the land of the living!"* (Psalm 27:13).

Read: 1 Peter 3:8-17

Meditate: What kind of community should we Christians be seeking to build? What should I be doing to help this come to pass?

Do I "regard Christ as holy" in my heart (v. 15)? How do I do that? How would I show someone else how to do that?

How should I answer those who want to know about the hope I have in Jesus? Am I prepared to do this? How can I be better prepared?

Journal: I wonder if people look at me as someone who has hope? I wonder if they see us Christians as having hope? Has anyone asked me about this lately? If someone does...

Pray: *"The LORD is my light and my salvation; whom shall I fear? The LORD is the stronghold of my life; of whom shall I be afraid?"* (Psalm 27:1).

ENDNOTES

[1] W. E. Vine, An Expository Dictionary of New Testament Words, W. E. Vine, Merrill F. Unger, and William White, Jr., Vine's Complete Expository Dictionary of Old and New Testament Words (Nashville, TN: Thomas Nelson Publishers, 1996) 61.

[2] Neil Anderson, Victory Over the Darkness, 2nd ed. (Ventura, CA: Regal Books, 2000) 51-53.

[3] Steve Znachko, "A Conversation with God," sermon at Grace Community Church 2005, copied with permission.

Recommended Reading

Key Books

A'Kempis, Thomas. The Imitation of Christ. Chicago: Moody Press, 1980.

Anderson, Neil. Victory Over the Darkness. 2nd ed. Ventura, CA: Regal Books, 2000.

Barna, George. Think Like Jesus. Brentwood, TN: Integrity Publishers, 2003.

Barna, George. Transforming Children into Spiritual Champions. Ventura, CA: Regal Books, 2003.

Bass, Diana Butler. Christianity after Religion: The End of Church and the Birth of a New Spiritual Awakening. New York: HarperOne, 2012.

Bonhoeffer, Dietrich. The Cost of Discipleship. 1937. New York: Touchstone Books, 1995.

Budziszewski, J. How to Stay Christian in College. Colorado Springs, CO: TH1NK Books, 2004.

Colson, Charles. Dare to Be Different, Dare to Be Christian. Wheaton, IL: Victor Books, 1987.

Colson, Charles W., and Harold Fickett. The Faith: What Christians Believe, Why They Believe It, and Why It Matters. Grand Rapids, MI: Zondervan, 2008.

Everts, Don. Jesus with Dirty Feet: A Down-to-Earth Look at Christianity for the Curious and Skeptical. Downers Grove, IL: InterVarsity Press, 1999.

George, Bob. Classic Christianity. Eugene, Or.: Harvest House, 1989.

Keller, Timothy. The Songs of Jesus: A Year of Daily Devotions in the Psalms. New York, NY: Vikings, 2015.

Kinnaman, David. Good Faith: Being a Christian When Society Thinks You're Irrelevant and Extreme. N.p.: n.p., n.d.

Lewis, C. S. Mere Christianity. 1952. San Francisco: HarperCollins, 2001.

McDowell, Josh. The Last Christian Generation. Holiday, FL: Green Key Books, 2006.

Moreland, James Porter. Scaling the Secular City: A Defense of Christianity. Grand Rapids, MI: Baker Book House, 1987.

Schaeffer, Francis A. The Mark of a Christian. Downers Grove, IL: InterVarsity Press, 1970.

Stott, John R. W. Authentic Christianity. Ed. Timothy Dudley-Smith. Downers Grove, IL: InterVarsity Press, 1995.

Tozer, A. W. The Pursuit of God: The Original Classic Edition. Newstead, Qld.: Emereo Pub., 2012.

Wallace, J. Warner. Cold-case Christianity: A Homicide Detective Investigates the Claims of the Gospels. N.p.: n.p., n.d.

Wilson, Todd A. Real Christian: Bearing the Marks of Authentic Faith.

Lesson 8: Did Life Just Happen or Were We Created?

(Note: The content in this lesson comes from Tom Foltz, Indianapolis, Indiana. He formerly worked for NASA, at the Kennedy Space Center, in Florida.)

I. Dissecting Evolution: from the Goo...to the Zoo...to You?

A. Seeing God's creative handiwork:

1. Genesis 1:1-3

2. See Job 12:7-10

3. Romans 1:19-20

B. Definitions

1. **Biblical Creation** – A foundation based on Genesis through Revelation

    a. Not scientifically verifiable

    b. That is, it is a non-repeatable event or series of events.

2. **Micro-evolution** – The offspring of pre-existing organisms capable of reproducing. Offspring within a population ... i.e. dogs from dogs, cats from cats

    a. No scientific issues with micro-evolution by either those who support macro-evolution or creation (Biblical creation or any type of creation)

    b. Scientifically verifiable

3. **Macro-evolution** – The origin of life, 'molecules to man'

    a. Lots of issues and disagreements between those who support macro-evolution and creation

    b. Macro-evolutionists EXTRAPOLATE micro into macro!

    c. Macro-evolution is not scientifically verifiable. That is, it is a non-repeatable event or series of events.

4. **Historical** – An event or series of events in the past with one or more eye witnesses. Sometimes an event or events without eye witnesses, but with sufficient verifiable evidence to corroborate its authenticity.

5. **Operational Science** – The aspect of science that relates to repeatable, verifiable and testable results.

C. What does the Bible say about creation?

1. Genesis 1:1 *"In the beginning God created..."*

2. 1 Corinthians 15:19 *"If only for this life we have hope in Christ, we are to be pitied more than all men."*

3. John 1:1 *"In the beginning was the Word..."*

4. Revelation 4:11 *"'You are worthy, O Lord, to receive glory and honor and power: for you have created all things, and for your pleasure they are and were created.'"*

5. SUMMARY: Uniquely, the Bible affirms creation and indicates who did it (God), who was there at the time of creation (Jesus), why the creation was done, how it was done, what was created and for whose purpose! Neither the word evolution nor any similar molecules-to-man process [macro-evolution] is found in the Bible.

D. What do scientists and others say about macro-evolution?

1. "Evolution of life ... is a fact." – *Life* magazine, 1982[1]

2. "It is absolutely safe to say that, if you meet somebody who claims not to believe in evolution, that person is ignorant, stupid, or insane (or wicked, but I'd rather not consider that)." – Richard Dawkins, evolutionist and atheist[2]

3. "The theory [Darwinian evolution] is about as much in doubt as the earth goes around the sun." – Richard Dawkins[3]

4. "The first point to make about Darwin's theory is that it is <u>no longer a theory, but a fact</u>... Darwinianism has come of age so to speak. <u>We are no longer having to bother about establishing the fact of evolution</u>..."(emphasis added) – Dr. Julian Huxley, evolutionist[4]

5. "As were many persons from Alabama, I was a born-again Christian. When I was fifteen, I entered the Southern Baptist Church with great fervor and interest in the fundamentalist religion; <u>I left at seventeen when I got to the University of Alabama and heard about evolutionary theory</u>." (emphasis added) – E. O. Wilson[5]

6. "I believe that there is no supreme being with human attributes – <u>no God in the biblical sense</u> – but that life is the result of timeless evolutionary forces having reached its present transient state over millions of years." (emphasis added)

   – Charles Templeton, former evangelist with Billy Graham[6]

7. "It was because Darwinian theory broke man's link with God and set him adrift in a cosmos without purpose or end that its impact was so fundamental. <u>No other intellectual revolution in modern times ... so profoundly affected the way men viewed themselves and their place in the universe.</u>" (emphasis added) – Dr. Michael Denton[7]

8. "Christianity has fought, still fights, and will fight science to the desperate end over evolution, because evolution destroys utterly and finally the very reason Jesus' earthly life was supposedly made necessary. Destroy Adam and Eve and the original sin, and in the rubble you will find the sorry remains of the Son of God. Take away the meaning of his death. If Jesus was not the redeemer who died for our sins, and this is what evolution means, then Christianity is nothing!" – Richard Bozarth[8]

Creator vs. Macro-evolution[9]

	Biblical Creation	Macro-evolution
Person	Creator ("God") – Genesis 1	No Person
God	Revealed – Genesis 1 ("In the beginning God")	Does not exist
Process	Orderly process – Genesis 1	Random process
Uniqueness	Each unique – Genesis 1 ("fearfully and wonderfully made")	Each an accident
Man Special?	Man special – Genesis 1 ("made in our image")	Man not special
Man and time	Man created near the BEGINNING of time – Genesis 1	Man evolved near the END of evolutionary time
Origin/Offspring	Living things (organisms) after own "kind" – Genesis 1	Living things (organisms) after same single cell
Distinctness	Each thing created distinct – Genesis 1	Each thing from same origin
Temperature	Cool ("water") – Genesis 1	Initially hot, then cooled
Environment	Life sustaining – Genesis 1	Initially harsh
Morality	Defined by Creator God – Exodus 20	Defined by masses and power
Rights	Come from God – Exodus 20	Come from government
Races	Single race, created in God's image – Genesis 1 & 8	Some 'races' more evolved
Who's involved	God's involved and cares – Genesis 1, John 3:16	Government involved
Involvement	Personal God – John 3:16	Impersonal chance
Love	Loving God (agape) "God so loved the world" – John 3:16	"Love" defined by society/culture – [eros/phileo]
Life approach	Positive approach [life after physical death] – John 3:16	Negative approach [death is the end]
Complexity	Decreases over time - Genesis 1	Increases over time
Change	Limited – Genesis 1	Unlimited
Death	Entered via one man's sin (Adam) – Genesis 1	Entered via random upward progression
Information Source	Source & provider – Genesis 1	No provider
Purpose	Purpose to fulfill – Matthew 28:18-20	No purpose to fulfill
Realm	Spiritual and physical – Genesis 1	Physical only
Foundation	Love - John 3:16 ("For God so loved the world...")	Racist (Darwin)
Creation	Created mature – Genesis 1	Single cell, then more complex
Sustained	All things sustained by Jesus Christ "in Him all things hold together" – Colossians 1:17	All things in random motion
Glory to...	God to receive glory and honor – Revelation 4:11	Science and man to receive glory and honor

E. Quotes on macro-evolution

1. Quote #1, from a non-Christian:

   "The inability of unguided trial and error to reach anything but the most trivial of ends in almost every field of interest obviously raises doubts as to its validity in the biological realm." – Dr. Michael Denton[10]

2. Quote #2, from a non-Christian:

   "The theory of life was assembled by an intelligence... Indeed, such a theory is so obvious that one wonders why it is not widely accepted as being self-evident. The reasons are psychological rather than scientific." – Dr. Fred Hoyle[11]

F. The Approach...

1. If you can't start the car engine, then you can't use the car to travel! If you can't get the car to move on its own, then you can't use the car to travel! If macro-evolution could not have started, then all the other "evidences" for macro-evolution would be **totally and completely** invalid!

2. **Questions to ask evolutionists or anyone who leans towards macro-evolutionism. These questions need to be answered from an operational science basis. Therefore, there can be NO**

   a. "Don't you **suppose**..."

   b. "Don't you **think**..."

   c. "Couldn't you **believe**..."

   d. "Wouldn't you **expect**..."

   e. "Can't you **see**" or "Doesn't it **seem**..."

   f. "**Shouldn't one know**..."

   g. "...**ly**" **words**. e.g.: "likely," "normally..."

If the macro-evolutionists cannot provide repeatable, verifiable, documented, double-blind analysis and studies for any **one or a combination or all of these questions**, then their position is one of a belief system, a religion, a philosophy totally without any operational science evidence and validation or mathematics.

Did God "use" macro-evolution after He initially created the 'heavens and the earth' in Genesis 1? **NO WAY!**

G. Questions to ask macro-evolutionists:

1. Question #1: Was there oxygen or no oxygen at the time the first cell evolved?

   a. **If "YES"...**

      i.   Then free-oxygen would reduce or tear down an organism. How could the first weak cell and organism survive an environment with oxygen?

      ii. If the early earth had free-oxygen in its atmosphere then "... the compounds (called amino acids) needed for life to evolve would have been destroyed by oxidation."– Dr. Walt Brown[12]

   b. **If "NO"...**

      i.   Then, life is without oxygen. How did it evolve?

      ii. Anaerobic organisms (bacteria, etc.): If these initially evolved, then how did they evolve to organisms that require oxygen for life?

      iii. The protective ozone layer would not exist without oxygen.

      iv. "Without ozone to shield the earth, the sun's ultraviolet radiation would destroy life."– Dr. Walt Brown[13]

   c. "If we have oxygen we have no organic compounds, but if we don't have oxygen we have none, either."– Dr. Michael Denton[14]

   d. **Either answer by a macro-evolutionist has very serious macro-evolutionary consequences!**

   e. **If either answer (a "yes" or a "no") leads to macro-evolution not being possible, then the solution promotes creation!**

2. Question #2: How did life come from non-life?

   a. Spontaneous generation: The belief that life comes from non-life.

      i.   In the mid-1800's, Louis Pasteur disproved contemporary theories of spontaneous generation and no viable evidence has been presented since then to support the claim.

   b. Law of Biogenesis – Life only comes from pre-existing life.

   c. "If thousands of scientists have designed carefully planned experiments to create life from something nonliving, and yet have failed miserably every time, how in the world can we be expected to believe that nature did it by using accidents, chance, and blind forces?"[15]

   d. **Since macro-evolution does not favor the weak and favors the strong, how did the first weak cell evolve in a harsh world? How DID it evolve...scientifically?**

3. **Question #3: How did sex evolve?**

   a. Which came first – asexual reproduction or sexual reproduction?

      i. Asexual reproduction – Reproduction in which an organism produces one or more clones of itself, such as by fission or budding.

      ii. Sexual reproduction – Need both a qualified male and female for reproduction. A mate **MUST** exist at the same time and place! Sexual reproduction takes more than biology.

   b. "The evolution of sex is one of the major unsolved problems of biology. Even those with enough hubris to publish on the topic often freely admit that they have little idea of how sex originated or is maintained. It is enough to give heart to creationists. – Michael Rose (Rose believes in macro-evolutionism)[16]

   c. "Sex is something of an embarrassment to evolutionary biologists. Textbooks understandably skirt the issue, keeping it a closely guarded secret." – Kathleen McAuliffe (McAuliffe believes in macro-evolutionism)[17]

   d. Darwinian/Neo-Darwinian issues: How do small, incremental, random events provide a solution to asexual or sexual reproduction?

   e. Punctuated Equilibrium issues: How do fast, discrete, random events provide a solution to asexual or sexual reproduction?

   f. "It turns out that sex is a big puzzle for Darwinian theory. In fact, a literal interpretation of the theory predicts that sexual reproduction should not exist. Here's the problem. Given two organisms, if both are asexual, both can reproduce. If both are sexual, only one (the female) can bear young. A little math shows that asexual organisms should rapidly outbreed sexual ones and dominate the world. But since sexual species actually dominate, Darwinism has some explaining to do. In the past century dozens of guesses have been made as to why, against straightforward expectations, sex predominates." (Emphasis added.) – Dr. Michael Behe[18]

   g. What about the sterile female ant worker and the sexual evolution issue? Same is true of the honey bee and termites!!

   h. In his 1859 book Origin of Species, Charles Darwin stated: "But with the working ant we have an insect differing greatly from its parents, yet absolutely sterile; so that it could never have transmitted successively acquired modifications of structure or instinct to its progeny. It may well be asked, how is it possible to reconcile this case with the theory of natural selection?"[19]

4. **Question #4: How did information evolve? How did it get into the cell if the cell evolved by random chance?**

    a. Definition of information: "Knowledge of specific events or situations that has been gathered or received by communications..."[20]

       i.   Implies an information giver or provider!

       ii. Implies an information receiver who can use the information, if progress is to be made.

       iii. Who is the information giver or provider?

       iv. Can't be a "what," for "what" can't communicate information.

    b. Random chance does not utilize nor have information to assist it in obtaining a goal, by definition. (Random: proceeding, made or occurring without definite aim, reason or pattern.)

    c. Doesn't information in a cell indicate an information giver or provider?

    d. Macro-evolutionists are then in a box:

       i.   If they *affirm* information existed at the time life evolved,

            a. Then they acknowledge an information provider and the aspect of randomness is lost.

       ii. If they *deny* information existed at the time life evolved,

            a. Then they cannot communicate information because it does not exist.

    e. Information has to exist! It is a *requirement* for life. But if information is a requirement, then life didn't come about via randomness or via an accident. There then exists an information giver.

    f. Information is needed for:

       i.   An information giver

       ii. An information receiver

       iii. An information processor

5. **Question #5: What is the probability of macro-evolution ever occurring?**

a. What is the definition of impossibility in science?

   i. In our study of the reliability of Scripture, we taught that the threshold for impossibility in science is 1 in 10^{50}. Any number beyond this is meaningless from the standpoint of human understanding.

   ii. William Dembski has stated with his Law of Small Probability[21] that specified events of small probability do not occur by chance. He would say that small probability is something that is worse than 10^{-150}. Alternatively one chance in 10^{150}.

   iii. 'Visually' a decimal point+149 zeros, then a 1.

b. Probabilities of an event or set of events are given as fully possible to fully impossible. Any time an event has a chance that gets closer and closer to zero as a probability (possibility), then that event is moving closer to a non-occurrence, an impossibility. Given the amount of time, from a macro-evolutionary perspective of supposedly 15-20 billion years for the universe or 4.5 billion years for the presumed age of the earth, biological evolution could never have occurred, on or off the earth, based upon the given probabilities in the chart below.

c. Using the macro-evolutionary time frame, there are about 141,912,000,000,000,000 seconds for the last 4.5 billion years (86,400 seconds/day * 365 days/year * 4,500,000,000 years). Listed in the chart below it shows the probability of getting 2000 properly functioning enzymes is 1 chance in $10^{-40,000th}$. Since 10 to the 40,000[th] power is substantially GREATER than the number of seconds for the last 4.5 billion years we can easily conclude that EVEN IF EACH AND EVERY macro-evolutionary step was successful WITH the proper information being transferred and the proper time, place and method that macro-evolution would never occur. Even if you presume each step took approximately 1 second, macro-evolution could NEVER occur. Keep in mind that this 10 to the 40,000[th] power is only a simple cell, not a complete human life or ANY viable organism!

d. Psalm 139:14: *"I praise you because I am fearfully and wonderfully made; your works are wonderful, I know that full well."*

e. Look at some examples on the following chart:

Mathematical Impossibility: 10^{-150}	Getting 2000 properly functioning enzymes in a cell [Hoyle][22]	To get a Simple Cell [Mastropaolo][23]
Probability	$10^{-40,000}$	$10^{-4,478,296}$
Dice[(A)]	51,400	5,755,000
Coin Flip[(B)]	132,875	8,302,775

Dice - The possibility that this number of people would be throwing dice and obtaining the same results simultaneously

Coin Flip - The possibility that this number of people would be flipping a coin and obtain the same results simultaneously

f. Areas NOT included in above calculations:

  i.   These probabilities ONLY focus on the components!

  ii. Energy needed for the formation and functioning of the cell

  iii. Functional differences of various cells

  iv. Life allowing environmental conditions outside the cell

  v.   Life allowing temperature outside the cell

  vi. Proper angular structure of each molecule

  vii. Proper three-dimensional structure of the molecules

  viii. Information!

  ix. Others... (Time is really an enemy of macro-evolution due to the dynamic nature of changing EXTERNAL situations which cannot be coped with within an entirely random process!)

g. Dr. Michael Denton states:

"The Darwinian claims that all the adaptive design of nature has resulted from a random search, a mechanism unable to find the best solution in a game of checkers, is one of the most daring claims in the history of science.

"Neither Darwin, Dawkins nor any other biologist has ever calculated the probability of a random search finding, in the finite time available, the sorts of complex systems which are ubiquitous in nature. (emphasis added)

"It is surely a little premature to claim that random processes could have assembled mosquitoes and elephants when we still have to determine the actual probability of the discovery of chance of one single functional protein molecule."[24]

i. Macro-evolution:

    (a) Never existed in the past

    (b) Does not exist in the present

    (c) Never will exist in the future

ii. Macro-evolution is now shown to be...

    (a) Scientifically impossible

    (b) Mathematically impossible

Small Group Discussion Guide

Lesson 8: Did Life Just Happen or Were We Created?

Small Group Objective:

The goal is to help the students begin to better understand the importance of these issues, and be better equipped to speak intelligently and constructively with others about why they believe in the Creator God.

✓ **Check Points**

☐ Bring 3 x 5 cards for your students to write down any questions they may have which aren't answered during the discussion.

☐ Enlist a student to share a brief personal testimony.

Discussion Questions:

1. Review prayer requests from the week before and ask how the students are doing.

2. Lead a time of discussion, asking the following questions:

(*Note: Work through as many of the following questions as possible. The goal is not to get through all of them, but to encourage each student to participate in the discussion as part of the learning process.*)

   a. What day of the devotional did you find most meaningful?

   b. How did last week's lesson impact your life? Did you share it?

   c. How many of you have ever had an opportunity to engage someone in conversation about macro-evolution? How did it go? Did you feel confident in what you were sharing, or not?

   d. Why is this subject of Creator versus Macro-evolution so important?

   e. Has this lesson changed your own ideas about macro-evolution in any way? If so, how?

   f. Of the different questions to ask macro-evolutionists that were presented, which one(s) did you find the most compelling?

   g. What did you learn about this subject that you found interesting or encouraging?

   h. Do you feel more confident to be able to talk with someone about this subject?

i.   In light of what you have learned, why is it important that you include "uniquely created" when framing someone?

j.   What questions, if any, come to mind as a result of this week's lesson?

3.   Ask for prayer requests and tell students that you will be faithful to pray for them during the week. Encourage students to record the prayer requests in the prayer request section of their handbooks, so they can pray for one another during the week. Begin the prayer time by sharing your own request. Spend the remaining time in prayer.

★ **After the Session**

1.   Contact small group members during the week. Ask them about their devotional time, a question they have raised, or how their week is going.

Prayer Requests

Student Devotionals written by T.M. Moore

Did Life Just Happen Or Were We Created?

The daily readings for this week concentrate on God's work of creating the world and all that is in it. The teaching of Scripture is crystal clear; the challenge to us is to receive the Word of God and to live in the world He has made as His creatures, seeking His ends for the world He has made.

Day 1: By the Word of His Power

Pray: *"Know that the LORD, he is God! It is he who made us..."* (Psalm 100:3).

Read: Colossians 1:15-17

Meditate: How much of "all that is" did the Word of God create? Why were these things made?

             What does it mean to say that the Word of God "is before all things?" In what sense does He "hold together" all that He has made?

             If He made it, and is before it, and if He holds it all together, how should I regard the various things of the world with which I will come into contact today?

Journal: The world I live in belongs to Jesus. Everything has its existence because and by Him. Today, I will show that I acknowledge this by...

Pray: *"Enter his gates with thanksgiving, and his courts with praise!"* (Psalm 100:4).

Day 2: Ignorance is No Excuse

Pray: *"He set the earth on its foundations, so that it should never be moved"* (Psalm 104:5).

Read: 2 Peter 3:1-7

Meditate: How does Peter regard those who do not believe that the Word of God created all things (v. 3)? What does that mean?

According to v. 5, why do these people hold this view of the world? What would make them do that?

Is it ever true of me that I "deliberately overlook" the true nature of the created world? How does that show up in me?

Journal: People who "deliberately overlook" the teaching of Scripture will most likely scoff at its teachings. I know some people like that. My responsibility toward them is...

Pray: *"Bless the LORD, O my soul! O LORD my God, you are very great!"* (Psalm 104:1).

Day 3: Wisdom Beyond Reason

Pray: *"Be not silent, O God of my praise! For wicked and deceitful mouths are opened against me..."* (Psalm 109:1, 2).

Read: Job 38:1-11

Meditate: Job had questioned the wisdom of God, because He would not give him a reason for his suffering. How did God regard Job's insistence that he be given a reasonable explanation of such mysteries (vv. 1-3)?

Creation is also a great mystery. Does this mean I should not expect to be able fully to understand how or why God made the world? But does this mean I should not believe that He made it? What's the difference?

The world God created has certain "boundaries," "limits," and "laws." What are some of these? What makes them work the way they do? If God should withdraw the upholding work of His Word on any of these things, what would happen?

Lesson 8: Did Life Just Happen or Were We Created? - Anchorsaway Worldview Handbook ©

Journal: What a mystery creation is! No one can fully understand it. But I can understand that God made it all, and that He keeps it going. Therefore...

Pray: *"With my mouth I will give great thanks to the LORD; I will praise him in the midst of the throng..."* (Psalm 109:30).

Day 4: And Everything in It!

Pray: *"The earth is the LORD's and the fullness thereof, the world and those who dwell therein..."* (Psalm 24:1).

Read: Psalm 24

Meditate: This psalm combines teaching about creation with teaching about seeking the Lord. How are these two things related?

Why is it logical for me – a creature – to be a seeker after God – the Creator? Can those who are not seeking the Lord hope to gain true knowledge about the world and everything in it – including themselves?

The Creator is also the King of Glory. He created the world, and me, for His glory. What does that mean? Does my life reflect this purpose? How?

Journal: As a creature of God, and a seeker after Him, I want to live for the glory of God. I need to make certain that all the "gates" of the city of my life are open to Him. I need to check to make sure that's the case; therefore...

Pray: *"Who shall ascend to the hill of the LORD? And who shall stand in his holy place?"* (Psalm 24:3).

Day 5: Right Before Their Eyes

Pray: *"By the word of the LORD the heavens were made, and by the breath of his mouth all their host"* (Psalm 33:6).

Read: Romans 1:18-32

Meditate: Do people know that God created the world? How do they know this? Does the fact that they don't admit it mean they don't know it?

Instead of honoring God as Creator, what do many people do? If they stopped to give Him thanks for His creation – or if they knew people who were more vocal in their thanksgiving – would this affect them in any ways? How?

People who, knowing God made them and the world, are not grateful, and turn instead to "idols" – all manner of created things – quickly find that God "gives them up" to sinful practices. What does this suggest about the importance of honoring God as Creator? Do I honor Him this way? How?

Journal: Sin, it seems, is flourishing in the world because people do not honor God as Creator. Surely, I can do something about this! Surely, I...

Pray: *"The LORD brings the counsel of the nations to nothing...the counsel of the LORD stands forever..."* (Psalm 33:10, 11).

ENDNOTES

1 "Was Darwin Wrong?" Life Apr. 1982: 48.

2 Richard Dawkins, as quoted by Josh Gilder, a creationist, in his critical review, "PBS's 'Evolution' series is propaganda, not science," WorldNetDaily.com 24 September 2001, WorldNetDaily 13 April 2005 <http://www.worldnetdaily.com/news/article.asp?ARTICLE_ID=24640>. For other related quotes by Richard Dawkins, see <http://www.positiveatheism.org/hist/quotes/dawkins.htm>.

3 Richard Dawkins, The Selfish Gene (Oxford, UK: Oxford University Press, 1976) 1.

4 Julian Huxley, "The Emergence of Darwinism," Evolution of Life ed. Sol Tax (Chicago: University of Chicago Press, 1960) 1. Quoted in Michael Denton, Evolution: Theory in Crisis (Bethesda, MD: Adler & Adler Publishers, 1985) 75.

5 Edward O. Wilson, "Toward a Humanistic Biology," The Humanist vol. 42 Sept.-Oct. 1982: 40.

6 Charles Templeton, A Farewell to God: My Reasons for Rejecting the Christian Faith (Toronto, Ontario, Canada: McClelland & Stewart, Inc., 1996) 232.

7 Michael Denton, Evolution: Theory in Crisis (Bethesda, MD: Adler & Adler Publishers, 1985) 67.

8 Richard Bozarth, "The Meaning of Evolution," The American Atheist vol. 20 #2 Feb. 1978: 30.

9 Foltz, Tom, Chart on Macro vs. Creation.

10 Denton, Evolution: Theory in Crisis, 314.

11 Fred Hoyle, The Intelligent Universe (London: Michael Joseph Ltd., 1983) 16.

12 Walt Brown, In the Beginning: Compelling Evidence for Creation and the Flood 7th ed. (Phoenix, AZ: Center for Scientific Creation, 2001) 13.

13 Walt Brown, In the Beginning: Compelling Evidence for Creation and the Flood 7th ed. (Phoenix, AZ: Center for Scientific Creation, 2001) 13.

14 Denton, Evolution: Theory in Crisis 261-262.

15 Kyle Butt, "Biogenesis – The Long Arm of the Law," ApologeticsPress.org 2002, Apologetics Press 13 April 2005 <http://www.apologeticspress.org/modules.php?name=Read&itemid=1769&cat=3>.

16 Michael Rose, "Slap and Tickle in the Primeval Soup," New Scientist vol. 112 Oct. 30, 1986: p. 55.

17 Kathleen McAuliffe, "Why We have Sex," Omni Dec. 1983: 18. Quoted in Walt Brown, In the Beginning, 65.

18 Michael J. Behe, "Darwin's Hostages: A decision in Kansas to question evolution dogma has given rise to hysteria and intolerance," The American Spectator Dec. 1999-Jan. 2000: Access Research Network 19 April 2005 <http://www.arn.org/docs/behe/mb_darwinshostages.htm>.

19 Charles Darwin, On the Origin of Species (1859; London: Penguin Books, 1985) 258.

20 "Information" Dictionary.com 14 April 2005 <http://dictionary.reference.com/search?q=information>.

21 William Dembski, The Design Inference: Eliminating Chance Through Small Probabilities (Cambridge, UK: Cambridge University Press, 1998) 5, 209-210.

22 Fred Hoyle, and C. Wickramasinghe, Evolution from Space (London: J. M. Dent and Sons, 1981) 24.

23 Joseph Mastropaolo, "Evolution is Biologically Impossible," Institute for Creation Research Impact no. 317 November 1999 14 April 2005 <http://www.icr.org/pubs/imp/imp-317.htm>.

24 Denton, Evolution: Theory in Crisis, 324.

Recommended Reading

Key Organizations:

- For up-to-date biblical research in the area of science and creation, Answers In Genesis: www.answersingenesis.org

- For up-to-date biblical research in the area of science and creation, Institute for Creation Research: www.icr.org

- For great scientific research debunking the Theory of Evolution and defending Intelligent Design, The Discovery Institute: www.discovery.org/csc/

Key Books:

Brown, Walt. In the Beginning: Compelling Evidence for Creation and the Flood. 7th Ed. Phoenix, AZ: Center for Scientific Creation, 2001.

Butt, Kyle. "Biogenesis – The Long Arm of the Law." ApologeticsPress.org. 2002 Apologetics Press. 13 April 2005

Colson, Chuck. Answers to Your Kids' Questions. Wheaton, IL: Tyndale House Publishers, 2000.

Copan, Paul, and William Lane. Craig. Creation out of Nothing: A Biblical, Philosophical, and Scientific Exploration. Leicester, England: Apollos, 2004.

Darwin, Charles. On the Origin of Species. 1859. London: Penguin Books, 1985.

Dawkins, Richard. The Selfish Gene. Oxford, UK: Oxford University Press, 1976.

Denton, Michael. Evolution: Theory in Crisis. Bethseda, MD: Adler & Adler Publishers, 1985.

Dembski, William A. The Design Revolution: Answering the Toughest Questions about Intelligent Design. Downers Grove, IL: InterVarsity, 2004.

Hoyle, Fred. The Intelligent Universe. London: Michael Joseph Ltd., 1983.

Hoyle, Fred and C. Wickramasinghe. Evolution from Space. London: J. M. Dent and Sons, 1981.

Huxley, Julian. "The Emergence of Darwinism." Evolution of Life. Chicago: University of Chicago Press, 1960.

Mastropaolo, Joseph. "Evolution is Biologically Impossible." Institute for Creation Research Impact no. 317 November 1999 14 April 2005 14 April 2005.

Moreland, James Porter, and John Mark Reynolds. Three Views on Creation and Evolution. Grand Rapids, MI: Zondervan Pub., 1999.

Strobel, Lee. The Case for A Creator. Grand Rapids, MI 49530, Zondervan, 2004.

Templeton, Charles. A Farewell to God: My Reasons for Rejecting the Christian Faith. Toronto, Ontario, Canada: McClelland & Stewart, Inc., 1996.

"TMR 048 : Dr. Michael J. Behe : Intelligent Design." TMR 048 : Dr. Michael J. Behe : Intelligent Design. N.p., n.d. Web. 23 Aug. 2016.

Vine, W. E. An Expository Dictionary of New Testament Words. Vine, W. E., Merrill F. Unger, and William White, Jr. Vine's Complete Expository Dictionary of Old and New Testament Words. Nashville, TN: Thomas Nelson Publishers, 1996.

Wald, George. "The Origin of Life." The Scientific American August 1954: 44-53.

"Was Darwin Wrong?" Life April 1982: 48.

Lesson 9: Who Is the god of Islam?

A. Introduction:[1]

1. Seven million Muslims live among us and more than 2 billion Muslims live worldwide, who still have not heard the good news of Jesus Christ. We have a historic opportunity to reach more Muslims than ever before with the Gospel.

B. What is Islam?

1. Islam is the name of the Muslim religion. It means, "to submit or surrender one's will." Traditionally, Islamic teachers claimed that Muslims are submitting to the will of Allah.

2. Muslim is the name of the followers of the religion of Islam.

3. Muhammad founded the religion in 610 AD, after the birth of Christ. Muhammad's life and actions embody, for a Muslim today, the perfect behavior and model.

4. Muslims follow the Qur'an, Hadith and the Imam's (Muslim Teacher) interpretation of Islamic teachings. The majority of Muslims have never studied the Qur'an or the New Testament.

C. Basic Beliefs of Islam:

1. Belief in "god"

a. Allah in Arabic means, "the only god."

b. Christian Arabs used the name, Allah, to refer to the God of Abraham, Moses, and Jacob.

c. According to the Qur'an, Allah is unknowable and uninterested in the daily lives of Muslims. He is a sovereign god that has the power to do good and evil.

d. This belief of god shows that the Quranic understanding of god is not the same as the Bible. God in the Bible is Holy and does not create sin and evil. Allah in the Qur'an is unknowable and transcendent. He is the Law giver and punisher of the disobedient. God in the Bible is the law giver, the just judge, the merciful and the Redeemer.

e. Muslim Imams or teachers, claim that Allah can be known through the 99 beautiful names. The Qur'an has 104 names of god, but the number 99 has a magical significance to Muslims. Many of the names of Allah are similar to the characteristics of God in the Bible.

f. However, there are attributes of the God of Scripture that are missing from the 99 names of Allah. They are agape love, justice, and mercy.

g. We disagree, as Christians, on the following names for God:

    i. Al Mumeet – The Source of Death

    ii. Al Muntaqem – God will come after you out of vengeance, not necessarily justice.

    iii. Al Macker – The Schemer, god can change his mind.

2. Belief in angels

a. Angels are created from light to do good on earth.

b. Demons, 'afrit,' are created from fire to do evil on earth.

c. Jinn are half demonic and half human. They tend to be regarded as demonic or controlled by Satan, known as Iblis.

3. Belief in prophets (Sura 2:136 – Sura 3:84)

a. Islam teaches that god sends prophets to enlighten men. They also believe in the prophets God sent to the Jewish people.

b. Adam, Noah, Abraham, Moses, Jacob, and Jesus are all respected equally. The Qur'an mentions Job and Jonah, although it does not record their story.

c. The Qur'an also requires Muslims to believe in John the Baptist, who is called the prophet, Yahya.

d. Orthodox Islam teaches that Muhammad is the seal or last of the prophets.

e. The Ahmadiyah sect teaches that Gholam Ahmad is the seal or last of the prophets.

f. The Bahai' religion claims that Baha'ulah was the seal or last of the prophets.

4. Belief in holy books

a. Islam teaches that god sent four holy books that must be read and studied by all Muslims.

    i. Tawrat: Book of Moses

    ii. Zabur: Book of David

    iii. Injeel: Book of Jesus

    iv. Qur'an: Book of Muhamad

b. The only book accessible to Muslims is the Qur'an. The Qur'an mentions the first three books but they are unavailable to Muslims due to oppressive government restrictions. Religious Imams claim that the first three revelations from god were corrupted, hence, god sent the Qur'an. When asked about the possibility of corrupting the Qur'an, Muslims emphatically deny the possibility, since god, Allah, is stronger than humans and does keep his revelation.

5. Belief in the judgment day

    a. The Qur'an teaches that god will judge all people one day for all their deeds in their life.

    b. There is no promise of salvation for women.

    c. A scale will weigh the good and evil works a person has committed. Whichever is more will tip the scale, determining whether a person is to spend eternity in paradise or hell.

    d. Islam teaches that Allah might change his mind on the judgment day and send a devout Muslim to hell. Allah, in Islam, is not bound by his character or word. Allah judges according to his whims, not according to justice.

    e. Salvation, in Islam, depends entirely on one's good works. Life is regarded as a test that can be passed through human efforts. Salvation of mankind is reduced to a system of good and bad works without a biblical understanding of sin. The Ten Commandments may be followed, but they must be applied by imitating Muhammad's life and teachings.

6. Belief in fate – This belief is on the rise.

    a. Islam teaches that whatever Allah decrees, either good or evil, must come to pass. God, in Islam, is the source of good and evil. Evil people have no way out since they were created in that manner. It is important to understand that the concept of grace is very foreign if you believe in fate. Fatalism is entrenched in the minds of many Muslims as a way to control their social and daily lives.

    b. Fear from Allah engulfs their daily life and moral conduct. Their obedience is a result of fear, and not of the power of the Holy Spirit.

D. Pillars of Diin – Islam has five basic pillars of faith that every Muslim must practice. (A smaller percentage of Muslims believe in a sixth pillar, Jihad):[2]

    1. Al-Shahadah (profession of faith): The recitation of: "I testify that there is no god except Allah, and I testify that Muhammad is the messenger of Allah."

        a. Reciting this creed in front of a Muslim makes you a Muslim.

        b. This creed becomes a power object to recite and control Allah's favor and blessing, Barakah. This creed is whispered in the ear of the newborn infant, proclaiming that Islam has been decided for him/her as a religion and political allegiance.

    2. Al-Salat (prayer): A prayer ceremony exercised in the mosque or alone five times a day.

a. The times of prayer are:

    i. Sunrise

    ii. Noon

    iii. Afternoon – usually 2 hours after the noon hour

    iv. Sunset

    v. Nighttime – usually 2 hours after sunset

b. All prayers must be preceded by ritual ablutions, after which a Christian, Jew, pagan or woman must not be touched, for fear of defilement. Muslims around the world must recite the first chapter of the Qur'an in Arabic regardless of whether or not they understand Arabic.

c. Muslims borrowed the prayer rug from Arabian Jews during the life of Muhammad.

d. Muhammad ordered his people to pray to Mecca instead of Jerusalem, once they migrated to Medina.

e. Women must never pray in front of men. Many men ask their wives to pray at home rather than in the mosque.

3. Al-Saum (fasting):

a. During the month of Ramadam or Ramazan, a Muslim is not allowed to eat, as long as there is daylight.

4. Al-Zakat (giving alms):

a. A percentage of a Muslim's income must be given as alms to needy Muslims.

5. Al-Hajj (pilgrimage): The Pilgrimage to Mecca and Medina

a. This pilgrimage is a must for every Muslim who is able to make the trip and can afford it.

b. A Muslim man or woman who has performed the Hajj ritual will be called a Hajji.

c. This was borrowed from Christian Arabs who made a pilgrimage to Jerusalem prior to Islam.

6. Al-Jihad (The belief in this sixth pillar is increasing.) Persevere and strive for implementing Islam even through force.

a. It is a term given to holy war. Since the institution of Jihad, Muhammad referred to those dying in Jihad as special martyrs. They were not praying in a mosque or reading the Qur'an, but they were implementing Islam by force. Whenever you hear or read about Jihad, it means fighting in the cause of Islam. This is clearly depicted in the history of the Middle East.

b. Today's Islam does not have a religious leader acting as the Caliph, successor of Muhammad. Therefore, holy war, Jihad, has been waged against anyone disagreeing with the whims of Muslim leaders.

c. Eight of ten Muslims have not read the Qur'an. Few know what is written and therefore do not know what or why they believe.

d. In 2006, there were 2.2 billion Muslims in the world. Five percent of that number are militant Muslims who wage war against anyone disagreeing with the whims of Muslim leaders.

e. There are several verses in the Qur'an that promote waging war (Sura 9:111, Sura 9:5, 5:33, 8:12-17, 9:73, 9:29, 5:51).

   i. Sura 56:12-40 (The companions of the right hand are promised virgins.)

   ii. Hadith - Vol. 1, Book 2, #24 (Allah's Apostle said: "I have been ordered (by Allah) to fight against the people until they testify that none has the right to be worshipped but Allah and that Muhammad is Allah's Apostle.")

f. Why do they hate Americans?

   i. They do not know us.

   ii. They watch selected American TV programs and see magazines and think that all Americans are like what they see through the media.

   iii. Materialism, freedom for women, and the power and influence of America do not sit well with the Muslim nations.

E. Comparison between Jesus and Muhammad:

1. Muhammad

   a. Was born of Aminah in AD 570.

   b. Abdallah is his earthly father.

   c. Married 13 + wives/concubines.

   d. Lived a pious life, at best.

   e. Prayed often for forgiveness for himself.

   f. Waged 66 battles.

   g. Ordered the deaths of many and approved assassinations.

   h. Showed little mercy, and used the sword in controlling people.

   i. Established the rule of Islam in Arabia.

   j. Died of pneumonia or poisoning at age 62.

    k. He is dead!

    l. Is never mentioned in the Bible.

    m. Is mentioned in the Qur'an 25 times.

    n. No prophecies given about Muhammad or his coming.

2. **Jesus**

    a. Was born of the virgin Mary.

    b. Had no earthly father.

    c. Never married.

    d. Lived a sinless life.

    e. Never prayed for forgiveness for himself.

    f. Waged no war.

    g. Ordered the death of no one.

    h. Established the kingdom of God in the hearts of men.

    i. Died by crucifixion at 33 years of age.

    j. Rose from the dead!

    k. Christianity rests on Christ and Christ alone.

    l. Is mentioned in the Qur'an 97 times.

    m. Over 300 prophecies given hundreds of years before His birth.

F. Verses in the Qur'an on believing in the New Testament:

1. The following verses clearly show that the Qur'an supports that Muslims read the message of Jesus. The Imams refuse to allow Muslims to think for themselves and study the teachings of Christ.

2. **Sura 2:136** "Say ye: 'We believe in Allah, and the revelation given to us, and to Abraham, Isma`il, Isaac, Jacob, and the Tribes, and that given to Moses and Jesus, and that given to (all) Prophets from their Lord. We make no difference between one and another of them, and we bow to Allah (in Islam).'"

3. **Sura 57:27** "Then, in their wake, We followed them up with (others of) Our messengers: We sent after them Jesus the son of Mary, and bestowed on him the Gospel; and We ordained in the hearts of those who followed him Compassion and Mercy."

4. **Sura 5:46** "And in their footsteps We sent Jesus the son of Mary, confirming the Law that had come before him: We sent him the Gospel: therein was guidance and light, and confirmation of the Law that had come before him: a guidance and an admonition to those who fear Allah."

5. **Sura 5:47** "Let the people of the Gospel judge by what Allah hath revealed therein. If

any do fail to judge by (the light of) what Allah hath revealed, they are (no better than) those who rebel."

6. **Sura 2:148** "For Allah Hath power over all things."

7. **Sura 5:68** "Say: 'O People of the Book! ye have no ground to stand upon unless ye stand fast by the Law, the Gospel, and all the revelation that has come to you from your Lord.'"

G. Witnessing to Muslims:

1. **Pray for the salvation of Muslims.** Pray for God to send an awakening on the Muslim world.

2. **Build friendships.**

3. **Be patient.**

4. **Take the initiative and begin a conversation.** Ask about their country and background.

5. **Do not witness to Muslims in a group.**

6. **Answer criticism,** if necessary, in order to expel false information about Christ and Christianity.

7. **Give Muslims a New Testament (Injeel) as a gift.**

8. **Expect results.**

9. **Invite them to a small group Bible study.**

10. **Build on similarities between Islam and Christianity.**

H. Recommended Training

It is difficult to give justice to the study of Islam and how to witness to Muslims in just one session. We recommend attending the one day seminar, "Sharing the Hope" an intensive training. Visit www.crescentproject.org for more information.

Conclusion

The more we understand Islam, the better equipped we will be to address the emerging issues in our culture today. It may be necessary, however, to work through our preconceived ideas about Muslims and their faith, in order for us to reach them for Christ.

Muslims are no different than any of us, in that, before accepting God's gift of saving grace, we are all lost in our sin. Given the growing interest in the Muslim religion and the great numbers of Muslims living in the world today, the harvest is becoming increasingly plentiful. As we build bridges with our Muslim neighbors, we will be able to ultimately help them cross the bridge to Christ.

Do our hearts break for Muslims? Do we feel an urgency to reach them with the truth of the Gospel? Never in our time have we been presented with a more unique moment to reach the Muslim world with the love and grace that can only be found in Jesus Christ. As Fouad Masri reminds us, the events taking place in the Muslim world, including increased Islamic militancy, suggest a growing thirst for truth.[4] The opportunity is before us. How will we respond?

For more information on how to effectively share the hope of Jesus Christ with Muslims, contact:
Crescent Project – P.O. Box 50986, Indianapolis, IN 46250 317-257-8870
www.crescentproject.org

Small Group Discussion Guide

Lesson 9: Who Is the god of Islam?

Small Group Objective:

The goal is to help the students begin to better understand Islam, in order that they might build friendships with Muslims, and, ultimately, introduce them to Jesus Christ.

✓ Check Points

☐ Bring 3 x 5 cards for your students to write down any questions they may have which aren't answered during the discussion.

☐ Enlist a student to share a brief personal testimony.

Discussion Questions:

1. Review prayer requests from the week before and ask how the students are doing.

2. Lead a time of discussion, asking the following questions:

(*Note*: Work through as many of the following questions as possible. The goal is not to get through all of them, but to encourage each student to participate in the discussion as part of the learning process.)

    a. What day of the devotional did you find most meaningful?

    b. How did last week's lesson impact your life? Did you share it?

    c. How many of you know someone who is Muslim? Have you ever had a chance to talk with them about their faith? Were you able to share your faith with them? How did it go?

    d. Is the god of Islam the same as the God of the Bible? Why/why not?

    e. How does the character of Allah differ from the character of the God of Scripture?

    f. Has this lesson changed your own ideas about Muslims in any way? If so, how?

    g. Frame a Muslim.

    h. What did you learn about this subject that you found interesting, or encouraging?

    i. How can a true understanding of Islam help us reach out to the Muslim world?

    j. How might you be able to share your faith with a Muslim? Is there a particular approach you would use?

    k. What questions, if any, come to mind as a result of this week's lesson?

3. Ask for prayer requests and tell students that you will be faithful to pray for them during the week. Encourage students to record the prayer requests in the prayer request section of their handbooks, so they can pray for one another during the week. Begin the prayer time by sharing your own request. Spend the remaining   time in prayer.

★ After the Session

1. Contact small group members during the week. Ask them about their devotional time, a question they have raised, or how their week is going.

<u>Prayer Requests</u>

Student Devotionals written by T.M. Moore

Who Is the god of Islam?

The Word of God is our authority on all matters of faith and practice. It guides us even in judging the claims of other worldviews and other religions. Scripture gives us examples of what can happen when people embrace false gods in the name of true religion, as we shall see in the devotionals for this week.

Day 1: No Substitutes

Pray: *"Why should the nations say, 'Where is their God?' Our God is in the heavens; he does all that he pleases"* (Psalm 115:2, 3).

Read: 1 Kings 12:25-33

Meditate: Why did Jeroboam set up this alternative religious system (vv. 26, 27)? Were his actions primarily spiritual or political? Whose interest was he serving?

           In what ways did Jeroboam's religious system mirror that of the true God?

           In what ways did Jeroboam compromise and corrupt central aspects of the true religion of Israel? What dangers were there for the people in this?

Journal: Maybe I need to check my motives in worshipping God the way I do. Just to make sure, today I will...

Pray: *"The counsel of the LORD stands forever, the plans of his heart to all generations"* (Psalm 33:11).

Day 2: The Folly of Idolatry

Pray: *"The idols of the nations are...the work of human hands...Those who make them become like them, so do all who trust in them"* (Psalm 135:15, 18).

Read: Isaiah 44:9-20

Meditate:	How does this passage characterize religions that are made up by human beings? In what ways can Islam be seen to fall into this category?

Meditate:	How does this passage characterize religions that are made up by human beings? In what ways can Islam be seen to fall into this category?
What is it about the false gods of man-made religions that makes it so foolish for people to embrace them (vv. 18-20)? How do people fall into such error (cf. Rev. 12:9)? How should I regard people who are trapped in false religions?

According to vv. 12-15, is there a certain "beauty" to false religions? What is it about people that makes them susceptible to the allure of false religions? Do I ever feel attracted to man-made systems of religion? In what ways?

Journal:	Surely, many of the people I know are captivated by false gods of one kind or another. I know they are deceived; I know they have directed the image of God in them to a false deity; nevertheless, I...

Pray:	*"Do not let my heart incline to any evil, to busy myself with wicked deeds in company with men who work iniquity, and let me not eat of their delicacies"* (Psalm 141:4).

Day 3: God Can Handle Himself

Pray:	*"Mark the blameless and behold the upright, for there is a future for the man of peace. But transgressors shall be altogether destroyed; the future of the wicked shall be cut off"* (Psalm 37:37, 38).

Read:	1 Samuel 5:1-12

Meditate:	How did God judge the false god of the Philistines? How did He judge them? Does God still do these kinds of things today?

During the last century, many people wrote that Marxism, which violently persecuted the Church, was just another man-made religion. Has Marxism, at least in many places, suffered the fate of Dagon? Was God involved in this?

Is it possible that "the hand of God" is resting "heavy" upon Islam and other false religions? What would that look like? Should I be encouraged by this? Why or why not?

Journal: Since God is able to act on His own against all false religions, I should...

Pray: *"Let them know that this is your hand; O LORD, you have done it"* (Psalm 109:27).

Day 4: Do I Encourage False Religion?

Pray: *"O God, you know my folly; the wrongs I have done are not hidden from you. Let not those who hope in you be put to shame through me"* (Psalm 69:5, 6).

Read: Leviticus 19:9-18

Meditate: How would I re-phrase this passage in language relevant to my own life situation? What do these verses require of me?

                    If those who worship false gods are "blind," is it possible that Christians in the West are guilty of putting a stumbling-block before them in any way? Can I think of any examples, based on what I see in this text?

                    Is it possible that people turn to false religions because they see so little of real substance in the lives of confessing Christians? Is that ever true of me? Do I truly love my neighbor (v. 18) in the kind of practical ways outlined in this passage?

Journal: Am I a stumbling-block to people who otherwise might come to faith in the one true God? Today, I'm going to examine my life carefully to see whether this is so. I'm going to...

Pray: *"For the LORD is righteous; he loves righteous deeds; the upright shall behold his face"* (Psalm 11:7).

<u>Day 5: Confronting False Religion</u>

Pray: *"Deliver my soul from the wicked by your sword, from men by your hand O LORD, from men of the world whose portion is in this life"* (Psalm 17:13, 14).

Read: Acts 17:22-34

Meditate: I see (vv. 16-21) that Paul took the time to learn about the religion of the Athenians (cf. also vv. 22, 23). How does this counsel me?

How did Paul try to show the Athenians that their religion was illogical (vv. 24-27)? That even some of their own writers pointed to the one true God (vv. 27, 28)? Am I able to do the same with my friends who are attracted to false religions?

How much of the Gospel was Paul able to inject into this message? What was the result (vv. 32-34)? If a Muslim friend, or a friend holding to any other false religion, were to come to faith in Jesus, what would I do with him/her?

Journal: Man, this stuff we're studying is important! From this point on, I...

Pray: *"Let me hear what God the LORD will speak, for he will speak peace to his people, to his saints; but let them not turn back to folly"* (Psalm 85:8).

ENDNOTES

* Unless otherwise indicated, this material was developed by Fouad Masri and has been adapted from the training manual for the "Sharing the Hope" seminar, sponsored by Crescent Project, P.O. Box 50986, Indianapolis, IN 46250 <www.crescentproject.org>. Used with permission.

[1] "Sixth pillar of Islam," Wikipedia: The Free Encyclopedia 7 April 2005 <http://en.wikipedia.org/wiki/Sixth_pillar_of_Islam>.

Recommended Reading

Key Sites:

- For a Christian-Muslim Dialogue: www.answering-islam.org

- For a ministry to Muslims, Fouad Masri – Crescent Project: www.crescentproject.org

Key Books:

Accad, Fouad Elias. Building Bridges: Christianity and Islam. Colorado Springs, CO: NavPress Publishing Group, 1997.

Bary, Rifqa. Hiding in the Light: Why I Risked Everything to Leave Islam and Follow Jesus. Place of Publication Not Identified: Waterbrook Pr, 2016.

Caner, Ergun Mehmet, and Emir Fethi Caner. Unveiling Islam: An Insider's Look at Muslim Life and Beliefs. Grand Rapids, MI: Kregel Publications, 2002.

Gabriel, Mark A. Islam and Terrorism. Lake Mary, FL: Charisma House, 2002.

Garrison, V. David. A Wind in the House of Islam: How God Is Drawing Muslims around the World to Faith in Jesus Christ. Monument, CO: WIGTake Resources, 2014.

Geisler, Norman L., and Abdul Saleeb. Answering Islam: The Crescent in the Light of the Cross. Grand Rapids, MI: Baker Book House, 1994.

Hourani, Albert. A History of the Arab Peoples, 2nd ed. Cambridge, MA: Harvard University Press, 2003.

Huntington, Stephen P. The Clash of Civilizations and the Remaking of World Order. New York: Simon & Schuster, 1998.

Love, Fran, and Jeleta Eckheart. Ministry to Muslim Women: Longing to Call Them Sisters. Pasedena, CA: William Carey Library Publishers, 2003.

Masri, Fouad. "Sharing the Hope" training manual. Crescent Project. P.O. Box 50986, Indianapolis, IN 46250. <www.crescentproject.org>.

McCurry, Don. Healing the Broken Family of Abraham: New Life for Muslims. Colorado Springs, CO: Ministries to Muslims, 2001.

McDowell, Josh. The Islam Debate. San Bernadino, CA: Here's Life Publishers, 1983.

Parshall, Phil. The Cross and the Crescent: Understanding the Muslim Heart and Mind. Gabriel Publishing, 2002.

Qureshi, Nabeel. Answering Jihad: A Better Way Forward. Grand Rapids, MI. Zondervan. 2016.

Qureshi, Nabeel. No God but One: Allah or Jesus?: A Former Muslim Investigates the Evidence for Islam and Christianity. Grand Rapids, MI Zondervan. 2016.

Qureshi, Nabeel. Seeking Allah, Finding Jesus: A Devout Muslim Encounters Christianity. Grand Rapids, MI: Zondervan, 2015.

Sheikh, Belquis and Richard H. Schneider. I Dared to Call Him Father: the Miraculous Story of a Muslim's Encounter with God. Grand Rapids, MI: Chosen Books, 2003.

Zacharias, Ravi K., and Kevin Johnson. Jesus among Other Gods. Nashville, TN: Word Pub., 2000.

Zacharias, Ravi. Light in the Shadow of Jihad: The Struggle for Truth. Sisters, OR: Multnomah, 2002.

Lesson 10: Covenant: What Is the Big Picture of God's Redemption of Man?

⚓ Anchor of the Week: God keeps His covenant promise.

I. What is a covenant?

A. Hebrew: berith means "to bind, to fetter, to cut, a binding obligation."[1]

B. Characteristics of a covenant:

a. Not a contract (exchange of goods, services, time, products) which can be negotiated/changed/canceled

b. The giving of self into a union for life and for death

c. Fullest expression of love and commitment

d. Complements strengths, not based on similarities

II. Covenant Types

A. Parity: An equal party covenant made primarily to complement strengths and weaknesses of both parties. This type of covenant typically provided a fair and equitable benefit to both parties and increased overall quality of life.

B. Suzerain—vassal: A unilateral covenant initiated by a person/tribe/nation vastly superior in power and authority to another party, graciously imposed for the lesser one's good.

A. Representative

B. Promises/Terms/Blessings

C. Blood Sacrifice

D. Seals

E. Oath/Vows

F. Exchanges

G. Meal

H. Memorials

I. Language/Word Clues

1. Hebrew word: hesed means "mutual responsibility that each party to a covenant has to the other, and the rights that each enjoys in the covenant relationship; covenant in action."[2]

2. Love (Greek word: agape "unconditional God-kind of love")

3. Peace

4. Friendship

5. Compassion

6. Remembrance

7. Oath or swearing

8. Blessings & curses

9. Treaty

IV. Illustration: David, Jonathan and Mephibosheth - a picture of God's covenant love

A. The Gospel message is illustrated in this account.

1. David — Lord Almighty (God the Father)

2. Jonathan — Jesus (God the Son)

3. Mephibosheth — You and I

V. The Covenant Connection

A. The Covenant Connection: Obligation to the body of Christ

1. Romans 12:10, 13

2. Galatians 6:10

Lesson 10: Covenant: What Is the Big Picture of God's Redemption of Man?

Small Group Objective:

Your goal is to help students begin to walk deeper in God's covenant love, understand the essential nature of covenant, and better understand the Bible, God's manual for living in this world.

✓ **Check Points:**

☐ Bring 3 x 5 cards for your students to write down any questions they may have which aren't answered during the discussion.

☐ Enlist a student to share a brief personal testimony.

Discussion Questions:

1. Review prayer requests from the week before and ask how the students are doing.

(*Note*: Have students give names of juniors that they would like to be invited for next year's Anchorsaway class. Give these names to the administrator.)

2. Lead a time of discussion, asking the following questions:

(*Note*: Work through as many of the following questions as possible. The goal is not to get through all of them, but to encourage each student to participate in the discussion as part of the learning process.)

    a. What day of the devotional did you find most meaningful?

    b. How did last week's lesson impact your life? Did you share it?

    c. Has this lesson on covenant opened your eyes to looking at God's Word from a new perspective? How so?

    d. What element of the covenant-making process of the Hittite culture, which was acted out during the session, made the deepest impression on you? Why? Which element surprised you the most?

    e. Many of God's names are actually "covenant names." Jehovah Jireh (Provider), Jehovah Rophe (Healer), Jehovah Shalom (Peace), Jehovah Rohi (Shepherd), Jehovah Tsidkenu (Righteousness). How does this help you frame your perception of God?

    f. Describe in your own words the "big picture" of God's redemptive plan through the person of Jesus Christ.

g. Besides the study of God's Word, what other ways can the filter of covenant be applied to your life? (Prayer, evangelism, meditation, relationships) How so?

h. If this lesson were to trigger you to study the Bible more, which section of the Bible would be your starting point? (History, Psalms, Prophets, Gospels, Epistles) Why?

i. What questions, if any, come to mind as a result of this week's lesson?

j. If marriage is a covenant, how seriously should we take it?

3. Ask for prayer requests and tell students that you will be faithful to pray for them during the week. Encourage students to record the prayer requests in the prayer request section of their handbooks, so they can pray for one another during the week. Begin the prayer time by sharing your own request. Spend the remaining time in prayer.

★ After the Session

1. Contact small group members during the week. Ask them about their devotional time, a question they have raised, or how their week is going.

<u>Prayer Requests</u>

Student Devotionals written by T.M. Moore

What Is the Big Picture of God's Redemption of Man?

Understanding God's covenant is an extremely important aspect of our callings as Christians. For the covenant consists of all that God has promised us and all that He is doing in, through, and for us. This week, as we meditate on God's covenant, ask the Lord to help you become more fully immersed in His glorious promises, and to know His covenant presence more continuously at all times.

Day 1: The Covenants of the Promise

Pray: *"He is the LORD our God; his judgments are in all the earth. He remembers his covenant forever..."* (Psalm 105:7, 8).

Read: Ephesians 2:11-22

Meditate: Let's revisit this passage from a different perspective. First, what does this passage say about those who are outside of God's covenant? What must that be like?

           Notice that the text says the covenants (plural) of the promise (singular). How many times in the Old Testament did God come to make his covenant with someone? Are these various covenants all part of one grand promise? What might that promise be?

           How does this passage point me to Jesus as the fulfillment of God's promise? Can Jesus really be the sum and substance of everything God has promised?

Journal: I know many people who are "strangers" to God's covenant. Is my attitude toward them what it ought to be? To find this out, today...

Pray: *"Oh give thanks to the LORD; call upon his name; make known his deeds among the peoples!"* (Psalm 105:1).

Day 2: Promises to Abram, Promises to Us

Pray: *"He sent redemption to his people; he has commanded his covenant forever. Holy and awesome is his name!"* (Psalm 111:9).

Read: Genesis 12:1-3; Romans 4:13-17

Meditate: How many promises can I see in God's word to Abram? If God came today and spoke those promises to me, how would I understand them? In what kinds of directions would they cause my mind to go?

             According to Paul in Romans 4, who are the recipients of God's promises to Abram? What can that possibly mean for me?

             Would it make any difference in my daily life if, every day, I thought about these promises as promises made to me? How?

Journal: I wonder what it would be like to rephrase God's promises to Abram as though He had actually spoken them to me. Let's see...

Pray: *"What shall I render to the LORD for all his benefits to me? I will lift up the cup of salvation and call on the name of the LORD"* (Psalm 116:12, 13).

Day 3: The Purpose of the Promises

Pray: *"I will offer to you the sacrifice of thanksgiving and call on the name of the LORD"* (Psalm 116:17.

Read: 2 Peter 1:3, 4

Meditate: What has God granted me? Which promises are these? How should I regard them?

             What does God intend to do through me by these precious and very great promises? What does that mean? How would I know when that was happening?

Can I say that I "have escaped the corruption that is in the world because of sinful desire?" If not, could that be keeping me from realizing the purpose of God's promises? How?

Journal: Today I get to choose: the corruption of the world or the precious and very great promises of God. I need to keep this in mind at all times, so...

Pray: "Open to me the gates of righteousness, that I may enter through them and give thanks to the LORD" (Psalm 118:19).

Day 4: The Realization of the Promises

Pray: "If you, O LORD, should mark iniquities, O Lord, who could stand? But with you there is forgiveness, that you may be feared" (Psalm 130:3, 4).

Read: Luke 1:67-75

Meditate: John the Baptist is about to be born, and his father, Zechariah, is singing about what his birth signifies. According to this prophet, what was God about to do?

             God was going to raise up "a horn of salvation for us in the house of his servant David." Who would that be? What is the connection between the promises (covenant) to Abram, the covenant with David, and the coming of this One?

             According to v. 74, what is the purpose of God's fulfilling His promises? How does that relate to what I saw yesterday? Am I living out that purpose? How?

Journal: Christ has come; God is fulfilling His promises, keeping His end of the deal. And me? I'm...

Pray: "I will make a horn to sprout for David; I have prepared a lamp for my anointed. His enemies I will clothe with shame, but on him his crown will shine" (Psalm 132:17, 18).

Day 5: The Fulfillment of God's Covenant

Pray: *"Praise the LORD, for the LORD is good; sing to his name, for it is pleasant!"* (Psalm 135:3).

Read: 2 Corinthians 1:12-22

Meditate: What did Paul boast about? Am I able to boast about this, as well?

                    Where do all the promises of God's covenant find their fulfillment (v. 20)? Can I participate in that fulfillment? How (v. 21)? Am I? Day by day?

                    What has God given me as a seal that I belong to Him, am safe in His covenant of promise, and can know the fulfillment of all His promises in Jesus (v. 22)? How do I know? How do I experience this each day?

Journal: If, in the power of God's Spirit, I am daily walking in Jesus, then all the promises to Abram, and David – all those precious and very great promises – should be mine, more and more. That being the case...

Pray: *"In God we have boasted continually, and we will give thanks to your name forever"* (Psalm 44:8).

ENDNOTES

[1] "Old Testament Hebrew Lexicon," crosswalk.com 11 April 2005 <http://bible.crosswalk.com/Lexicons/OldTestamentHebrew/>.

[2] Malcolm Smith, The Lost Secret of the New Covenant (Tulsa: Harrison House, 2002) 41-42.

Recommended Reading

Key Books:

Drumbrell, W. J. Covenant and Creation: A Theology of Old Testament Covenants. Carlisle, UK: Paternoster Press, 1984, 1997.

Garlow, James L. The Covenant: A Study of God's Extraordinary Love for You. Kansas City, MO: Beacon Hill of Kansas City, 2007.

Hahn, Scott. A Father Who Keeps His Promises: God's Covenant Love in Scripture. Ann Arbor, MI: Charis, 1998.

"Old Testament Hebrew Lexicon." crosswalk.com 11 April 2005 <http://bible.crosswalk.com/Lexicons/OldTestamentHebrew/>.

Robertson, O. Palmer. Christ and the Covenants. Phillipsburg, NJ: Presbyterian and Reformed Publishing Co., 1980.

Smith, Malcolm, The Lost Secret of the New Covenant. Tulsa: Harrison House, 2002.

Vine, W. E., An Expository Dictionary of New Testament Words. Vine, W. E., Merrill F. Unger, and William White, Jr. Vine's Complete Expository Dictionary of Old and New Testament Words. Nashville, TN: Thomas Nelson Publishers, 1996.

Key Audio:

Missler, Chuck. "The Legacy: Israel in Prophecy." Audio CD. Koinania House Ministries. <www.khouse.org>

Smith, Malcolm. "The Blood Covenant." Audiocassette. Unconditional Love Ministries. 11 April 2005 <www.malcolmsmith.org>

Lesson 10: Covenant: What Is the Big Picture of God's Redemption of Man?
-Anchorsaway Worldview Handbook ©

Lesson 11: Who Is Satan and How Does He Work?

⚓ **Anchor of the Week: Satan is real and active in the world.**

I. Is Satan Real?

A. Logic demands it; Scriptures declare it, and experiences support it.

1. Logic demands it. If there is evil, then there must be a source for that evil.

2. Scripture declares it (Ezekiel 28:11-19; Isaiah 14:12-20; Genesis 3:1-5).

3. Experiences support it. – We have all experienced the effects of evil in the world (i.e. disease, physical/emotional suffering, death ...).

B. The implications of the Big Lie – *"... you will be like God"* (Genesis 3:5).

1. The Birth of doubt happened in Eve's conversation with the serpent (Genesis 3:1-5).

   a. Doubt can lead us in a positive direction = questioning, searching, studying, faith and belief.

   b. On the other hand, not to act on one's doubt leads one to deny truth, to unbelief and destruction ... buying into Satan's lie ... Jesus is not God.

2. You can become a God. Do it your way, not God's way.

3. What does God say in Scripture? He takes His place as the one God very seriously.

   a. In Hosea 11:9, God says, *"'I am God and not man.'"*

   b. 2 Corinthians 3:18 – We are being transformed into His likeness. This is to say we are to bear the image of God; we are not to be God.

   c. See King Herod's ruin in Acts 12:21-23.

II. From where did Satan originate?

A. Satan is not God. He is not eternal. He was created and as a creature has a beginning and an end.

B. Scripture indicates that he was a chief angel who led a large number of the angels in a rebellion against God (Isaiah 14:12-15; Ezekiel 28:11-19).

C. Satan and his angels (who we now refer to as "demons") were cast down from heaven and eventually will be punished for all eternity (Luke 10:18; 2 Peter 2:6; Jude 6; 2 Peter 2:4; Revelation 12:7-9).

    A. The name Satan is a Hebrew word that means "adversary." [1]

    B. Tempter: (Luke 4:1-13 – The devil tempted Jesus.)

    C. Angel of Light: (2 Corinthians 11:14)

        1. Counterfeit:

            a. Christians: (Matthew 13:36-43)

            b. Gospel: (Galatians 1:6-7)

            c. Righteousness (by works and the law): (Romans 9:30-32)

            d. Ministers: (2 Corinthians 11:13-15)

            e. Counterfeit christs: (2 Thessalonians 2:3-4)

        2. Subtle and deceiver: (2 Corinthians 4:4; Matthew 7:15)

    D. The Enemy: (Matthew 13:28-29, 39; 1 Peter 5:8)

    E. Destroyer: (John 10:10; Revelation 9:11)

    F. Adversary, A Roaring Lion: (1 Peter 5:8)

    G. Accuser: (Revelation 12:10)

    H. Liar and a Murderer: (John 8:44)

    I. Prince of Demons: (Matthew 12:24)

    J. Prince of this World: (John 12:31, 14:30, 16:11)

    K. Prince of the Power of the Air: (Ephesians 2:2)

    L. God of this Age: (2 Corinthians 4:4)

M. Lawless One: (2 Thessalonians 2:8)

N. Devil: (Luke 4:2; Hebrews 2:14)

O. Blinds Minds: (2 Corinthians 4:4)

P. Unclean Spirit: (Matthew 12:43)

Q. Serpent: (Genesis 3:1-5; Revelation 12:9)

R. Beelzebub: (Luke 11:15)

S. The Evil One: (Matthew 6:13; 1 John 5:19)

IV. How does the lie spread?

A. Satan is *"'the father of lies'"* (John 8:44).

B. Satan was not content to keep this lie to himself. He wants to pass on this concept that, *"'... you will be like God.'"* When you sin, you share it (Genesis 3). We are still suffering as a result of the original sin.

V. How can we escape him?

A. Satan is a formidable adversary. He is an enemy who is as subtle as a serpent and as strong as a lion, who is able to appear as an angel of light.

B. When we are faced with temptation from Satan, God promises to provide a way of escape (1 Corinthians 10:12-13).

C. Nothing is impossible with God (Mark 10:26-27). The concept here is that whatever God desires for you or from you, He will enable you to do.

D. When we focus on Christ, Satan has no power (1 John 4:4).

VI. Satan's Helpers

A. Lying, Anger, Stealing, Pride, Slander, Guilt, Unbelief, Discouragement, Hopelessness, Worry, Anxiety

B. Dabbling in the occult: séances, Ouija boards, occult paraphernalia...(Deuteronomy 18 and Leviticus 18 & 19).

VII. Satan's Ploys

A. Satan has set out to use whatever means necessary to turn people away from God and toward their own eventual destruction.

B. He always mixes his lies with some truth, even quoting Scripture, if necessary. Note the following examples:

C. He will speak in your voice and lie to you about who you are and about the situation you are experiencing.

D. <u>Important point</u>: Satan will always attack the person, while God will attack the sin.

VIII. How do we fight Satan?

A. Recognize the enemy (I Peter 5:8-9; Ephesians 6:12-13; John 8:44; 2 Corinthians 11:14).

B. Give him no credit (Ephesians 4:27; James 4:7).

C. Do not play into his hand by becoming a "helper."

D. When tempted, follow Christ's example (See Matthew 4:1-11; Luke 4:1-13).

   1. He did not even entertain Satan's suggestions, but responded firmly and immediately.

   2. He responded to Satan with truth from God's Word.

   3. He rebuked Satan and commanded him to leave (Matthew 4:10). We can also, in the name of Christ, rebuke Satan (Luke 9:1).

E. Stay focused on God through prayer and study of the Scriptures (2 Timothy 3:16; 1 Peter 2:11; Romans 13:14; Galatians 5:16; 1 John 4:4; Colossians 1:12-14).

F. Set up an accountability partner.

   1. Find a friend who is willing to really hold you accountable.

IX. Closing Questions

    A. Is Satan incapable of doing 'good' in order to deceive?

    B. What is Satan's prime desire?

    C. Can a Christian be impacted by Satan?

        1. A chrisitan can not be possessed of Satan. They can however be oppressed.

            a. Oppression – demonic influence

            b. Possession – demonic control

Lesson 11: Who Is Satan and How Does He Work?

Small Group Objective:

Your goal is to help the students begin to better understand the reality of Satan and his influence over the world, in order to stand firm in resisting his presence in our lives. This involves developing a greater awareness of Satan's presence, as well as deepening our reliance on God, in order to resist the Devil's schemes.

✓ Check Points:

☐ Bring 3 x 5 cards for your students to write down any questions they may have which aren't answered during the discussion.

☐ Enlist a student to share a brief personal testimony.

Discussion Questions:

1. Review prayer requests from the week before and ask how the students are doing.

2. Lead a time of discussion, asking the following questions:

(Note: Work through as many of the following questions as possible. The goal is not to get through all of them, but to encourage each student to participate in the discussion as part of the learning process.)

    a. What day of the devotional did you find most meaningful?

    b. How did last week's lesson impact your life? Did you share it?

    c. How do you see Satan impacting lives in your world?

    d. How does Satan keep you from praying and doing your devotionals?

    e. Do we have power over Satan? How?

    f. Does your life aid Satan in his plan to cause people to doubt that there is a God of love?

    g. How are you like Matt Abernethy?

    h. Do you know someone like Matt?

    i. How might you help him/her?

    j. How does Satan try to mess with your mind?

    k. What is one strategy you can use this week to overcome Satan's temptations?

    l. What questions, if any, come to mind as a result of this week's lesson?

3. Ask for prayer requests and tell students that you will be faithful to pray for them during the week. Encourage students to record the prayer requests in the prayer request section of their handbooks, so they can pray for one another during the week. Begin the prayer time by sharing your own request. Spend the remaining time in prayer.

★ After the Session

1. Contact small group members during the week. Ask them about their devotional time, a question they have raised, or how their week is going.

Prayer Requests

Who Is Satan And How Does He Work?

The enemy of our souls is active and determined. His goal is to rob us of our joy and power and to deny God the glory which is due Him. By understanding his wiles and knowing how to resist him, we can share in Christ's defeat of the devil and continue to walk in the light of Christ consistently and victoriously.

Day 1: Resisting the Devil

Pray: *"Truly God is good to Israel, to those who are pure in heart"* (Psalm 73:1).

Read: Matthew 4:1-11

Meditate: What condition was Jesus in when the devil came to tempt Him? How did Satan try to deter Him from God's purpose and plan?

               What did Jesus do to resist the devil? What can I learn from His example about dealing with temptation? Am I prepared to do this?

               How can I know when the devil is tempting me?

Journal: I will surely face numerous temptations from the devil today. Therefore, I...

Pray: *"But for me it is good to be near God..."* (Psalm 73:28).

Day 2: The Tempter Bound

Pray: *"The LORD will keep you from all evil..."* (Psalm 121:7).

Read: Matthew 12:22-29

Meditate: What did Jesus mean when He said He had "bound" the "strong man?" How was that evident in this situation?

If Jesus has bound the devil for me, should he be able to defeat me in my walk with the Lord? Do I understand what walking with Jesus requires of me today?

Jesus was not afraid of Satan. Should I be? He is like a roaring lion (1 Peter 5:8), but Jesus has him on a chain. How can I keep from not being "devoured" by the devil today?

Journal: Satan is bound, and can only hurt me if I "get too close" to him. I'm going to be vigilant today, as Peter says, so...

Pray: *"The LORD will keep your going out and your coming in from this time forth and forevermore"* (Psalm 121:8).

Day 3: The Warfare Rages

Pray: *"Contend, O LORD, with those who contend with me..."* (Psalm 35:1).

Read: Ephesians 6:10-18

Meditate: What does spiritual warfare look like? Where should I expect to encounter spiritual warfare today?

What does it mean to "stand against the schemes of the devil?" Am I consistent in doing this? How can I tell when I am not?

Am I using all the weapons available to me in this spiritual warfare? Do I need to learn how to use any of these better? Which ones?

Journal: I'm heading off to battle, so I'd better "suit up." Let's see, today I'll especially need to be sharp in using...

Pray: *"Rescue me from their destruction, my precious life from the lions!"* (Psalm 35:17).

Day 4: Looking for a Fight?

Pray: *"Guard me, O LORD, from the hands of the wicked..."* (Psalm 140:4).

Read: Revelation 12:13-17

Meditate: Against whom is the devil making war (v. 17)? Would he recognize me as one of the enemy? How?

                  Why does he attack those who "keep the commandments of God?" Or those who "hold to the testimony of Jesus?" Why are these people particularly the object of his deceptive ways?

                  If I go out today in obedience to God's commandments and resolved to hold to the testimony of Jesus, am I just asking for a fight? What do I have to help me be victorious in this struggle?

Journal: I know the devil is out there today, looking for someone to attack. I'm ready for him, though, because Jesus has bound him, God is guarding me, and I have all the weapons of warfare ready to deploy. So in spite of his threats, I'm...

Pray: *"I say to the LORD, You are my God; give ear to the voice of my pleas for mercy, O LORD!"* (Psalm 140:6).

Day 5: Ever Vigilant

Pray: *"Do not let my heart incline to any evil, to busy myself with wicked deeds..."* (Psalm 141:4).

Read: Ephesians 5:15-21

Meditate: Hmm... "the days are evil." Do I agree with Paul's assessment? How can I see that Paul was right?

                  Paul seems to say that if I don't "make the best use of my time" for Christ and His Kingdom, I might become open to evil. Why is that so?

What does "making the most of my time" require of me? Do I understand the will of God for my life? Am I pursuing it? Do I know how to be filled with the Holy Spirit? Why should I? What's the alternative to being filled with Him and making the best use of my time for Jesus?

Journal: I want to make the best use of all my time today, so that Jesus will show through in my life. Therefore...

Pray: *"Keep me from the trap they have laid for me and from the snare of the evildoers!"* (Psalm 141:9).

ENDNOTES

[1] Wayne Grudem, *Systematic Theology: An Introduction to Biblical Doctrine* (Grand Rapids, MI: Zondervan, 1994) 414. See also Merrill F. Unger, and William White, Jr., *Nelson's Expository Dictionary of the Old Testament*, W. E. Vine, Merrill F. Unger, and William White, Jr., *Vine's Complete Expository Dictionary of Old and New Testament Words* (Nashville, TN: Thomas Nelson Publishers, 1996) 213-214.

Recommended Reading

Key Books:

Anderson, Neil. *Victory Over the Darkness*. 2nd Ed. Ventura, CA: Regal Books, 2000.

Barna, George. "Teenagers." The Barna Group. <https://www.barna.org/researches search?q=Teenagers>.

Grudem, Wayne. *Systematic Theology: An Introduction to Biblical Doctrine*. Grand Rapids, MI: Zondervan, 1994.

Kennedy, D. James. *Why I Believe*. Nashville, TN: W Publishing Group, 1999.

McCallum, Dennis. Satan and His Kingdom: What the Bible Says and How It Matters to You. Minneapolis, MN: Bethany House, 2009.

Rohdes, Ron. *Angels Among Us*. Eugene, OR: Harvest House Publishers, 2001.

Stone, Perry F. Exposing Satan's Playbook. Lake Mary, FL: Charisma House, 2012.

Stone, Perry F. There's a Crack in Your Armor. Lake Mary, FL: Charisma House, 2014.

Lesson 12: What Is a Cult?

I. What is a Cult?

A. Definition of a cult:

   1. From a Christian perspective, a cult is a group of people centered on the false teachings of a leader who claims that he/she is uniquely called of God.

   2. A cult requires at least two people: A leader and a follower.

   3. It is a counterfeit of the true faith of the Bible.

      a. Christians: 2 Peter 2:1-3

      b. Gospel: Galatians 1:6-12

      c. Righteousness: Romans 9:30-32

      d. Ministers: 2 Corinthians 11:13-15

      e. Christ: 2 Thessalonians 2:3-4

B. What is the Occult?

   1. Occult means "secret." It is the belief that an infinite force pervades the universe. Those initiated into its secrets can use it to their own ends.[1]

   2. It is blatantly the work of Satan and his demons.

   3. The person involved in an occult practice can do this by himself/herself or with a group of people.

   4. Tools used in the Occult: Tarot cards, crystals, Ouija boards, charms, secret oaths, spirit guides, astrology, Transcendental Meditation, yoga, labyrinths, ...

   5. Occultic groups: Wicca/Witchcraft, Vampirism, Shamanism, New Age, ...

   6. Many of those in a <u>cult</u> practice the <u>occult</u> in some way.

C. Characteristics of a cult:

1. A strong leader who professes to have been uniquely called of God to be a spiritual leader.

2. The leader claims to have had a miraculous experience in this calling.

3. The group requires the study of books other than the Bible. Revealed truths supersede or contradict the Bible.

4. They reject all translations of the Bible as "incorrect" and only use their own translations or commentaries by their leader in order to "understand the Bible."

5. They claim that theirs is "the only true church" or organization on the face of the earth today.

6. They speak ill of all Christian churches.

7. There is excessive control imposed.

8. Severe discipline is exercised by the leaders of the group.

9. Persons who leave the cult must be shunned by the rest of the members. They may not even be addressed on the street.

10. Jesus is not considered to be God of the Scriptures.

11. The gospel of God's grace is absent.

12. Cult leaders often claim new revelations from God. Beliefs change with the new revelations.

II. The cardinal keys of the Christian faith

A. There is only one God. He is eternal, omnipresent, omnipotent, and omniscient. He created all things from nothing (Isaiah 43:10; Psalm 90:2).

B. God consists of three Persons: God the Father, God the Son, and God the Holy Spirit. These three Persons <u>are</u> the one true God. We call this the holy Trinity (Matthew 28:19).

C. Jesus Christ is God the Son (Matthew 3:17; John 1:1; Hebrews 1).

D. Eternal life comes as a free gift to anyone who believes the gospel of Jesus Christ *alone* for salvation (Ephesians 2:8-10). The Gospel is this: He died on the cross for our sins; He was resurrected in an incorruptible body of flesh and bone on the third day; He now lives to intercede (mediate) for us in Heaven with the Father, <u>*according to the Scriptures*</u> (The gospel is clearly defined in 1 Corinthians 15:1-4.)

E. The Bible is our *only* source of authority. It is inerrant, sufficient and *complete* (Proverbs 30:5-6; 2 Timothy 3:17).

F. Those who do not possess eternal life will be in an *eternal* hell; separated for all eternity from God (Matthew 25:46).

G. Mormons <u>deny</u> most of these key doctrines of the Christian faith.

III. What are the religious works of the Mormon religion?

A. *The Book of Mormon*

B. *Doctrine and Covenants*

C. *Pearl of Great Price*
  1. Contains the *Book of Abraham* and selections from the *Book of Moses.*
  2. The *Book of Moses* is taken from Joseph Smith's translation of the Bible.
  3. The *Book of Abraham* was claimed to have been translated from Egyptian papyri that contained the writings of Abraham. The documents have been examined and verified to be nothing more than Egyptian funeral texts.[2]

D. *The King James Version "as far as it is translated correctly."* (Some of the sects still use Joseph Smith's The Inspired Version.)

E. Authoritative teachings of Mormon prophets and other Latter Day Saints "authorities."

F. Who was Joseph Smith?

Four Deadly Questions

As you listen to the testimony, use the four deadly questions to ask the speaker for clarification of an idea.

1. What do you mean by that?

2. How do you know that is true?

3. Where do you get your information?

4. What happens if you are wrong?

IV. What Mormons Teach

(Note: The following information about Mormonism comes primarily from Agusta Harting, a former Mormon who is now a Christian. She and her husband, Dan, founded "Families Against Cults of Indiana," a Christian ministry in Indianapolis, Indiana dedicated to raising awareness about cults, and helping those who have come out of cults.).

A. As a Mormon I believe that "I am a Christian because Mormons are the only TRUE Christians."

B. As a Mormon I believe that:

1. God is my Father in Heaven.
2. Jesus Christ is God's Son.
3. The Holy Ghost is the third member of the Godhead.
4. Jesus Christ is my Savior and Lord.
5. Jesus was born of a virgin.
6. Jesus Christ is God.
7. Salvation is by God's grace through faith.
8. I believe in Heaven and Hell.
9. I believe the Bible is true, as far as it is translated correctly.
10. I believe in all the gifts of the Holy Ghost.

C. All of the preceding statements have <u>DIFFERENT MEANINGS</u> in Mormonism than in Christianity.

1. "God is my Father in Heaven."

Mormon meaning: The Mormon god is a 6-foot, physical "exalted man." His name is "Elohim." Once only a mere human, he <u>had to learn to become god</u>. He has a father, and there are many gods above him. He is *only* the "god of this universe."[3]

Christian meaning: Even though He is a personal Being, God the Father has never been human. He is the Creator, and we are the created. God has created the entire universe. He is the head of the Trinity and all things are subject to Him; there is nothing, and no one, who is above Him (Genesis 1:1; Psalm 90:2; Isaiah 43:10; Isaiah 44:6; John 4:24; John 8:24 1 Corinthians 15:27-28).

2. "Jesus Christ is God's Son."

Mormon meaning: The Mormon Jesus Christ was a spirit baby born to Heavenly Father and one of his goddess wives, "Heavenly Mother." They named him "Jehovah." The Mormon god is married to many women, and he cannot create anything from nothing. He <u>had to have sex</u> with his wife in order to produce Jesus pre-mortally, as well as *all* of humanity by the same method. Lucifer, the Devil, is also one of Jesus' "spiritual brothers."[4]

Christian meaning: Jesus, as God's Son, shares all of the qualities of God Himself. He lacks nothing. As such, He never came into being because He has always been. In addition, Jesus has power over the Devil. The Devil has never been a spiritual equal of Jesus, as he is a fallen angel, and all angels are subject to Christ (Matthew 28:18; Luke 10:18-19; John 8:58; Colossians 1:15-18; Revelation 12:7-9).

3. "The Holy Ghost is the third member of the Godhead."

Mormon meaning: The Mormon Holy Ghost is a <u>different god</u> than Heavenly Father (Elohim). He has no physical body, and we do not know his name. He must not be confused with "The Holy Spirit" which is only like an <u>impersonal electrical current</u>.[5]

Christian meaning: In the history of Christianity, the title, "Holy Ghost," has frequently been interchangeable with the more common title, "Holy Spirit," when referring to the third member of the Trinity. They are not two separate entities, but instead, references to the same Being. The doctrine of the Trinity tells us that "God eternally exists as three persons, Father, Son, and Holy Spirit, and each person is fully God, and there is one God."[6] Therefore, the Holy Spirit is not a different God; He is God. He is a personal Being who has been sent to give us regeneration and help us live in obedience to God. (Matthew 28:19; John 3:5-8; Ephesians 4:30 – Note: Only a personal Being can be "grieved.")

4. "Jesus Christ is my Savior and Lord."

Mormon meaning: The Mormon Jesus (Jehovah) had to come to Earth to complete his test of godhood. While here, he was married (possibly a polygamist)[7] and sweat blood in Gethsemane in order to "atone" for mankind and assure that we would *all* "gain resurrection bodies" someday. He is our "elder brother,"[8] and we must imitate him in order to earn and merit eternal life.

Christian meaning: Jesus did not earn His deity; He has always been God (Genesis 1:1; John 1:1-3). Yes, 1 John 2:6 tells us we must imitate Jesus by walking as He did, but our obedience to Christ is not a means to salvation. Salvation is a *gift of God*, which comes through our faith in Jesus' atoning sacrifice of Himself on the cross for our sins (Ephesians 2:8-9; 1 John 2:2).

5. "Jesus was born of a virgin."

Mormon meaning: The Mormon god (Elohim) came down to Earth and had literal sexual intercourse with his virgin daughter, Mary. She thus conceived the earthly body for Jesus (Jehovah).[9]

Christian meaning: The Bible tells us that the Holy Spirit, not God the Father, was the One who impregnated the virgin, Mary (Matthew 1:18-21; Luke 1:30-35). This was not a physical act of intercourse, but rather a miraculous act of conception through the Holy Spirit.

6. "Jesus Christ is God."

Mormon meaning: The Mormon Jesus Christ is a god, one of possibly billions of gods. Mormons are forbidden to worship or pray to him. They are *not* to have a "personal relationship" with him.[10]

Christian meaning: The Trinity doctrine tells us that there is only one God, not multiple gods. As a part of the Trinity, Jesus possesses the same divine characteristics of God the Father (John 8:58, 10:30). We are called to bow before Christ in worship and demonstrate our love for Him through our obedience to His commands (Philippians 2:9-11). Our personal relationship with Jesus is cultivated as we follow Him, in much the same way as He had a personal relationship with the twelve disciples during His three years of ministry on earth (John 10:27).

7. "Salvation is by God's grace through faith and works."

Mormon meaning: The Mormon god only gives us the "grace" to be resurrected in a body of flesh and bone through Christ's sweating blood and death on the cross. Eternal life, however, must be EARNED and merited through personal worthiness.[11] This is called *Eternal Progression to godhood*. This is every Mormon's goal. The slogan in Mormonism is: *"As man is, God once was; as God is, man may become!"*[12]

Christian meaning: Scripture tells us that we have been saved through faith in God's gift of grace (Ephesians 2:8-9). We are not saved through our own merits. Our worth, therefore, is found in our being created in God's image (Genesis 1:26-27). God has called us to come under His authority. When we seek to elevate ourselves above God, we sin against Him. (See Eve in Genesis 3:1-6 and the Tower of Babel in Genesis 11:1-9.)

8. "I believe in heaven and hell."

Mormon meaning: "Heaven": There are three heavens for the Mormon. They are called the Celestial, Terrestrial and Telestial Kingdoms.[13] Most Christians and *unworthy* Mormons only qualify for the second, or the Terrestrial.[14] Worthy Mormons, who have become gods and goddesses, inherit the Celestial Kingdom. They will beget spirit children and populate their own

Earths and planets, just like Heavenly Parents did. The Telestial Kingdom is for the wicked, but still "glorious," according to Joseph Smith.

"Hell" is only a temporary prison for all non-Mormons until the resurrection. Great missionary work is being performed there right now.[15]

"Outer Darkness" is where the Devil and the demons go, as well as apostates who have left Mormonism and have become "Sons of Perdition." They remain there forever.

Christian meaning: The Bible speaks of only two eternal destinations for humanity – heaven or hell. They are both literal places, and Scripture does not suggest that there is more than one heaven. Hell is the place of eternal punishment for the wicked, while the righteous will enjoy eternal life in heaven (Matthew 25:46).

9. "I believe the Bible is true, as far as it is translated correctly."

Mormon meaning: The Bible was *not* translated correctly and there are many "plain and precious truths" missing in it, including whole books. According to Mormon Prophet Ezra T. Benson, it is not *"big enough, nor good enough, to lead this* [the Mormon] *Church."*

Christian meaning: The Bible is not only true, it is also without error. The three common tests for works of antiquity (Bibliographic, Internal, and External) confirm the authenticity of the Bible. More importantly, Scripture itself proclaims that every word has come from God Himself (2 Timothy 3:16-17; 2 Peter 1:20-21). Therefore, it is pure, perfect, and true[16] (Psalm 12:6, 119:96; Proverbs 30:5). There is nothing that needs to be added or taken away from God's Word; it is all we need for salvation (Deuteronomy 4:2, 12:32; Proverbs 30:5-6; Revelation 22:18-19).

10. "I believe in all the gifts of the Holy Ghost."

Mormon meaning: All spiritual gifts must be given from Joseph Smith, Jr. through the General Authorities of the Mormon Church, channeled down to the recipient by the laying on of hands by Mormon priests.[17]

Christian meaning: Scripture tells us that all gifts come from God and are bestowed upon us by the Holy Spirit Himself (James 1:17; 1 Corinthians 12:1-11).

Key Tips for Sharing the Gospel with a Mormon

1. Know what Mormons believe.

2. Develop a relationship with them.

3. Ask them to tell their life story.

4. Because Mormonism is based on works, when the time comes that you feel the Holy Spirit asking you to share the gospel you might ask them: " If you were to die in 5 minutes where would you go?"

A QUICK SUMMARY OF MORMONISM

History

The Church of Jesus Christ of Latter Day Saints was founded by Joseph Smith, Jr. in 1830.

The Book of Mormon was also published in 1830. *The Doctrine and Covenants, The Pearl of Great Price,* and *The King James Bible* are also considered "The Standard Works" by Mormons.

Mormonism boasts over eleven million members worldwide, with an estimated 800 conversions per day.

There are currently over 63,000 full-time Mormon missionaries worldwide, and the current Mormon prophet is Gordon B. Hinckley.

Main Teachings of Mormonism

The gospel of Jesus Christ was lost in the first century A.D. It had to be "restored" by Joseph Smith, Jr. in 1830.

The Bible is an insufficient guide to lead god's church. We must have *The Book of Mormon, The Doctrine and Covenants,* and *The Pearl of Great Price.* Most importantly, a living oracle, the (Mormon) Prophet, is needed to lead the church today.

Mormons alone have the "priesthood authority" to act for god on the Earth.

There exist multiple gods in this universe and others. Our heavenly father (Elohim) is only one of them. He is the "god of this world."

God is a former human. He had to learn how to become a god through obedience, death, resurrection, and marriage to a godly wife or wives (goddesses.) He never had the power to create our spirits, because he is not able to create matter from nothing. God can be surprised; he could possibly be "voted out" of the Mormon church, should he do something wrong.

The Mormon Jesus Christ (Jehovah) is god's sexually begotten spirit son. He was begotten on Earth by Mary and the heavenly father by literal, sexual intercourse.

Lucifer, the Devil, was Jesus' spirit brother.

All humans were sexually conceived by god and one of his wives, and lived as "spirit children" in the "Pre-mortal Existence" before coming to Earth.

Men are here in order to have "happiness" and to eternally progress to godhood. This is possible through personal worthiness, secret Temple rituals, membership in the LDS Church, and by keeping all the commandments of god.

As man is, God once was; as God is, man may become." – Mormon prophet, Lorenzo Snow

Lesson 12: What Is a Cult? - Anchorsaway Worldview Handbook ©

WHAT MORMONS DON'T DARE TELL YOU AT THE DOOR!

Did you know that Mormons teach that all churches other than their own are from Satan?

Did you know that Joseph Smith was a false prophet and predicted the end of the world for 1891? That a Mormon temple would be built in Independence, Missouri, before the generation of 1832 passed away? That the LDS church doesn't even own this Temple Lot, and it stands vacant to this day?

Did you know that over fifty other false prophecies of Joseph Smith have been fully documented? (God demands 100% accuracy from his prophets. See Deuteronomy chapters 13 and 18.)

Did you know that Mormons teach that if you drink alcohol, coffee, or tea, or use tobacco products you can never be "worthy" to meet god? This teaching is known as the "Word of Wisdom."

Did you know that if you become a Mormon, you are required to attend a minimum of 156 meetings per year at the Ward Chapel?

Did you know that if you become a Mormon, you will be required to give ten percent of your income to the Mormon Church (tithing), plus contribute to building funds and "fast offerings?"

Did you know that if you become a Mormon, you or your children will be encouraged to be baptized, confirmed, married, and go through hours-long "sealing" and "endowment" ceremonies in the Mormon temple for all of your dead relatives? That is why Mormons are so interested in genealogy.

Did you know that Mormons teach that Jesus and Lucifer are spirit brothers? That god is just an exalted man? That there are many gods and goddesses, and that god is married to many wives? That you are the sexually begotten offspring of god and one of his wives?

Mormons teach that Jesus was sexually begotten by the father with Mary, who was his daughter, and was no longer a virgin after the father "overshadowed" her.

Did you know that Mormons teach that you can't go to heaven (the "Celestial Kingdom") unless you are a "worthy" Temple Mormon? You can become a god, too, if you are a "worthy" Mormon. You must be married, and married in a Mormon Temple to be a god. (The Bible says, "Before me there was no God formed, neither shall there be after me." Isaiah 43:10)

Did you know that non-Mormon and "unworthy" Mormon friends and relatives will not be able to attend your celestial marriage ceremony in the temple?

Did you know that Mormons teach that the United States Constitution "will hang by a thread" and the Mormon Church will establish a theocracy (religious government) in America?

Mormons coming to your door will ask you to read the *Book of Mormon*, and then pray to know whether it is true. Ask them why there is not one historical or archaeological fact to support the *Book of Mormon*, in spite of the lofty claims of Mormon laymen. If the *Book of Mormon* is scripture, why have there been thousands of material changes since the original 1830 version? Why pray about the *Book of Mormon*?

The truth is:

You do not need an organized religion to go to heaven. Eternal life in heaven is a free gift from God based on Jesus' sacrifice on the cross (I John 5:11-12, Colossians 1:19-20, 2:13-15).

People often ask us why we have our ministry. We love the Mormon and Jehovah's Witness people, and have many family members still in these and other cults. We pray that others will be spared the anguish we have experienced.

WHAT JEHOVAH'S WITNESSES DON'T DARE TELL YOU AT THE DOOR!

Jehovah's Witnesses teach that all churches other than their own are from Satan.

Jehovah's Witnesses teach that god is going to destroy you and your family and everyone that does not become a Jehovah's Witness at Armageddon.

Jehovah's Witnesses are false prophets and have predicted the end of the world in 1914, 1918, 1925, 1941, and 1975. They will deny this or make excuses for it when talking with you. (God demands 100% accuracy from his prophets. See Deuteronomy chapters 13 and 18.)

If you become one of Jehovah's Witnesses, you will never again celebrate Christmas, Easter, Thanksgiving, your own or any relatives' birthdays, or Mother's Day.

Jehovah's Witnesses teach that the penalty for smoking is eternal damnation.

Jehovah's Witnesses have written their own translation of the Bible, and have changed and added words to agree with their teachings.

If you become a Jehovah's Witness, you are required to attend 260 meetings a year at the Kingdom Hall.

Jehovah's Witnesses are required to die rather than accept a blood transfusion. Anyone accepting a transfusion will be destroyed by Jehovah.

Jehovah's Witnesses built a house in 1925 near San Diego, California and deeded it to Abraham, Isaac, and Jacob. They taught that these patriarchs would be resurrected in that year.

Jehovah's Witnesses teach that Jesus already came the second time in 1914. They said the date was 1874, and taught that for 40 years.

Jehovah's Witnesses teach that all governments are from Satan, so you may not vote, go into the military, or run for public office.

Jehovah's Witnesses break up families if all do not become (or remain) JW's.

Ask Jehovah's Witnesses:

Why they cannot say "My Lord and my God" to Jesus, as the Apostle Thomas did. If this was a blasphemy, why did Rabbi Jesus not rebuke Thomas, as it would be his duty to do (John 20:26-29)?

Why they will not pray to Jesus for redemption from sin, when the Bible commands us to. John 14:14 says we are to ask Jesus anything in his name. Acts 22:14-16 tells us that we are to wash away our sins by calling on Jesus' name.

The truth is:

You do not need an organized religion to go to heaven. Eternal life in heaven is a free gift from God based on Jesus' sacrifice on the cross (1 John 5:11-12, Colossians 1:19-20, 2:13-15).

Why not ask Jesus for forgiveness and eternal life today? We love the Mormon and JW people and have many family members still in these and other cults. We pray that others will be spared the anguish we have experienced.

Cults and the Occult[18]

Many times people are confused by the difference between a cult and the occult. This chart will make some of those distinctions a little more clear. There are over 5,000 cults in the U.S. While the specifics for each cult differ, the underlying concepts are the same. If you will learn the biblical concepts in each of these areas, you will be able to defend the Scriptures against these attacks. You will then be able to provide answers to hurting people in need of the true Savior.

Christianity	Mormonism	Jehovah's Witnesses	Scientology[19]	Wicca[20]
God	Once a man as we are now. He is now an exalted man. Literally our heavenly father. He and his many wives have sex to produce spirit babies that eventually become the human race.	One person god, called Jehovah. There is no other name for god. Jesus is not god, he is the first thing that Jehovah created.	Does not define god or supreme being, but rejects the biblical God. Everyone is a "thetan," an immortal spirit with unlimited powers over its own universe, but all are not aware of this.	The supreme being is called the goddess, sometimes the goddess and god, or goddess and horned god. The goddess can be a symbol, the impersonal force in everything, or a personal being.
Jesus Christ John 1:1-3, 14; 8:58 Colossians 1:16-20	Jesus Christ, spirit brother of Lucifer, received a body of flesh and bone and is now elevated to deity. He is referred to as our "elder brother," one of many gods.	Jesus is a god, not God the Son. He is represented as the first creation of Jehovah. Before his incarnation he was Michael, captain of Jehovah's hosts.	Jesus is rarely mentioned. Jesus was not Creator, nor was he an "operating thetan" (in control of supernatural powers, cleared from mental defects). Jesus did not die for our sins.	Jesus is either rejected altogether or sometimes considered a spiritual teacher who taught love and compassion.
Tri-Unity Luke 3:21-22, 1 Peter 1:2 Matthew 28:19 John 15:26	Mormon theology is henotheistic. It exalts one god (the father god) above the other gods in the universe. The Holy Spirit is a spiritual impersonal "force."	The doctrine of the Tri-Unity is denied emphatically. The deity of the Holy Spirit is denied—he is likened to a radar beam.	The doctrine of the Tri-Unity is denied. The Holy Spirit is not part of their belief.	The doctrine of the Trui-Unity is denied. The Holy Spirit is not part of their belief. Some Wiccans may refer to "spirit" as a kind of divine energy.
Everyone has an eternal spirit Matthew 25:46 Daniel 12:2 Ecclesiastes 12:7 Revelation 20:11-15	Yes	They argue for painless extinction, indicating man does not possess an immortal soul, just a combination of breath and flesh. That is, unless you become part of the Organization or the 144,000.	There are no particular human incarnations of god, as the universal life force (Theta) is inherent in all. All humans are immortal spiritual beings (thetans), capable of realizing a nearly godlike state.	Values are part of our social paradigms, as well. Tolerance, freedom of expression, inclusion, and refusal to claim to have the answers are the only universal values.

	Christianity	Mormonism	Jehovah's Witnesses	Scientology[21]	Wicca[22]
Born a Lost Soul Psalm 51:5 James 1:15 Romans 5:12-21 I Corinthians 15: 21 -22		Mormons deny the doctrine of original sin and teach that the fall of man was a good and necessary thing. There is no imputed sin nature.	Adam's sin imputed to mankind, as federal head of the race. However, a sin nature apparently not inherited by the race.	No sin and no need to repent. Hell is a myth. People who get clear of "engrams" become operating "thetans."	Definitely not.
Suggested Approaches For Presenting The Christian Faith		1. Confront with the "pillars" of Mormonism: god, works, salvation. 2. Compare beliefs with Bible. 3. The archaeology of the New World refutes the Book of Mormon. 4. Ask where they would go if they died in 5 minutes.	1. Present a clear biblical case of Christ's and Holy Spirit's deity. 2. Present the case of the Tri-Unity. 3. Challenge them to look at the whole of Scripture.	1. Ask why they think the world is in such a mess? 2. Ask how they know for sure that what they believe is true. 3. Present the gospel and the gift of eternal life.	1. Wicca is an occultic "nature religion." Explain the origins of this belief. 2. Ask them how they know that there is no God who loves. 3. Share with them the gospel of eternal life.
Other Beliefs		No alcohol, tobacco, coffee or tea. Baptism on behalf of the dead. Two year missionary commitment encouraged. Extensive social network.	Known as the Watchtower Bible and Tract Society. Meet in Kingdom Halls. Do not observe holidays or birthdays. Forbidden to vote, salute flag, work in military.	Highly controversial. Publication of *Dianetics*. Organizations related: Narconan, Criminon, Way to Happiness Foundation, WISE, Applied Scholastics.	Wiccans practice divination and spell-casting, with most rituals performed in a circle. Many Wiccans are part of a coven. Extremely occultic.

Charts for Cults and the Occult within urban settings available in Appendix A.

Small Group Discussion Guide

Lesson 12: What Is a Cult?

Small Group Objective:

The goal is to help the students begin to better understand cults, and, specifically, Mormonism, in order to be able to witness to those who are struggling in a cult.

✓ **Check Points:**

☐ Bring 3 x 5 cards for your students to write down any questions they may have which aren't answered during the discussion.

☐ Enlist a student to share a brief personal testimony.

Discussion Questions:

1. Review prayer requests from the week before and ask how the students are doing.

2. Lead a time of discussion, asking the following questions:

(Note: Work through as many of the following questions as possible. The goal is not to get through all of them, but to encourage each student to participate in the discussion as part of the learning process.)

    a. What day of the devotional did you find most meaningful?

    b. How did last week's lesson impact your life? Did you share it?

    c. Who thinks that you would never get into a cult?

    d. Why do "Christians" sometimes get deceived into a cult?

    e. What is the key question to ask anyone who invites you to anything spiritual? Who is Jesus Christ?

    f. What would be your response if your friend came to you and invited you to the Mormon Church?

    g. Why is it so important to have a secure foundation in what you believe?

    h. Frame a Mormon.

    i. Take time to pray for any friends who are Mormons.

3. Ask for prayer requests and tell students that you will be faithful to pray for them during the week. Encourage students to record the prayer requests in the prayer request section of their handbooks, so they can pray for one another during the week. Begin the prayer time by sharing your own request. Spend the remaining time in prayer.

Prayer Requests

Student Devotionals written by T.M. Moore

What Is A Cult?

There have always been cults threatening the Gospel and the well-being of the Church. They tend to be personality-driven and legalistic, all the while using the language of Scripture and Christianity to attract followers. Our devotionals this week will help us in determining which movements in our day are cults and in becoming equipped to respond to them.

Day 1: The Bonds of Legalism

Pray: *"The wicked are estranged from the womb; they go astray from birth, speaking lies"* (Psalm 58:3.

Read: Galatians 3:1-14

Meditate: According to Paul, what is the condition of those who try to be right with God through any kind of works of law (vv. 1, 10)? What does this suggest about the *spiritual* origin of cultish, legalistic teachings?

How would I be able to recognize if someone were proclaiming a gospel of works rather than the Gospel of grace?

I'm not saved by keeping laws – either God's or those of some human design. But does this mean I have no responsibility for keeping God's Law? How should I approach the holy, righteous, and good Law of God (Romans 7:12), if not to *gain* salvation?

Journal: Some of my "religious" friends may be trapped in a cult of legalism and not even know it. If I'm going to be able to help them see that I need to...

Pray: *"O God...let them vanish like water that runs away; when he aims his arrows, let them be blunted"* (Psalm 58:6, 7.)

Day 2: They Like to Put Themselves First

Pray: *"My soul is in the midst of lions; I lie down amid fiery beasts – the children of man, whose teeth are spears and arrows, whose tongues are sharp swords"* (Psalm 57:4).

Read: 3 John: 9-12

Meditate: What does it "look like" when someone is enjoying putting himself first in spiritual matters? Am I ever guilty of this?

How could I tell if someone who seemed to be prominent in religious and spiritual circles was acknowledging the authority of Christ's apostles (vv. 9, 10)?

What is the difference between Demetrius and Diotrephes in this passage? Both seemed to have some prominence, but John commended one and condemned the other. Why?

Journal: The leaders I am following seem to be prominent in matters of faith. I need to make sure I can trust them, therefore (Acts 17:11)...

Pray: *"My heart is steadfast, O God, my heart is steadfast!"* (Psalm 57:7).

Day 3: Infiltrating the Church

Pray: *"I trust in the steadfast love of God forever and ever"* (Psalm 52:8).

Read: Revelation 2:18-29

Meditate: How was this "Jezebel" able to attract people to her false teaching? How did Jesus respond to her (vv. 21, 22)? How does one encourage a person to repent of false teaching?

How does false teaching like this get into a church or group of Christians? How does the Lord counsel us when such is the case (vv. 24-26)? What does He promise if we will do this?

Do cults sometimes attract followers because their views are more agreeable to our natural, fleshly desires? Does their approach to faith sometimes seem "easier?" Can I think of any examples?

Journal: The law of sin is still at work in me, which means that I'm still susceptible to the allure of fleshly, easy ways. I need to guard against this, so...

Pray: "I will wait for your name, for it is good, in the presence of the godly" (Psalm 52:9).

Day 4: Wreaking Havoc in the Church

Pray: "All day long they injure my cause; all their thoughts are against me for evil. They stir up strife..." (Psalm 56:5, 6).

Read: Titus 1:10-16

Meditate: How did Paul describe those who were trying to introduce false teaching into the churches? How would I be able to recognize such people?

It seems this particular person was using secular philosophy to "wow" unsuspecting Christians. Do cults do this? Do they blend Christianity and unbelieving thought to attract followers? Can I think of an example?

How am I to respond to such false teachers, who threaten to disrupt the peace of my community (vv. 13, 14)? Am I equipped to do this? How would I do this with grace (Colossians 4:6)?

Journal: Hmmm...responding to false teaching with gracious speech...I think this means...

Pray: "In God, whose word I praise, in the LORD, whose word I praise, in God I trust; I shall not be afraid" (Psalm 56:10, 11).

Day 5: Teaching the Truth for the Sake of Love

Pray: "He declares his word to Jacob, his statutes and rules to Israel. He has not dealt thus with any other nation; they do not know his rules" (Psalm 147:19).

Read: 1 Timothy 1:3-7

Meditate: What does it mean to "promote speculations rather than the stewardship from God that is by faith?" How do cults do this?

True teaching does not aim merely at enlisting followers or establishing one's views or positions. What does Paul say the true end of teaching must be (v. 5)? How would I be able to tell if someone's teaching were honestly directed toward this?

What seems to be the moral trap the false teachers in vv. 6 and 7 had fallen into? Does that particular sin have any pull on me? How can I guard against it?

Journal: If the goal of all teaching is love, then I need to make sure that I'm really learning God's truth, and not just seeking out speculations for the sake of pride. Here's how I can continuously guard myself against falling into this trap:

Pray: "Great is our Lord, and abundant in power; his understanding is beyond measure.. The LORD lifts up the humble; he casts the wicked to the ground" (Psalm 147:5, 6).

ENDNOTES

[1] Dave Hunt, *Occult Invasion* (Harvest House, 1998).

[2] Charles M. Larson, *...by his own hand upon papyrus* (Grand Rapids: Institute for Religious Research, 1992).

[3] Joseph Smith, *Journal of Discourses* Volume 6, (Salt Lake City, UT: The Church of Jesus Christ of Latter Day Saints, 1844) 3-5. Also see: Bob Witte, *Where Does It Say That?* (Grand Rapids: Gospel Truths).

[4] Joseph Smith, *Journal of Discourses* Volume 6, (1844) 8. Also see: Brigham Young, *Journal of Discourses*, Volume 8 (1860) 268.

[5] Joseph Fielding Smith, *Doctrines of Salvation* Volume 1, (Salt Lake City, UT: The Church of Jesus Christ of Latter Day Saints, no date) 39.

[6] Wayne Grudem, *Systematic Theology: An Introduction to Biblical Doctrine* (Grand Rapids: Zondervan, 1994) 226, 231.

[7] Orson Pratt, *The Seer* (1853) 172.

[8] Bruce McConkie, *The Mortal Messiah* (Salt Lake City, UT: Deseret, 1984) 434.

[9] Orson Pratt, *The Seer* (1853) 158. Also see: Bob Witte, *Where Does It Say That?* (Grand Rapids, Gospel Truths) 4-7.

[10] Bruce McConkie, *Speech given at BYU* devotional (March 2, 1982).

[11] *Book of Mormon* (Salt Lake City, UT: The Church of Jesus Christ of Latter Day Saints, no date) II Nephi 25:23.

[12] Joseph Smith, *Journal of Discourses* Volume 6, (Salt Lake City, UT: The Church of Latter Day Saints, 1844) 3-4.

[13] Joseph Smith, *History of the Church* Volume 1, (Salt Lake City, UT: The Church of Latter Day Saints, no date) 283.

[14] Joseph Fielding Smith, *Doctrines of Salvation* Volume 2, (Salt Lake City, UT: The Church of Latter Day Saints) 133.

[15] Joseph Fielding Smith, *Doctrines of Salvation* Volume 2, 183. Also see: Jerald & Sandra Tanner, *Mormonism-Shadow or Reality?* (Salt Lake City: Utah Lighthouse Ministry, 1987, Fifth Edition) 198-199.

[16] Joseph Fielding Smith, 93.

[17] The Mormon meanings associated with the previous ten different doctrinal expressions come from Agusta Harting.

[18] Boa, Kenneth, *Cults, World Religions and the Occult,* (Wheaton, IL: Victor Books, 1990)

[19] Rose Publishing, <u>Christianity, Cults & Religions</u> chart. Compares 17 religions and cults

[20] Ibid.

[21] Ibid.

[22] Ibid.

Recommended Reading

Key Organizations:

- For a ministry to Masons, Ephesians 5:11: www.ephesians5-11.org .

- For additional Christian organizations dealing with theology and cults: www.watchman.org, www.ronrhodes.org, www.thebereancall.org.

Key Books:

Abanes, Richard. *One Nation Under Gods: A History of the Mormon Church.* New York: Four Walls Eight Windows Publishers, 2002.

Beckwith, Francis. *The Counterfeit Gospel of Mormonism.* Eugene, Or.: Harvest House, 1998

Beckwith, Francis, and Stephen E. Parrish. *See the Gods Fall: Four Rivals to Christianity.* Joplin, MO: College Pub., 1997.

Boa, Kenneth. *Cults, World Religions and the Occult.* Wheaton, IL: Victor Books, 1990.

Decker, Ed, and Dave Hunt. *The God Makers.* Eugene, OR: Harvest House Publishers, 1997.

Flynn, Brian. *Running Against The Wind.* Silverton, OR: Lighthouse Trails Publishing, 2005.

Geisler, Norm, and Ron Rhodes. *Correcting the Cults: Expert Responses to Their Scripture Twisting.* Grand Rapids, MI: Baker Books, 2005.

Grudem, Wayne. *Systematic Theology: An Introduction to Biblical Doctrine.* Grand Rapids: Zondervan, 1994.

Halverson, Dean. *The Compact Guide to World Religions.* Minneapolis, MN: Bethany House Publishers, 1996.

Martin, Dr. Walter. *The Kingdom of the Cults.* Minneapolis, MN: Bethany House Publishers, 2003.

McDowell, Josh, and Don Stewart. *Handbook of Today's Religions.* Thomas Nelson, Inc., 1992.

Sire, James. *Scripture Twisting: Twenty Ways the Cults Misread the Bible.* Downers Grove, IL: InterVarsity Press, 1980.

Tanner, Jerald, and Sandra. *Mormonism, Shadow or Reality?* Salt Lake City, UT: Utah Lighthouse Ministry, 1992.

Key DVDs / Videos:

- "The GodMakers." Hemet, CA: Jeremiah Films, 2003. 25 April 2005 <www.jeremiahfilms.com>.

- "The Secret World of Mormonism." Hemet, CA: Jeremiah Films, 2004. 25 April 2005 <www.jeremiahfilms.com>.

Lesson 13: Why Don't the Jews Believe in Jesus?

I. Understanding the Jewish people

(Note: The content of this lesson comes primarily from Jeff Adler, a Messianic Jew and the Rabbi of the Ahavat Yeshua Messianic Jewish Congregation in Indianapolis, Indiana. The information designated with an asterisk(*) comes largely from Sherry Miley, a Messianic Jew from Indianapolis, Indiana.)

A. What does the Old Testament have to say about the coming of the Messiah through Israel?

1. Scripture predicts many different aspects of Jesus' coming:

   a. Daniel 9, Isaiah 53, Psalm 22

   b. The Old Testament prophecies are pointing to Jesus as the Messiah, and He is the Messiah because of what God's Word says.

2. Jesus is not just the God of the Gentiles – He is the Jewish Messiah.

   a. Before Jesus could be the Savior of the world, He had to be the Messiah of the Jews.

   b. His being the Jewish Messiah fulfilled Scripture, which then qualified Him to be the Savior of the world.

   c. No matter what the stereotypes or ideas are about who Jesus is, the most important thing is what the God of Israel says. If God says that Jesus is the Messiah, then He is the Messiah.

3. Why is it so important to know Scripture?

   a. There are all kinds of people believing all kinds of things; there are scholars, pastors in churches, and others who stand up and teach that Moses did not write Genesis, that Isaiah did not write Isaiah and that the Bible is not the Word of God.

   b. These same people still say God loves us. How is that possible?

B. What are the different types of Jews?

  1. Orthodox Jews (20% in US)

     a. They still keep the dietary laws.

     b. They believe that the Torah (the five books of Moses) and the Prophets (in the Old Testament) are the Word of God. We can speak to them directly from these portions of Scripture.

  2. Conservative Jews (35%)

     a. This branch of Judaism is more of an American development.

     b. Conservative Jews will drive on the Sabbath and make some other accommodations, but generally keep kosher.

  3. Reformed Jews (35%)

     a. This group started in Europe as a result of Jewish people being persecuted.

     b. To avoid continued persecution, they took the approach of being like those who were persecuting them. The Jews became one of them.

     c. Their theology became more and more liberal.

  4. Reconstructionist Jews (<10%)

     a. Reconstructionism is very American.

     b. Their degree of observance will vary.

        i. Practices will be very traditional, and their services will appear almost conservative.

        ii. Their theology is almost reformed. They believe it is good to practice those things to keep Jewish people together as a body.

  5. Non-observant Jews (<10%)

     a. They don't belong to a synagogue.

     b. They might support Jewish social causes, but they are not religious.

C. Are the Jews God's chosen people?

  1. Yes! The Jewish people are God's chosen people.

  2. God wanted to reveal Himself to mankind.

     a. God was determined to show His mercy, faithfulness, compassion and justice to them. When the nations would see how God related to them, they would understand that God meant to have that personal relationship with them.

     b. God called on Abram (Abraham) and made a covenant with Him...and God showed Himself to be faithful.

D. How has God shown His faithfulness to the Jews?

   1. The amazing thing about God is that our sins are plastered all over the pages of the Bible. We broke all of God's laws, and we still do. And yet, God is still willing to keep His promises to His people.

   2. Paul says about the Jews that God's gifts and his call are irrevocable (Romans 11:29).

   3. God shows His faithfulness in the promise to cause the desert to blossom like a rose (Isaiah 35:1 and Isaiah 27:6).

   4. God's faithfulness is seen in different modern military conflicts.

      a. The Six Day War

      b. The enemies of Israel were fighting God.

      c. Moses is speaking to the Israelites about the Egyptians in Exodus 14:13-14.

   5. Our understanding of God's relationship with the Jews helps us rest secure in who He is with us.

II. Jewish Beliefs:

A. Do the Jews believe in Jesus?

   1. Many do!

      a. This means that the Jewish response to Jesus was greater than any nation in history at that time.

      b. Jewish people today, and down through history, accept Jesus at about the same rate that everyone else does.

   2. Rabbinic theology teaches a Two-Messiah theory. It is believed that there are two strands of prophecy that talked about the Messiah:

      a. Messiah, the Son of David – A Messiah who comes and establishes a kingdom that brings peace; this Messiah comes to rule.

      b. Messiah, the Son of Joseph – Talked about as a Messiah who comes to suffer and die (Isaiah 42, 49, 50, 53; Daniel 9; Psalm 22; Genesis 3:15)

      c. If we believe God, we get the Messiah who comes and brings peace; if we do not obey God, we get the Messiah who comes to suffer.

3. What do the Scriptures say?

    a. The prophecy says, "He was despised and rejected by men, a man of sorrows, and familiar with suffering" (Isaiah 53:3).

    b. The Scriptures confirm that God prophesied the Messiah would come to die.

    c. God put such prophecies in Scripture in order to fulfill His will, namely, that Jesus "must suffer many things and be rejected by this generation [first-century Jews]" (Luke 17:25).

    d. It was necessary for Jesus to be rejected so that He might carry out God's will. If the Jews had recognized Him as the Messiah, they would never have allowed Him to die.

4. How is God able to satisfy both His mercy and His justice?

    a. God, in His genius, is the only One who can bring mercy and justice together. He satisfied them, not through man, but through Jesus. He paid for it completely!

    b. Isaiah 53:10-11 tells us that God has already been satisfied through the suffering of Christ's soul on the cross. Christ has already made mankind righteous, because He has borne our guilt.

    c. Because Jesus was only going to die once, God had to build into that act enough payment to satisfy the debt, both principal and damages, not only for you and me, but also for everyone who has ever lived, and will live, on the earth.

    d. That is why Paul says in Romans 8:1, *"Therefore, there is now no condemnation for those who are in Christ Jesus."*

5. There were four major sacrifices in Mosaic Law:

    a. Burnt offerings and Peace offerings – sacrifices for general guilt

    b. Sin offerings and guilt offerings – sacrifices for specific sins

        i. A guilt offering was a sacrifice for cheating someone, for depriving someone of an obligation that you could be legitimately expected to fulfill.

        ii. This principle says that when we sin we must pay for what we have done and also for damages.

6. What is the significance of God's gift of forgiveness?

    a. There are many people today who believe that they have done something so terrible, that they have to suffer for what they have done.

    b. There is more atonement, more payment, in the blood of Jesus than we will ever need or be able to use.

B. What do the Jews believe about Scripture?

1. Both conservative and orthodox Jews believe in the Old Testament and the Torah (the first five books of the Old Testament).

2. Reformed Jews discount both the historicity of any Scriptures and their inspiration by God.

3. Most of them are agnostics with a growing interest in maintaining Jewish culture.

C. What do the Jews believe about death?

1. Orthodox Jews believe in heaven and hell. Those two concepts are well-developed Jewish ideas.

2. Modern Jews believe that when you die, that's it: dust to dust.

3. The Bible teaches that there will be a resurrection from the dead.

4. Psalm 16:9-10 and Daniel 12:1b-2

5. We can point Jewish people to their own Jewish Bible to support this idea of heaven and hell and counter the "dust to dust" misconception.

D. Do the Jews believe in the Trinity?

1. Jews tend to believe that God is one person with no distinctions. To them, "one God" means one God, the Father.

2. How can we respond to those Jews who believe this idea of God?

3. Deuteronomy 6:4 and Isaiah 48:12-16 ·

E. Is anti-Semitism an issue today? If so, how can Christians address it effectively?

1. Anti-Semitism does take place today.

2. How is anti-Semitism addressed?

   a. Love is the key!

   b. Christians need to "feel the pain" of Jews who have suffered, or are suffering.

III. Witnessing to Jews

A. Keys to witnessing to Jews:

    1. Address and dispel their misconceptions:

        a. Remember, the Jew does not want to be a Christian, because in his mind, that means he has to stop being Jewish.

        b. We need to show him that his Bible calls for him to believe in Jesus, because Jesus is the Jewish Messiah.

        c. Also remember that he thinks you (as a Christian) hate him. He thinks you believe that "He killed Jesus."

        d. Use the Jewish Bible (the Torah and the Prophets in the Old Testament) to build a bridge with him/her.

        e. When speaking about Jesus, use the word Yeshua. It is an easier term for a Jewish person to accept. It is a Hebrew name. We can tell them, "It is a name of your Messiah."

B. How do we witness to a Jew who doesn't believe in God or the Torah?

    1. These kinds of people make up the majority of our Jewish friends, because they have been taught that the Bible is not God's Word.

    2. Refer to the arguments that support the reliability of Scripture as God's Word:

        a. Bibliographic Test

        b. Internal Evidence Test

        c. Prophecy

        d. Archaeology

        e. External Evidence Test

    3. Point to the writings of others.

        a. Highlight specifically the writings of the Jewish historian, Josephus, that referred to Jesus.

C. What does it cost a Jew to come to Christ?

    1. Everything!

    2. Most especially, his/her family.

    3. One is considered a traitor to not only his/her heritage by accepting Christ, but also to every living family member.

    4. Most Jewish believers are considered outcasts by the Rabbi, synagogue and friends.

Lesson 13: Why Don't the Jews Believe in Jesus?

Small Group Objective:

Your goal is to help students gain a better understanding of the Jewish people and their connection to the Christian faith, with the hope that their own relationship with God will be strengthened. Also, it is important that the students apply what they have learned, as they pursue opportunities to witness to Jews.

✓ **Check Points:**

☐ Bring 3 x 5 cards for your students to write down any questions they may have which aren't answered during the discussion.

☐ Enlist a student to share a brief personal testimony.

Discussion Questions:

1. Review prayer requests from the week before and ask how the students are doing.

2. Lead a time of discussion, asking the following questions:

(Note: Work through as many of the following questions as possible. The goal is not to get through all of them, but to encourage each student to participate in the discussion as part of the learning process.)

   a. What day of the devotional did you find most meaningful?

   b. How did last week's lesson impact your life? Did you share it?

   c. How many of you have ever had an opportunity to interact with a Jewish person?

   d. What were some preconceived ideas you had about Jewish people prior to that experience?

   e. What did you learn this week about the Jewish people and their beliefs that you did not know before?

   f. How would you describe the Jews' understanding of Jehovah God?

   g. What might be the reason why they would reject Jesus?

   h. What are some of the ways we can talk to Jews about Jesus?

   i. Frame a Jew.

   j. How can we share with a Jewish person about the "Jewishness" of Christianity?

   k. How has your understanding of the Jewish people/history affected your own faith?

Lesson 13: Why Don't the Jews Believe in Jesus? - Anchorsaway Worldview Handbook ©

Student Devotionals written by T.M. Moore

Why Don't Jews Believe In Jesus?

There are many reasons why the Jews did not receive Jesus when He came among them to proclaim the Kingdom of God. In fact, we may suffer from some of those obstacles, as well.

Day 1: Misguided Expectations

Pray:　　　*"Hear my cry, O God, listen to my prayer; from the end of the earth I call to you when my heart is faint. Lead me to the rock that is higher than I" (Psalm 61:1, 2.)*

Read:　　　John 6:15-41

Meditate:　What kinds of expectations of Jesus did these Jews seem to have? Why did they grumble about Jesus?

Is it possible that people seek to follow Jesus for the wrong reasons, with the wrong kind of expectations? What might be some examples of this?

Do I ever find any of these expectations cropping up in my own relationship with Christ? Which ones? How do I deal with them?

Journal:　　It's clear that Jesus will only have me follow Him on His terms, not mine. I'd better be careful here, because...

Pray:　　　*"Let me dwell in your tent forever! Let me take refuge under the shelter of your wings! "* (Psalm 66:4).

Day 2: Petty Jealousy

Pray:　　　*"I will ponder the way that is blameless. Oh when will you come to me?" (Psalm 101:2).*

Read: Matthew 12:22-32

Meditate: How is it apparent that the Jews were jealous of Jesus here? What were they jealous about (v. 23)?

How did the Jews express their jealousy? Whom were they trying to influence by their words? To what end?

Do I ever feel jealous about someone else's relationship with Jesus? Why? What should I be careful about whenever I feel this way? What should I do?

Journal: I know there are many people whose faith in Jesus far outstrips my own – even some of my friends. I need to guard against becoming jealous, so that I don't do or say something really stupid. So...

Pray: *"I will look with favor on the faithful in the land, that they may dwell with me; he who walks in the way that is blameless shall minister to me"* (Psalm 101:6).

Day 3: Misunderstanding the Word

Pray: *"I desire to do your will, O my God; your law is within my heart"* (Psalm 40:8).

Read: Matthew 22:23-33

Meditate: Jesus was speaking with Jewish theologians. How could He say that they did not know the Scriptures? What did He mean?

How would I describe Jesus' reading of the Old Testament in v. 31? Careful? Detailed? Thoughtful? Is this the way I read the Scriptures?

Knowing the Scripture and knowing the power of God seem to go together in Jesus' mind. Do I know the power of God? How is that evident in my life?

Journal: It is very important that I know the Scriptures *and* the power of God. Maybe I need to rethink my approach to the Bible. Maybe I need to...

Pray: *"I waited patiently for the LORD; he inclined to me and heard my cry"* (Psalm 40:1).

Day 4: Hardness of Heart

Pray: *"Create in me a clean heart, O God, and renew a right spirit within me."* (Psalm 51:10)

Read: Romans 11:25-36

Meditate: What is a "partial hardening" (v. 25)? How can I see that the Jews in Jesus' day suffered from this? Do I know any people suffering from this today?

                    What is the status of those who are hardened of heart with respect to the Gospel (v. 28)? Does this mean, according to Paul, that God doesn't love them any more? Does this release me from having to love those who have hardened hearts?

                    This is a great mystery – this hardness of heart. How did Paul explain this (vv. 33-35)? It seems I need to leave the mysteries to God to sort out; but what is *my* responsibility toward even the most hardened of heart?

Journal: I know some people with hardened hearts toward God. In fact, I'm pretty sure I'll see some of them today. I'd better get ready, so that I...

Pray: *"Then I will teach transgressors your ways, and sinners will return to you"* (Psalm 51:13).

Day 5: Simple Unbelief

Pray: *"I have not hidden your deliverance within my heart; I have spoken of your faithfulness and your salvation"* (Psalm 40:10).

Read: John 1:1-12

Meditate: What does it mean to "receive" Jesus? How do people receive Him? If someone has not received Him, it's simply because...

John says that Jesus is the true light. How does He shine His true light on others? Am I a part of that? In what ways?

Looking at me, would people conclude that I believed in Jesus, that I had received Him? Do they see His light in me? Is His light shining through me to the people around who yet do not believe in Him?

Journal: Jesus is the Light of the world, and He intends to shine His light through me, so that others will believe in Him. Well, if that's the case, today...

Pray: *"I have not concealed your steadfast love and your faithfulness"* (Psalm 40:10).

Key Organizations:

- For Jews who have recognized the Messiah: www.jewsforjesus.com
- For great teaching in regard to the Jews, Koinania House: www.khouse.org

Key Books:

Brown, Michael L. 60 Questions Christians Ask about Jewish Beliefs and Practices. Bloomington, MN: Chosen, 2011.

Brown, Michael L. Answering Jewish Objections to Jesus. Grand Rapids, MI: Baker, 2000.

Burge, Gary M. Jesus and the Jewish Festivals. Grand Rapids, MI: Zondervan, 2012.

Carson, D. A. Matthew. Frank E. Gaebelein. *The Expositor's Bible Commentary with the New International Version.* Grand Rapids, MI: Zondervan, 1995 *(Chapters 13 Through 28).*

Chernoff, David. *Messianic Judaism: Questions and Answers.* Havertown, PA: Kesher Ministries International

Chernoff, David. *Yeshua the Messiah.* Havertown, PA: Kesher Ministries International, 2001.

Glaser, Mitch and Zhava. *The Fall Feasts of Israel.* Chicago: Moody Press, 1987.

Juster, David C. *Jewishness and Jesus.* Downers Grove, IL: InterVarsity Press, 1999.

Rosen, Moishe. *Y'shua: The Jewish Way to Say Jesus.* Chicago: Moody Press, 1983.

Schaeffer, Edith. *Christianity is Jewish.* Carol Stream, IL: Tyndale House Publishers, 1975.

Shafiroff, Ira L. Every Christian's Book on Judaism: Exploring Jewish Faith and Law for a Richer Understanding of Christianity. Torrance, CA: Noga, 1998.

Telchin, Stan. *Betrayed!* Grand Rapids, MI: Chosen Books, 1981.

Key Audio:

- Missler, Chuck. "The Legacy: Israel in Prophecy." Audio CD. Koinania House Ministries. <www.khouse.org>

Lesson 14: How Does God View the Homosexual?

⚓ Anchor of the Week: God hates sin but loves the sinner.

I. What does Scripture say about homosexuality?

A. Many will say that homosexuality is not a sin and is not found in Scripture. Look at the following verses to see if that is true: Romans 1:20-32; 1 Corinthians 6:9-11, 18-20; Leviticus 18:22-28; Revelation 21:8.

 1. Things to remember when dealing with the issue of homosexuality:

 a. Yes, homosexuality is a sin with very severe consequences.

 b. Take a moment to look over these Scripture verses and see what other sins are grouped in with the sin of homosexuality.

 c. God hates all sin. We, too, are to hate all sin. God loves the sinner and proved it by dying for all of us. We, too, are called to love the sinner and that includes the homosexual.

 d. Too often, believers are quick to point a finger at someone else's sin, while overlooking their own. As with all those who do not know Christ, we are to listen and then reach out with the good news of Jesus Christ. The issue is salvation and holiness. It is more than simply not "doing that sin any more."

II. Background - What are those experiences or other influences that have shaped the life of the homosexual? Five common factors in people struggling with homosexuality:[1]

A. Early childhood development

B. Family background

 1. The role of the father

 2. The role of the mother

 3. The role of the community

C. Temperament and interests

D. Peer Pressure

E. Abuse

    1. Verbal

        a. Greg's experience was much like this. He says, "When I was eleven, I began to take a lot of ridicule for my speech impediment. There was a lot of verbal abuse that took place in my life, a lot of labeling and shaming that got poured into my heart. There were a lot of words that got applied to me that labeled me as worthless, and inadequate, and damaged and no good. Those were the kind of things that got poured into my heart and I took them onto myself."

            i. We should think before we speak. As the Bible says, *"The tongue has the power of life and death, and those who love it will eat its fruit"* (Proverbs 18:21).

    2. Physical

    3. Sexual

        a. Sexual abuse is one of the most prevalent factors that influences people toward the homosexual lifestyle. As Bob Davies and Lori Rentzel point out, "Sexual abuse is common in the backgrounds of women and men struggling with homosexual attractions."[2]

            i. Upwards of 85 percent of gay women

            ii. Between 50-60 percent of gay men[3]

    4. Emotional

    5. Religion

F. Is there really a "gay gene?"

    1. When it comes to the idea that people are either born gay or not, "...the evidence is inconclusive, and a growing body of critics believes that there is evidence to the contrary."[4]

    2. Greg Wallace describes homosexuality as a "neurosis," because "there is no genetic connection. I know that's a very popular thing in our culture today, to try and prove the genetic link, because it takes all the burden off of the choices that we make. It takes all the burden off the responsibility we have to live our lives the way God designed them. If we're born that way, it's not a choice, and we don't have anything to say about it. If we're born that way, we shouldn't have to change. If we're born that way, we shouldn't even *want* to change.")

III. How can we as Christians reach out to those who are struggling with homosexuality?

A. Too often we think the goal in helping people who struggle in this area is that they should get married, that the goal is simply "not homosexuality." That is not the goal.

B. The goal is holiness. That is what we strive for - not heterosexuality.

IV. How would Jesus frame the homosexual?

    A. Loved by God

    B. Created in His image

    C. Broken as all people are.

    D. Christ died for all their sins.

    E. Made with the purpose to love God and others to His glory.

(Note: The following space should be used for notes on this important subject. As you watch the DVD presentation by Mr. Greg Wallace or Mr. Brad Grammer, write down points that you have in common with their story so that you can better understand that these people are human beings that desperately need love and healthy relationships!)

V. Tips for Sharing the Gospel

    A. See a person and not a homosexual.

    B. Remember that the Gospel means "good news."

    C. Know what you are offering.

    D. Actively love that person.

    E. Share your life.

    F. Do not make sexual brokenness the focal point of your relationship.

    G. Share relevant Scripture when appropriate.

Is Homosexuality Genetic?

Recent studies indicate that there is no evidence people are born gay or transgender.
http://www.wnd.com/2016/08/johns-hopkins-shrinks-warn-against-going-transgender-with-kids/
https://pjmedia.com/trending/2016/08/23/johns-hopkins-research-no-evidence-people-are-born-gay-or-transgender/--
http://www.christianpost.com/news/no-scientific-evidence-that-people-are-born-gay-or-transgender-johns-hopkins-researchers-say-168263/

Three Studies

1. LEVAY STUDY

Simon LeVay, "A Difference in Hypothalamic Structure Between Heterosexual and Homosexual Men," reported in *Science* magazine on August 30, 1991, professed to have found a group of neurons in the hypothalamus (called INAH3) that appeared to be twice as big in heterosexual men than in homosexual men. LeVay theorized that this part of the hypothalamus has something to do with sexual behavior. Therefore, he concluded, sexual orientation is somehow biologically determined.

Brief critique of the LeVay study:

All 19 homosexual subjects died of AIDS, and we know that HIV/AIDS may affect the brain, causing chemical changes. Therefore, rather than looking at the cause of homosexuality, we may be observing the effects of HIV/AIDS.

LeVay did not verify the sexual orientation of his control group. "Two of these subjects (both AIDS patients) had denied homosexual activity. The records of the remaining 14 patients contained no information about their sexual orientation. They are assumed to have been mostly or all heterosexual." It is poor science to "assume" anything about your subjects.

Three (3) of the 19 homosexual subjects had a larger group of neurons in the hypothalamus than the average heterosexual subject. Three (3) of the 16 heterosexual subjects had a smaller group of neurons in the hypothalamus than the average homosexual subject. That means 6 out of 35 male subjects disproved his hypothesis. These results, then, are not statistically significant or reliable.

There is no proof that this group of neurons affects sexuality. Dr. Charles Socarides, Professor of Psychiatry at Albert Einstein College of Medicine in New York City said, "The question of a minute section of the brain, sub-microscopic almost, as deciding sexual object choice is really preposterous. A cluster of the brain cannot determine sexual object choice."

LeVay himself stated, "It's important to stress what I didn't find. I did not prove that homosexuality is genetic, or find a genetic cause for being gay. I didn't show that gay men are born that way, the most common mistake people make in interpreting my work. Nor did I locate a gay center in the brain... Since I look at adult brains, we don't know if the differences I found were there at birth or if they appeared later."

2. BAILEY AND PILLARD STUDY

John M. Bailey and Richard Pillard, "A Genetic Study of Male Sexual Orientation," reported in the Archives of General Psychiatry, December 1991. They studied the prevalence of homosexuality among twins and adopted brothers where at least one brother was homosexual. They found that 52% (29 pairs out of 56) of the identical twins were both homosexual; 22% (12 pairs out of 54) of the fraternal twins were both homosexual; and 11% (6 of 57) of the adoptive brothers were both homosexual. They also found 9% (13 of 142) of the non-twin biological siblings were both homosexual. The authors therefore concluded that there is a genetic cause to homosexuality.

Brief Critique of the Bailey-Pillard study:

The biggest flaw is the interpretation of the researchers. Since about 50% of the identical twins were not homosexual, we can easily conclude that genetics does not play a major part in their sexual orientation. If it had, then 100% of the twins should be homosexual since identical twins have the same genetic makeup. We might just as easily interpret the findings to mean that environmental influences caused their homosexuality. Biologist, Anne Fausto Stirling, of Brown University stated, "In order for such a study to be at all meaningful, you'd have to look at twins raised apart. It's such badly interpreted genetics."

This was not a random sample, but a biased sample, as the twins who volunteered were solicited through advertisements in homosexual newspapers and magazines, as opposed to general periodicals. Therefore, the subjects were more likely to resemble each other than non-homosexual twins.

Dr. Simon LeVay stated, "In fact, the twin studies ... suggest that it's not totally inborn [homosexuality], because even identical twins are not always of the same sexual orientation."

Dr. Bailey stated, "There must be something in the environment to yield the discordant twins."

The researchers failed to investigate the roles that incest or sexual abuse and other environmental factors play in determining same-sex attractions. If they had found that incest was more common among identical twins than fraternal twins or non-twin blood brothers, this could have helped explain the varying rates of homosexuality.

3. <u>HAMER STUDY</u>

Dean Hamer, et al., of the National Cancer Institute, "A Linkage between DNA markers on the X Chromosome and Male Sexual Orientation," reported in *Science* magazine, July 1993. The media reported that the "gay gene" was discovered as a result of this study. The researchers studied 40 pairs of homosexual brothers and suggested that some cases of homosexuality are linked to a specific region on the X chromosome (Xq28) inherited from the mother to her homosexual son. Thirty-three (33) pairs of brothers shared the same pattern variation in the tip of one arm of the chromosome. Hamer estimated that the sequence of the given genetic markers on Xq28 is linked to homosexuality in 64% of the brothers.

Brief critique of the Hamer, et al. study:

Dr. Kenneth Klivington, assistant to the president of the Salk Institute in San Diego states, "There is a body of evidence that shows the brain's neural networks reconfigure themselves in response to certain experience. Therefore, the difference in homosexual brain structure may be a result of behavior and environmental conditions."

There was no control group. This is poor scientific methodology. Hamer and associates failed to test the heterosexual brothers. What if the heterosexual brothers had the same genetic markers?

It has not been proven that the identified section of the chromosomes has a direct bearing on sexuality or sexual orientation. One of Hamer's fellow research assistants brought him up on charges, saying that he withheld some of the findings that invalidated his study. The National Cancer Institute is investigating Hamer. (To date, they have not released the results of this investigation.)

A Canadian research team using a similar experimental design was unable to duplicate the findings of Hamer's study. Hamer states, "These genes do not cause people to become homosexuals ... ultimately, it is the environment that determines how these genes will express themselves."

Comments by other scientists:

"Evan S. Balaban, a neurobiologist at the Neurosciences Institute in San Diego, notes that the search for the biological underpinnings of complex human traits has a sorry history of late. In recent years, researchers and the media have proclaimed the `discovery' of genes linked to alcoholism and mental illness, as well as to homosexuality. None of the claims, Balaban points out, have been confirmed." (*Scientific America*, November 1995)

"Recent studies postulate biologic factors as the primary basis for sexual orientation. However, there is no evidence at present to substantiate a biologic theory, just as there is no compelling evidence to support any singular psychological explanation. While all behavior must have an ultimate biologic substrate, the appeal of current biologic explanations for sexual orientation may derive more from dissatisfaction with the present status of psychosocial explanations than from a substantiating body of experimental data. Critical review shows the evidence favoring a biologic theory to be lacking. In an alternative model, temperamental and personality traits interact with the familial and social milieu as the individual's sexuality emerges." (Archives of *General Psychiatry*, March 1993)

"Reports of morphological differences between the brains of humans with different sexual orientation or gender identity have furthered speculation that such behaviors may result from hormonal or genetic influences on the developing brain. However, the causal chain may be reversed; sexual behavior in adulthood may have caused the morphological differences... It is possible that differences in sexual behavior cause, rather than are caused by, differences in brain structure." (*Nature*, October 1997)

"The myth of the all-powerful gene is based on flawed science that discounts the environmental context in which we and our genes exist, many modern researchers continue to believe that sexual preference is to some extent biologically determined. They base this belief on the fact that no single environmental explanation can account for the development of homosexuality, but this does not make sense. Human sexuality is complex and affected by many things. The failure to come up with a clear environmental explanation is not surprising, and does not mean that the answer lies in biology. Such studies are bound to come up with plenty of meaningless correlations which will get reported as further evidence of genetic transmission of homosexuality." (*Exploding the Gene Myth*, Harvard 1993)

"In the early 90's, three highly publicized studies seemed to suggest that homosexuality's roots were genetic, traceable to nature rather than nurture... More than five years later the data have never been replicated. Moreover, researchers say, the public has misunderstood `behavioral genetics.' Unlike eye color, behavior is not strictly inherited; it needs to be brought into play by a daunting complexity of environmental factors... The existence of a genetic pattern among homosexuals doesn't mean people are born gay, any more than the genes for height, presumably common in NBA players, indicate an inborn ability to play basketball ... admits biologist Evan Balaban, `I think we're as much in the dark as we ever were.'" (*Newsweek*, August 17, 1998)

"Like all complex behavioral and mental states, homosexuality is multifactorial. It is neither exclusively biological nor exclusively psychological, but results from an as-yet-difficult-to-quantitate mixture of genetic factors, intrauterine influences (some innate to the mother and thus present in every pregnancy, and others incidental to a given pregnancy), postnatal environment (such as parental, sibling, and cultural behavior), and a complex series of repeatedly reinforced choices occurring at critical phases in development." (*Homosexuality and the Politics of Truth*, 1996)

Conclusion to Studies

Repeated sexual behavior and environmental conditions change brain structure and body chemistry, which means the genetic/biological characteristics observed in these studies may be the result of homosexual behavior, rather than the cause of it.

All of these studies lack consistency and replication. Their results are inconclusive and speculative at best. Simon LeVay, Richard Pillard, and Dean Hamer are all self-proclaimed homosexuals. Therefore, I suggest that behind their work is a strong motivation to justify their same-sex attractions. If homosexuality is a normal sexual orientation, why is only 1% to 3% of the population homosexual and not 50%? Why are there more male homosexuals than female homosexuals?

Masters and Johnson, leading sex researchers in America state, "The genetic theory of homosexuality has been generally discarded today... No serious scientist suggests that a simple cause-effect relationship applies."

There is a preponderance of scientific evidence conducted over the past eighty years that shows homosexuality to be an acquired condition. Dr. Irving Bieber, Dr. Charles Socarides, Dr. Joseph Nicolosi, Dr. Elizabeth Moberly, Dr. Lawrence Hatterer, Dr. Robert Kronemeyer, Dr. E. Kaplan, Dr. Edith Fiore, Dr. Gerard van den Aardweg, Dr. Earl Wilson, Dr. Jeffrey Satinover - these are but a few of the psychiatrists and psychologists who have substantiated these findings through years of clinical research and empirical studies.

The best evidence to disprove a theory is experience. Thousands of men and women throughout the world have changed from homosexual to heterosexual. Masters and Johnson claim about a 65% success rate in helping people change. Other therapists who report successful treatment are Drs. Bieber, Socarides, Nicolosi, Hatterer, Gershman, Hadden, Hamilton, van den Aardweg, Barnhouse, Ellis, and many others.[20] The National Association for Research and Therapy of Homosexuality (NARTH) conducted a survey of 860 respondents and found that those who want to change their sexual orientation may succeed.

Small Group Discussion Guide

Lesson 14: How Does God View the Homosexual?

Small Group Objective:

The goal is to help the students begin to walk deeper in God's love in all areas of life. This goal concerns their interactions with all people they meet in life, including those in the homosexual lifestyle.

✓ Check Points

☐ Bring 3 x 5 cards for your students to write down any questions they may have which aren't answered during the discussion.

☐ Enlist a student to share a brief personal testimony.

Discussion Questions:

1. Review prayer requests from the week before and ask how the students are doing.

(*Note: Have students give names of juniors that they would like to be invited for next year's Anchorsaway class. Give these names to the administrator.*)

2. Lead a time of discussion, asking the following questions:

(*Note: Work through as many of the following questions as possible. The goal is not to get through all of them, but to encourage each student to participate in the discussion as part of the learning process.*)

a. What day of the devotional did you find most meaningful?

b. How did last week's lesson impact your life? Did you share it?

c. What stereotypes do people often have of homosexuals? How might those stereotypes affect those who struggle with homosexuality?

d. What is the real issue with being a homosexual?

e. What kinds of influences may affect a person's becoming a homosexual?

f. How do many homosexuals view Christians? Does their perspective have any merit?

g. How can you, as a Christian, reach out to the homosexual in healthy love?

h. How would Jeus frame a homosexual?

i. In what ways may a homosexual be wounded and broken?

j. Are there areas in our own lives that have brokenness

k. How can we effectively share the gospel with those who are struggling with homosexuality?

l. What kind of "Good News" does the Bible give to the homosexual (and to us)?

m. What questions, if any, come to mind as a result of this week's lesson?

3. Ask for prayer requests and tell students that you will be faithful to pray for them during the week. Encourage students to record the prayer requests in the prayer request section of their handbooks, so they can pray for one another during the week. Begin the prayer time by sharing your own request. Spend the remaining time in prayer.

★ After the Session

1. Contact small group members during the week. Ask them about their devotional time, a question they have raised, or how their week is going.

<u>**Prayer Requests**</u>

Lesson 14: How Does God View the Homosexual? - Anchorsaway Worldview Handbook ©

Student Devotionals written by T.M. Moore

How Does God View The Homosexual?

The Scriptures consistently condemn the practice of homosexuality (cf. Genesis 18:20; 19:1-11; Leviticus 18:22; 20:13; Romans 1:18, 26, 27; 1 Corinthians 6:9, 10; 1 Timothy 1:10). But then, the Scriptures consistently condemn the practice of every sin, and of any sin, and command the people of God to live in love toward Him and their neighbors. The challenge to us, therefore, in the face of whatever sin may be confronting us, is to learn how to fulfill what is required of us while keeping ourselves free from the taint of wickedness.

Day 1: The Love Mandate

Pray: "O taste and see that the LORD is good! Blessed is the man who takes refuge in him!" (Psalm 34:8).

Read: 1 John 4:13-21

Meditate: What does it mean to abide in Jesus? What should I expect to see happening in me if I am abiding in Him? Is this what I see?

What is love able to cast out fear? How can the love God has for me, and is "perfecting" in me, help me to love those whom I otherwise might fear?

How do people experience the love of God from me? How can I improve my ability to love God and others?

Journal: In a world where many people are searching for love in all the wrong places, God has placed me as a beacon of *His* love. Therefore...

Pray: "The eyes of the LORD are toward the righteous and his ears hear their cry" (Psalm 34:15).

Day 2: Take Time to Understand

Pray: *"Save, O LORD, for the godly one is gone; for the faithful have vanished from among the children of man"* (Psalm 12:1).

Read: Acts 17:16-21

Meditate: What was Paul doing in Athens? Why was he doing this? How did it make him feel (v. 16)?

Does it trouble me to see people trapped in sin, or do I just look down on them and move on? Do I understand what it is that makes people fall into sin? Do I care to try to find out?

How would I describe Paul's contacts with the people in Athens? Was he doing all the talking? Was he listening (cf. vv. 22, 23)? What can I learn from him about understanding other people?

Journal: The Apostle James says we're supposed to be "quick to hear, slow to speak, slow to anger" (James 1:19). If I'm going to understand why some people get trapped in sin, I need to...

Pray: *"The words of the LORD are pure words, like silver refined in a furnace on the ground, purified seven times. You, O LORD, will keep them..."* (Psalm 12:6, 7).

Day 3: Words That Edify

Pray: *"Set a guard, O LORD, over my mouth; keep watch over the door of my lips!"* (Psalm 141:3).

Read: Ephesians 4:25-5:4

Meditate: How am I supposed to be using my tongue? Is this the way I use it? Am I ever tempted to make light of someone else's sins?

Do people experience my words as building them up? Who builds me up with his or her words? How might I begin to use my words more like that?

Is there much thanksgiving in my conversation with others? Why or why not? Should there be more than there is? How might that serve to build others up?

Journal: A lot of how others think of me is a result of what they hear me say. Hmm... I think I could begin to change the way others think of me by...

Pray: *"Do not let my heart incline to any evil, to busy myself with wicked deeds..."* (Psalm 141:4).

Day 4: Resisting Temptation

Pray: *"Truly God is good to Israel, to those who are pure in heart"* (Psalm 73:1).

Read: Psalm 73

Meditate: With what was the psalmist tempted (vv. 2-14)? Why was that such a strong temptation for him?

How did he resist that temptation? How did he resist it in vv. 16 and 17? In vv. 18-20? In vv. 23 and 24? In vv. 25-28? How might his example help me in resisting temptation?

How do I know when I am being tempted? What does it feel like? What do I typically do at that moment? How can I help those who are beset by temptation?

Journal: Sin begins with temptation, the Apostle James reminds us (James 1:13-15). I need a strategy for recognizing and dealing with temptation that includes...

Pray: *"But for me it is good to be near God; I have made the Lord GOD my refuge, that I may tell of all your works"* (Psalm 73:28)

Day 5: Guarding Yourself Day by Day

Pray: *"I will not set before my eyes anything that is worthless..."* (Psalm 101:3).

Read: Psalm 101

Meditate: Here is a psalm I could pray at the beginning of every day. How does it guide me to use my words (v. 1)? What kind of "mindset" does it recommend (v. 2)? To what kind of lifestyle ("walk") does it commit me (v. 2)?

                  How does this psalm lead me to use my eyes (v. 3)? To set my heart (v. 4)? To resist the sins of others (I'm not going to "destroy" or "cut off" anyone, but how might I practice what I read in vv. 5 and 8, beginning with myself?)

                  How does this psalm lead me to deal with my Christian friends (v. 6)? To respond to the lies and half-truths of the sinful world around me (v. 7)?

Journal: I need a "whole-life" strategy for keeping myself pure from sin and for reaching out to others with the love of Jesus. I'll begin that strategy today by...

Pray: *"I will sing of steadfast love and justice; to you, O LORD, I will make music"* (Psalm 101:1).

            Lesson 14: How Does God View the Homosexual? - Anchorsaway Worldview Handbook ©

ENDNOTES

[1] These five influential factors commonly found in people struggling with homosexuality are adapted from Bob Davies and Lori Rentzel, *Coming Out of Homosexuality: New Freedom for Men & Women* (Downers Grove, IL: InterVarsity Press, 1993) 43.

[2] Davies, 123.

[3] Davies, 123-124.

[4] Don Schmierer, and Lela Gilbert, *An Ounce of Prevention: Preventing the Homosexual Condition in Today's Youth* (Santa Ana, CA: Promise Publishing Co., 2002) 51.

Recommended Reading

Key Websites:

- http://www.wnd.com/2016/08/johns-hopkins-shrinks-warn-against-going-transgender-with-kids/
- https://pjmedia.com/trending/2016/08/23/johns-hopkins-research-no-evidence-people-are-born-gay-or-transgender/--
- http://www.christianpost.com/news/no-scientific-evidence-that-people-are-born-gay-or-transgender-johns-hopkins-researchers-say-168263/

Key Books:

Brown, Michael L. Can You Be Gay and Christian? N.p.: n.p., n.d.

Comiskey, Andrew. *Pursuing Sexual Wholeness: How Jesus Heals the Homosexual.* Lake Mary, FL: Creation House, 1989.

Davies, Bob, and Lori Rentzel. *Coming Out of Homosexuality: New Freedom for Men & Women.* Downers Grove, IL: InterVarsity Press, 1993.

McDowell, Josh, and Sean McDowell. The Beauty of Intolerance: Setting a Generation Free to Know Truth & Love. N.p.: n.p., n.d.

Riley, Mona, and Brad Sargent. *Unwanted Harvest.* Nashville, TN: Broadmand & Holman, 1995.

Schmierer, Don, and Lela Gilbert. *An Ounce of Prevention: Preventing the Homosexual Condition in Today's Youth.* Santa Ana, CA: Promise Publishing Co., 2002.

Sprigg, Peter, and Timothy Dailey. *Getting It Straight: What the Research Shows about Homosexuality.* Washington DC: Family Research Council, 2004.

Thompson, Chad. *The Homophobia Stops Here: Addressing the Ex-Gay Perspective In Public Schools.* Grand Rapids, MI: Brazos Press, 2004.

Thompson, Chad. *Loving Homosexuals As Jesus Would.* Grand Rapids, MI: Brazos Press, 2004.

Worthen, Anita, and Bob Davies. *Someone I Love Is Gay.* Downers Grove, IL: InterVarsity Press, 1996.

Yarhouse, Mark A. Homosexuality and the Christian:. Bloomington, MN: Bethany House, 2010.

Lesson 15: What Is The Christian Role In Cultural Reconciliation?

⚓ **Anchor of the Week: Love your neighbor as yourself.**

A. As a Christian, our idenity must be firmly secured in Christ. We may participate in other communities; but our identity should primarily be in Christ and secondarily in community.

B. Using an example of a culturally segregated society, why is the body of Christ so racially and culturally segregated?

C. Are we prepared for an effective scriptural ministry in an increasingly diverse society? In this lesson, we will focus on how to peacefully bring people groups together while celebrating differences. The conflicts between people groups are not limited to skin color; many times prejudice and discrimination are just as divisive within a group.

D. What do we mean by the word race and racism?

1. The Bible does not use the word "race" as a group of people, but it does in Acts 17:26 make reference to all human beings being of "one blood."

2. All people are related in that we are all descendants of Adam (1 Corinthians 15:45).

E. What does science have to say about race?

1. Upon the acceptance of Darwinian evolution, people began to think in terms of different people groups (races). This was the beginning of comparing one group to another, thus the birth of racial prejudices, or racism, as we know it today.

2. The racial characteristics that make us look different from one another are extremely minor variations, typically around 0.2 percent. "These so called 'racial' characteristics that many think are major differences (skin color, eye shape, etc.) account for only 6 percent of this 0.2 percent variation, which amounts to a mere 0.012 percent difference genetically."[1]

3. "Overall, there is more variation *within* any group than there is *between* one group and another. If a white person is looking for a tissue match for an organ transplant, the best match may come from a black person, and vice versa."[2]

F. What is the definition of the word "culture?"

　1. The totality of socially transmitted behavior patterns, arts, beliefs, institutions, and all other products of human work and thought.

　2. Those patterns, traits, and products considered as the expression of a particular period, class, community or population.

　3. The predominating attitudes and behavior that characterize the functioning of a group or organization.

G. The role that cultural differences play in our lives:

　1. Cultural differences affect people's lives in a variety of ways.

H. Cultural Reconciliation is a critical part of the Christian worldview.

　1. Cultural reconciliation exists when believers of differing ethnic origins and/or cultural backgrounds have authentic relationships with each other based upon the biblical principles of unity, righteousness and acceptance in Christ, rather than ethnic or cultural preference, heritage and/or pride.

　2. Multiethnic ministry – Believers from various ethnic and/or cultural backgrounds who are engaged in Christian ministry together according to the clear principles of Scripture

I. Some challenges for becoming a generation of reconciliation:

　1. The reconciliation generation must understand key terms:

　　a. Multiculturalism – Is similar in meaning to cultural 'pluralism,' referring to the maintenance of ethnic subcultures with their traditions, values and styles. This is in contrast to the definition that is taught by many professors in college. Often times they use this term to mean the all-inclusiveness of religions and spirituality as being true and acceptable.

b. Pluralism – Groups live side by side with different languages and cultures, and with a minimum of social interaction, integration, or assimilation.

c. Prejudice – A set of attitudes that causes, supports and justifies discrimination; an emotionally rigid attitude or predisposition to respond toward a group of people; and an antipathy based upon a faulty and inflexible generalization.

d. Discrimination – Consists of the action or practices carried out by members of one group, or their representatives, which have a differential and harmful impact on members of another group.

e. Classism – Prejudice or discrimination against or in favor of people belonging to a particular social class.

f. Sexism – Discrimination against women; behavior, conditions, or attitudes that foster stereotypes of social roles based on discrimination against women.

J. The reconciliation generation must deal with the American history of prejudice and its consequent effects upon cross-cultural relationships.

1. The concept of white superiority and privilege was not only prominent in American society, but in much of the church, as well.

K. The reconciliation generation must reject the wisdom of the world. (Psalm 1:1-3; Romans 12:1-2; James 3:13-18)

1. The world, in general, has done a better job than the evangelical/fundamental church in seeking to correct past errors.

2. The world fails to understand the bottom line issue, which is sin and the fallen nature of humanity.

3. The world's philosophy lacks moral wisdom and discernment.

a. Tolerance vs. Truth – The world is telling us that unless we accept everyone and every religion as being true, we are bigoted and intolerant. They seem to be tolerant of all people and religions, except for Christians and Christianity. Christians must realize that there is truth, and all religions could not possibly be the same, as they contradict one another. (See the chart on *Comparisions of Other Religions* and the chart on *Cults and the Occult* found in Appendix B at the back of this handbook.)

b. The world believes that how one feels is a greater factor in establishing moral absolutes than the objective truth of Scripture.

L. The reconciliation generation must receive God's wisdom. (Proverbs 1:3-7; 2:3-15; 3:3-4, 13-18; James 3:13-18)

M. The reconciliation generation must understand the issue of leadership. (Philippians 2:3)

N. The reconciliation generation must understand the issue of inconsistency. (Proverbs 11:1; 21:2-3; 24:23)

1. Historical events must be reported with consistency of moral principle.

2. Descriptive language

3. Allowing one people group over another to obtain jobs or entrance into schools, regardless of the qualifications of the individual

4. Offending others

O. The reconciliation generation must understand the issue of compassion. (Acts 20:28; I Corinthians 12:12-14, 18-23, 25-27; Ephesians 4:11-16; I John 3:16-18; 4:7-12)

1. Service: Missionaries, pastors, professors and teachers

P. The reconciliation generation must exercise critical thinking. (Proverbs 21:3; 24:26; Philippians 1:9-11; Colossians 1:9-12)

1. Watch for stereotypes. (Jews, Asians, Whites, Blacks, Latinos)

2. Watch for extremes.

3. Watch your pride/anger. (Jonah, Peter)

4. Seek to know the heart and head. (Proverbs 4:23; 25:12; 27:5-6; 29:23-25)

5. Watch your communication.

6. Seek to win individuals, not people groups. (John 4)

Q. The reconciliation generation must understand the principles of reconciliation. (Breaking Down Walls)

1. Committment to Relationship

2. Intentionality (John 4 " I must...")

3. Sincerity, Sensitivity, Interdependency- Listen to their story

4. Sacrifice, Empowerment, Call

R. The reconciliation generation must understand the pathway to love.
(2 Peter 1:3-9)

1. Faith – (John 17:11, 21, 22; Ephesians 2:11-15; I Corinthians 12:13)

2. Virtue – (James 2:1-3; Acts 10:9-34; Galatians 2:11-14; Ephesians 4:3)

3. Knowledge – (Acts 10:9-34; 11:1-18; 3:13-18)

4. Temperance – (James 2:19-25; Psalm 1)

5. Patience – (James 1:2-12; 5:7-12)

6. Godliness – (Romans 5:3-5)

7. Brotherly Kindness – (Romans 1:7-12; Philippians 1:3-8; 2:1-18)

8. Love – (John 3:16; Matthew 5:43-48)

Lesson 15: What Is the Christian Role in Cultural Reconciliation?

Small Group Objective:

The goal is to help the students begin to understand some of the cultural barriers that have been erected, and, how, as Christians, we are called to dismantle these barriers. We are all sons and daughters of Adam and Eve, and the gospel is to be shared with everyone.

✓ Check Points

☐ Bring 3 x 5 cards for your students to write down any questions they may have which aren't answered during the discussion.

☐ Enlist a student to share a brief personal testimony.

Discussion Questions:

1. Review prayer requests from the week before and ask how the students are doing.

2. Lead a time of discussion, asking the following questions:

(Note: Work through as many of the following questions as possible. The goal is not to get through all of them, but to encourage each student to participate in the discussion as part of the learning process.)

  a. What day of the devotional did you find most meaningful?

  b. How did last week's lesson impact your life? Did you share it?

  c. Are there scriptural answers to cultural reconciliation issues being raised both nationally and internationally today? (Acts 17:26; Galatians 3:23-28).

  d. How can the church fulfill its mandate in Matthew 28:18-20 within a culturally diverse society?

  e. How can we effectively minister the Scriptures in a culturally confrontational society? (1 Corinthians 9:18-23).

  f. How can we effectively minister the Scriptures in the most ethnically diverse nation in the world, that is committed to "tolerance?" (Ephesians 4:11-16).

  g. Frame the group, community, or person you fear.

3. Ask for prayer requests and tell students that you will be faithful to pray for them during the week. Encourage students to record the prayer requests in the prayer request section of their handbooks, so they can pray for one another during the week. Begin the prayer time by sharing your own request. Spend the remaining time in prayer.

Student Devotionals written by T.M. Moore

What Is The Christian Role In Cultural Reconciliation?

In Jesus Christ everything is being made new – our attitudes, views, hopes, and ways of relating to others. In a day when racial prejudice continues to plague our society, Christians have a unique opportunity to demonstrate the power of Christ's love to bring newness to this area of life, as well. But we shall have to give ourselves deliberately and daily to the task of being agents of grace in the work of cultural reconciliation.

Day 1: Just Like Jesus

Pray: *"My soul clings to you; your right hand upholds me"* (Psalm 63:8).

Read: John 4:1-30

Meditate: In Jesus' day the Jews despised the Samaritans, whom they regarded as "half-breeds" with pagan peoples. NO self-respecting Jew would ever have walked through Samaria if he could avoid it. So what's Jesus doing here?

Does Jesus appear to be prejudiced toward this woman? How can you tell? Does He show her respect? Does He seem to care about her?

Jesus knew He had been sent by the Father to seek and to save the lost, wherever He found them (Luke 19:10). In the same way, He has sent me (John 20:21). What does this imply about my relationship with people of other cultures?

Journal: Jesus has sent me to seek the lost wherever I might find them. How do I feel about this? How do I feel about this with respect to people from other people groups? I need to take some first steps in reaching out, so this week I'm going to...

Pray: *"May all who seek you rejoice and be glad in you; may those who love your salvation say continually, 'Great is the LORD!'"* (Psalm 40:16).

Day 2: One in the Gospel

Pray: *"And now, O Lord, for what do I wait? My hope is in you"* (Psalm 39:7).

Read: Galatians 3:23-29

Meditate: What does it mean to say that "in Christ Jesus you are all sons [children] of God? If I have "put on Christ" what should others be seeing in me? If others have "put on Christ," what should I be seeing in them?

In one sense, are people from all people groups and social classes "one in Christ?" How can I help to make that oneness a reality?

Only the Gospel gives people the power to overcome cultural and class barriers and prejudices. How does it do that? Have I experienced that? How should others expect to see the Gospel at work in me to break down cultural and class barriers?

Journal: Are there any attitudes in me that are keeping me from "putting on Jesus" toward members of other people groups? Here's how I'm going to get rid of those attitudes and let the power of the Gospel begin to make me an agent of unity:

Pray: *"Power belongs to God, and to you, O Lord, belongs steadfast love"* (Psalm 62:11).

Day 3: No More Barriers

Pray: *"We have thought on your steadfast love, O God, in the midst of your temple"* (Psalm 48:9).

Read: Ephesians 2:11-22

Meditate: We have visited this text before, but this time we'll take a little different look at it. In Paul's day, portions of the Law of God had erected a barrier separating Jews and Gentiles, and creating hostility between them. What kinds of ethnic or cultural distinctives create barriers between me and people from other cultures?
By bringing Jews and Gentiles together in Himself, Jesus broke down those barriers and made one new person out of former adversaries. Have I experienced that kind

of newness with believers from other cultures? Does being "in Christ" really make a difference in how I look at people from other cultures? How?

Paul seems to think that, when we focus on growing up into Jesus (vv. 20-22), we work together to become more like Him and less like the things that divide us. Have I experienced this? Do people from other cultures experience this? Whom could I ask?

Journal: I think I need to get to know some believers from other cultures – maybe they can help me understand how this "being one in Jesus" really works. This week I'm going to talk to...

Pray: *"Lead me, O LORD, in your righteousness...make your way straight before me"* (Psalm 5:8).

Day 4: Working Together

Pray: *"Those who know your name put their trust in you, for you, O LORD have not forsaken those who seek you"* (Psalm 9:10).

Read: Acts 13:1-3

Meditate: The names of these people suggest that they were from various people groups – Jews (Saul, Barnabas), a Gentile (Manaen, probably an Edomite, of Herod's court), perhaps even an African (Simeon, called Niger, or Black). What do we find them doing in this passage? What do they have in common? Did working together like this help them overlook their cultural differences? How?

They were worshiping and fasting...hmmm...that means they were seeking something together. What? Do I ever do this with other believers? With believers from other cultures?

How did God show that He approved the work of this little group?

Journal: What if I wanted to do some project for the Lord together with people from other cultures? What might I like to do? Whom could I ask to join me? Maybe I'll talk with some folks about this. Like, for instance...

Pray: *"Your face, LORD, do I seek. Hide not your face from m." (Psalm 27:8-9).*

Day 5: Get Ready for Trouble

Pray: *"Oh, how abundant is your goodness, which you have stored up for those who fear you and worked for those who take refuge in you, in the sight of the children of mankind!"*
(Psalm 31:19).

Read: Acts 15:1-21

Meditate: So, OK, you go out with the Gospel to people from other cultures, and other believers get upset and take swipes at you. Well, if it happened to Peter and Paul, should I expect otherwise? What might that look like?

Look at how James used the Scriptures here (vv. 12-17): What did he prove? Was he trusting in God or the opinions of others? Did he fear God or men?

It's interesting to see that, in the face of a potential racial problem, Christian people came together, talked it out, shared their experiences, and looked at the Word together. Is there a pattern here for dealing with cultural misunderstandings? What might that be?

Journal: Let's face it: I'm a little bit afraid of getting involved with people from other cultures. My fears are of various kinds, such as...

Pray: *"When I am afraid I put my trust in you. In God, whose word I praise, in God I trust; I shall not be afraid" (Psalm 56:3-4).*

ENDNOTES

[1] Cameron and Wycoff, "The Destructive Nature of the Term Race: Growing Beyond a False Paradigm," (*Journal of Counseling & Development* 1998) v76 n3 pp. 277-85

Recommended Reading

Key Books:

Anderson, David A. *Multicultural Ministry*. Grand Rapids, MI: Zondervan, 2004.

DeYoung, Curtis Paul, Michael O. Emerson, George Yancy, Karen Chai Kim. *United By Faith: the Multi-racial Congregation*. New York, NY: Oxford University Press, 2003.

Emerson, Michael O. and Christian Smith. *Divided By Faith*. New York, NY: Oxford University Press, 2000.

Ham, Ken and Carl Wieland and Don Batten. *One Blood The Biblical Answer to Racism* Green Forest, Arizona: Master Books, 1999.

Katongole, Emmanuel, and Chris Rice. *Reconciling All Things: A Christian Vision for Justice, Peace and Healing*. Downers Grove, IL: IVP, 2008.

Maynard-Reid, Pedrito U. *Diverse Worship*. Downers Grove, IL: InterVarsity Press, 2000.

McNeil, Brenda Salter. *Roadmap to Reconciliation: Moving Communities into Unity, Wholeness, and Justice*. N.p.: n.p., n.d.

Pocock, Michael and Joseph Henriques. *Cultural Change and Your Church*. Grand Rapids, MI: Baker Books, 2002.

Schlesinger, Arthur M. *The Disuniting of America*. New York, NY: W.W. Norton, 1998.

Ware, Charles. *Prejudice and the People of God*. Grand Rapids, MI: Kregel Publications, 2001.

Ware, Charles and Eugene Seals. *Reuniting The Family of God*. Indianapolis, IN: Baptist Bible College of Indianapolis, 2000.

Washington, Raleigh and Glen Kehrein. *Breaking Down Walls: A Model for Reconciliation in an Age of Racial Strife*. Chicago, IL: Moody Press, 1993.

Yancey, George A. *Beyond Racial Gridlock: Embracing Mutual Responsibility*. Downers Grove, IL: InterVarsity, 2006.

Yancey, George. *One Body One Spirit*. Downers Grove, IL: InterVarsity Press, 2003.

Lesson 16: What Are The Moral Implications Of Bioethics?

A. What is Ethics?

1. **Ethics** in the Greek is "Ethos," which means custom or character. It is the distinguishing character, sentiment, moral nature or guiding beliefs of a person or group.

   a. A system of beliefs assessing right and wrong.

   b. "A set of moral principles and values"[1]

B. Biblical Principles

1. The Christian worldview bases right and wrong from:

   a. God's character

   b. God's direction as stated in Scripture

   c. The person of Jesus Christ

2. Biblical principles do not change because of situations that might look good on the outside. This is called situational ethics.

3. Does God exist to make us happy?

4. Our morals are to be absolute (unchanging) because God's Word and His character do not change. Because God's morals are absolute, our morals should reflect God's character. Christians should mirror Christ.

5. It is irrelevant what we think or how we feel about a particular moral or value. What matters is how God views it and what He has to say about it (Isaiah 55:8-9, Isaiah 58:2).

C. The Christian moral order

1. "Christian morality is founded on this belief in an absolute moral order existing outside of, and yet somehow inscribed into, man's very being. God does not make up new values according to any whim."[2]

   a. Romans 2:14-15 *"Indeed, when Gentiles, who do not have the law, do by nature things required by the law, they are a law for themselves, even though they do not have the law, since they show that the requirements of the law are written on their hearts, their consciences also bearing witness, and their thoughts now accusing, now even defending them."* (Emphasis added)

2. Christian theologian, Francis Schaeffer, states, **"If there is no absolute beyond man's ideas, then there is no final appeal to judge between individuals and groups whose moral judgments conflict. We are merely left with conflicting opinions."** [3]

3. For those who do not follow a biblical, moral approach to living, will they see it by the way you live, dress, talk and make decisions?

D. Basics in Secular Ethics (Ethical Relativism)

"The fundamental question of ethics is, who makes the rules? God or men? The theistic answer is that God makes them. The humanistic answer is that men make them. The distinction between theism and humanism is the fundamental division in moral theory."

Max Hocutt, Humanist[4]

1. Since those who embrace the worldview of naturalism, spiritism, post-modernism and pantheism have no source of ultimate truth, other than man or an impersonal force, they must accept ethical relativism as their foundation for ethics.

2. Paul Kurtz, humanist, admits similarly, "I can find no ultimate basis for 'ought.'"

3. Conclusion

   a. If there is no ultimate basis for what we ought or ought not to do, then there is no basis for determining right or wrong. This would mean Adolph Hitler, Jeffrey Dahmer and the September 11th, 2001, terrorists are innocent of   any wrongdoing.

   b. Christian theologian, David Noebel, makes this observation, "Without this code [absolute], what standard does mankind have for judging its actions right or wrong, or its moral beliefs true or false?

   c. "The biggest problem with ethical relativism is still that basically anything can be constructed as "good" or "bad" under the assumption that it is all relative to the situation in which a man finds himself.

   d. "...relativism means that no one may decide whether another's actions are right or wrong.

   e. "Tolerance is the buzzword: ... Humanists must tolerate all other views regarding morality because ethics is relative to the truth within each individual."[5]

I. Bioethical Issues

A. What is Bioethics?

1. The study of ethical problems arising from scientific advances, especially in biology and medicine[6]

2. A discipline dealing with the ethical implications of biological research and applications, especially in medicine[7]

3. Current bioethical issues include: abortion, cloning, embryonic stem cell research, and physician-assisted suicide, end of life decisions, and euthanasia.

B. Cloning

1. Definitions:

   a. Cloning is asexual reproduction in which an exact genetic copy of another plant, animal, or human is made through a laboratory process. With humans, the method being used is to insert the nucleus from an adult cell into a human egg, from which the nucleus has been extracted. The egg can then be stimulated to divide and grow without fertilization. This procedure is also called "somatic cell nuclear transfer."

b. By definition of the National Academy of Sciences, a clone is an exact genetic replica of another organism.[8]

2. Why clone a human?

3. Issues:

a. Destruction of Life – At least 29 states recognize that fertilization initiates the life of a human being. But, most of the clones fail to survive.

b. Ethical: It's a means to an end, makes a human being a commodity – either to get human parts and organs – or to get a human with specific traits or characteristics. There is also the possibility of abusing women via coercion to obtain eggs.

c. Parentage: Who are the parents? Is it the person who donated the genetic material, the woman who donated the egg, or the woman who gestated the baby?

d. Scientific: Genes can mutate with age, so a clone starts with a flawed cell.

4. Reproductive cloning versus therapeutic cloning:

a. They are the same process – but with different goals – both "reproduce" a living person...but for different purposes.

b. Reproductive, to achieve the goal of having a cloned child...therapeutic, to destroy for its embryonic stem cells, parts, or organs

5. Scripture:

a. Genesis 1:26, Genesis 9:6, Job 33:4, Ecclesiastes 11:5, Psalm 139:13-15

6. Answering the Arguments:

   a. It is only a mass of cells, not a human being.

      i. Scientific texts, congressional testimony, and scientific consensus says life begins at the one cell embryo stage.

      ii. A zygote is the beginning of a new human being.[9]

   b. Pregnancy begins at implantation.

      i. Human pregnancy begins with the fusion of an egg and a sperm.[10]

      ii. State laws recognize the embryo as a human being.

   c. The potential for curing disease outweighs the problem of destroying embryos.

      i. The poor availability of human oocytes (eggs), the low efficiency of the nuclear transfer procedure, and the long doubling time of human embryonic stem cells make it difficult to envision therapeutic cloning becoming a routine clinical procedure.[11]

      ii. The use of human life merely as a means to an end is morally unacceptable.

      iii. One should not oppose cloning because of bad outcomes, but because the process itself has inherent moral problems.

      iv. WARNING: Be alert to those who are changing the definition of "cloning" to pass laws in favor of cloning (e.g. New Jersey and Missouri). They are defining cloning as a live birth; while legalizing "somatic cell nuclear transfer," which is the scientific definition of cloning. By this change of definition, it is illegal to give birth to a clone (thereby making it a legal obligation to kill it prior to birth), but it is legal to make one.

C. Stem Cell Research

1. Definition: Stem cells are master cells that can turn into many different types of specialized cells. All 210 different tissues in the human body grow from stem cells of an embryo.

2. Sources of stem cells:

   a. Life threatening sources – Embryonic or fetal stem cells are extracted by destroying a days-old human embryo, the smallest component of human life.

   b. Life honoring sources – Umbilical cord blood, placenta or adults

3. Adult stem cells have the ability to turn into many types of tissues in the human body and are easy to extract. <u>Harvesting adult or non-embryonic stem cells does not destroy a human life</u>.

4. Uses of stem cells:

   a. Studies using non-embryonic stem cells derived ethically and safely from umbilical cord blood or adult bone marrow, brain tissue, and fat have moved well beyond theory to application. They offer solid benefits to patients suffering from heart disease, blood disorders, and other afflictions[12] and aid in cancer treatments.

   b. Embryonic stem cells have yet to demonstrate a single human therapeutic benefit.[13]

5. Issues:

   a. The problem of semantics: The purpose of cloning and stem cell research is to develop human tissue and human organs for use in human beings. Scientists try to dehumanize the embryo by referring to it as a "clump of cells." If human embryos are not human beings, then what are they?

   b. Embryonic stem cell research is immoral because it destroys life.

   c. Embryonic stem cell research is unethical. – As a result of Nazi war crimes the Nuremberg Code of Research Ethics states, "No experiment should be conducted where there is a prior reason (i.e. prospective reason) to believe that death or disabling injury will occur."[14]

   d. Any research that destroys life is unethical under the World Health Organization Code of Ethics.[15]

6. Scripture – Know what the Bible says: Genesis 1:26, Genesis 9:5-7, Deuteronomy 5:17, Jeremiah 10:23.

D. Physician-Assisted Suicide (PAS), and Decisions Regarding the End of Life (Euthanasia)

1. Definitions:[16]

   a. Physician-Assisted Suicide – occurs when a physician helps a person take his or her own life by giving advice, writing a prescription for lethal medication, or assisting the individual with some device which allows the person to take his or her own life. The physician lends expertise; the person does the act.

   b. Euthanasia – occurs when another person, out of compassion, does an action with the intention of ending the life of a suffering patient, either with or without the patient's request.

2. What you should know:

   a. Frequently, the request for PAS reflects the patient's misunderstanding about his or her options for end-of-life care. Patients who ask for PAS may actually be requesting aggressive symptom control should their suffering become intolerable. They may not understand that medications can be increased to whatever levels are required to relieve physical symptoms...or other physical and emotional suffering. Even if death is hastened in the process...such actions are morally permissible and legal when the intent of treatment is to relieve symptoms and not to cause the patient's death.[17]

b. Hippocratic Oath for physicians: Doctors pledge that "I will neither give a deadly drug to anybody if asked for it, nor will I make a suggestion to this effect."[18]

c. The proponents of "hastened death" speak of compassionate solutions to painful illness through "death with dignity." Combine these powerful ideologies with an impersonal and technological health care system and the result has proven to be horrifying.[19]

3. Scripture: 1 John 4:9-10, 1 Corinthians 6:19, Romans 8:35-39, John 3:16

E. Reproductive Technology

1. A better understanding of reproductive technology combined with advances in medical technology has led to the development of several methods of assisted reproductive technology.

a. Most of these methods involve the union of sperm and egg outside the womb (in vitro fertilization).

b. Definition of embryo: a human being in the earliest stage of development in the uterus or a dish – microscopic in size: per Donald Cline, MD, infertility specialist

c. Definition of fetus: the unborn while still in the uterus, especially in its later stages and specifically in humans from the time the heartbeat is detected or seen on ultrasound, as early as six weeks after conception – macroscopic in size: per Donald Cline, MD, infertility specialist

2. Issues:

a. What to do with fertilized eggs (embryos) that are not implanted, but stored? Should they be discarded?

i. The Food & Drug Administration estimates approximately 400,000 frozen embryos are in storage. Most are reserved for future attempts to have a baby; some are set aside for research or adoption.[20]

ii. Legal papers are often unknowingly signed that give the laboratory the right to discard fertilized eggs.

b. When does life begin? Two differing opinions:

i. Conception is defined by the American College of OB-GYN to mean implantation of the embryo in the uterus.

ii. The biblical worldview confirms that life begins at conception or fertilization of the egg (fusion of sperm and egg). Two examples from Scripture are that both

Jesus and John the Baptist were announced, named, and ministries proclaimed at conception.

3. New Techniques:

   a. Donald Cline, MD, Indianapolis, and Tom Boldt, MD, Indianapolis, helped develop a process by which eggs are harvested from the ovary and then stored frozen until needed.

   b. Third-party reproduction – the process of using donor eggs, donor sperm, or a surrogate to carry the baby is opposed by many religions, including many Jewish, Islamic, Protestant and Catholic authorities. A statement from the Vatican says that third-party reproduction "violates the rights of the child. It deprives him of his filial relationship with his parental origins and can hinder the maturity of his personal identity. Consequently, fertilizations of a married woman with the sperm of a donor different from her husband and fertilization with the husband's sperm of an ovum not coming from his wife are morally illicit."[21] Additionally, some feel that this arrangement violates the marriage relationship by introducing a third party into the union.

4. Scripture:

   a. Jeremiah 1:5 "'Before I formed you in the womb I knew you, before you were born I set you apart.'"

   b. Proverbs 6:16-19 "There are six things the LORD hates, seven that are detestable to him: haughty eyes, a lying tongue, hands that shed innocent blood, a heart that devises wicked schemes, feet that are quick to rush into evil, a false witness who pours out lies and a man who stirs up dissension among brothers."

II. Conclusion

Why should these issues of bioethics matter to me?

1. Bioethical issues are all connected with the beginning of life, truth telling, valid consent, surrogacy, and the end of life.

2. These issues are foundational to the definition of what it means to be human.

3. Bioethics will touch our lives in very significant ways because we all have to deal with life and death.

4. As we look at the Naturalistic/Humanistic worldview, we see that science and the pursuit of knowledge are their only hope. The pursuit becomes a "god" and reflects the belief that they can be like God.

5. The ends do not justify the means in God's economy; and a utilitarian philosophy violates the Hippocratic oath to "do no harm."

6. The possible implications for the future in the fields of reproductive technology, cloning and stem cell research could lead to complications with insurance companies and what they will cover.

7. As Christians, we must be ready to respond to those who are hurting, to reach out to them and point them to Christ, by prayer, encouragement, or ethical advice. Therefore, we must equip ourselves to enter the ethical debate. We must also be informed enough to know when to not participate personally in an offered treatment or procedure.

Scripture: Proverbs 1:7 *"The fear of the Lord is the beginning of knowledge; fools despise wisdom and instruction."*

Why should the Christian become involved?

What is the BIG picture?

The sanctity of human life, by Gary P. Stewart:[22] "The determination of right and wrong is not always easy. However, starting from the viewpoint that each human being is a creature of God with inestimable value provides a guard rail that prevents each of us from straying from decision-making based on faith and losing ourselves in the wilderness of finite human reason alone. Bioethical issues typically involve life and its limit. How we live and how we die should be understood from the Creator's point of view. This perspective gives us the best framework for answering questions about issues such as the use of donor eggs and sperm to have children 'on one's own,' the appropriateness of initiating or withdrawing life support, the purpose and management of suffering, and the appropriate use of alternative medicines. These questions and others cannot adequately be answered apart from a perspective that recognizes the sanctity and inestimable value of human life."

Questions of Life and Death
By Chuck Colson - 4/9/2003

The Activist and the Professor

How would you characterize someone who denies that you, and people like you, were persons when you were born, and says that your mother should have been free to kill you for being who you are?

This was the question facing Harriet McBryde Johnson, a prominent disabilities rights activist, when she was invited to debate Princeton ethicist, Peter Singer. Singer believes in infanticide and that it is okay under certain circumstances to kill, at any age, individuals with physical impairments so severe they are no longer "persons."

Ms. Johnson is a leading member of Not Dead Yet, an organization of disabled Americans opposed to physician-assisted suicide and other "disability-based killing." If Not Dead Yet has a public enemy number one, it is Peter Singer.

Johnson is seriously impaired, unable to function on her own—just the kind of person Singer regards as an "avoidable mistake." But with some trepidation, she traveled to Princeton for the exchange with Singer before one of his classes, and later before the entire university—an exchange she described in a brilliantly written Sunday *New York Times Magazine* piece.

Johnson wrote poignantly of her emotions when meeting the man whom she expected to be a "monster" and the "ultimate evil." Instead Singer surprised her by his graciousness. She described him as "easy to talk to and good company." Of course, the issue is not whether Singer is a monster— the line between good and evil runs through every human heart. The issue is where his ideas, beginning with his premises, lead.

And this is where Johnson ran into her problems. She repeatedly reminds readers that she is an atheist. In fact, she approves Singer's desire to ground ethics on "fact and reason" as opposed to religious beliefs. She referred to this as a "grand, heroic undertaking."

But the problem for people like Johnson is that, historically speaking, the alternative to what they dismiss as just a religious belief is the kind of utilitarianism that provides the foundation for Singer's ideas—that is, the goal is to maximize happiness in the world, by doing the greatest good for the greatest number.

People like Johnson, who require substantial resources to maintain what Singer regards as an inferior quality of life, would, by Singer's logic, be eliminated as early as possible.

No wonder Ms. Johnson, obviously an able advocate, wrote that she doubted whether she had bested Singer in the exchange. The reason is that, as an atheist, she is at a moral dead end; she has no moral basis to refute Singer's deadly logic so long as she embraces his premises about the origins of life.

Only the Christian ideal, that all life is sacred because it is created in the image of God, provides an unassailable answer to Singer's reasoning. It's the only sure basis for protecting people like Harriet McBryde Johnson from a moral calculus that reduces them to non-persons.

Ms. Johnson writes movingly, and the reader can feel her anguish over her difficult encounter with Singer. Though not the author's intent, the article in the *New York Times*—of all places—makes a powerful case for the Christian understanding of life.

Small Group Discussion Guide

Lesson 16: What Are the Moral Implications of Bioethics?

Small Group Objective:

The goal is to help the students develop a foundational understanding of the bioethical issues. As the students consider these issues, it is critical that they see the bottom line issue: the value of a human life. Too often, we think that if something works, then it must be "good." The Christian worldview maintains that God values all life, be it a fertilized egg, a child, or someone critically ill. We must be willing to stand for life, at all costs.

✓ **Check Points:**

☐ Bring 3 x 5 cards for your students to write down any questions they may have which aren't answered during the discussion.

☐ Enlist a student to share a brief personal testimony.

Discussion Questions:

1. Review prayer requests from the week before and ask how the students are doing.

2. Lead a time of discussion, asking the following questions:

(Note: Work through as many of the following questions as possible. The goal is not to get through all of them, but to encourage each student to participate in the discussion as part of the learning process.)

    a. What day of the devotional did you find most meaningful?

    b. How did last week's lesson impact your life? Did you share it?

    c. Why or why isn't it important to have a biblical worldview?

    d. If someone were to clone another person with no ill effects, would it be right? What are some of the problems associated with cloning?

    e. If stem cells were harvested from adults, or the umbilical cord of a born infant, would you have a moral problem with such a procedure? Why?

    f. When do you understand life to begin? Why is that a critical issue when it comes to reproduction technology?

    g. Frame an evolutionist.

3. Ask for prayer requests and tell students that you will be faithful to pray for them during the week. Encourage students to record the prayer requests in the prayer request section of their handbooks, so they can pray for one another during the week. Begin the prayer time by sharing your own request. Spend the remaining time in prayer.

Student Devotionals written by T. M. Moore

What Are The Moral Implications Of Bioethics?

Be sure to set aside the time you will need each day for the following devotionals. The combination of prayer, reading, meditation, and journaling will help you to let the Word of Christ dwell in you richly (Colossians 3:16). Take your time and do a thorough job in each section. Remember to let the beginning and ending prayers be a "starter" for you, and use them for a more extended time of talking with God about the subject of the day's reading.

We would not expect the Bible to have anything direct to say about issues that were, at the time of Scripture's writing, completely unknown and unforeseeable. Yet we would expect, since the Scriptures have been given to equip us for every good work (2 Timothy 3:15-17), that they would outline a framework for our learning to think biblically about any and every issue that might arise, whether foreseen in Scripture or not. Therefore, as we turn our attention to the subject of bioethics, we must look to the Word of God to outline the parameters within which we must approach thinking and acting in this realm.

Day 1: The Limits of Human Knowledge

Pray: *"O LORD, you have searched me and known me...You search out my path and my lying down and are acquainted with all my ways...Such knowledge is too wonderful for me; it is high; I cannot attain it" (Psalm 139:1, 3, 6).*

Read: Ecclesiastes 3:10-13

Meditate: What does Solomon mean by saying God has made everything beautiful "in its time?" Could he mean something like, "when it is properly used and understood?" What are the implications of this for bioethical issues?

       What can human beings *not* know (vs. 11)? Do people sometimes act as though they do not believe this? How?

       Life is a gift, and God intends people to enjoy it and to "do good" with all He gives us. How can we know what "good" is? Is there a danger that, if we ignore this source of "good," we might not enjoy life, even though we think we will? Explain.

Journal: I want people to see me as a person who receives God's gifts, enjoys life fully, and does what is good. I might need to pay a little more attention to this, so, today...

Pray: "How precious to me are your thoughts, O God! How vast is the sum of them!"
(Psalm 139:17).

Day 2: Letting God Be God

Pray: *"The LORD will fulfill his purpose for me; your steadfast love, O LORD, endures forever. Do not forsake the work of your hands"* (Psalm 138:8).

Read: Psalm 100

Meditate: Why are we to worship God? How? Who should worship Him?

One way of translating v. 3b is, "It is he who made us, and not we ourselves." Why would this interpretation of this verse seem to have something to say about bioethical issues today?

Our text tells us that the Lord is good, loving, and faithful. Therefore, if we want to know what the good, loving, and faithful thing to do is – in any situation – where should we look? How do we do that? How do we encourage others to join us in doing that?

Journal: If I want people to worship God, and to look to Him for every good thing, then I need to be someone who *attracts* others to God by the joy, praise, and gratitude they see in my life. Hmmm...I might need to do a little work here. I need to remove some things keeping me from living this way more consistently, so...

Pray: *"I give you thanks, O LORD, with my whole heart..."* (Psalm 138:1).

Day 3: Regarding Life

Pray: *"I praise you, for I am fearfully and wonderfully made. Wonderful are your works; my soul knows it well"* (Psalm 139:14).

Read: Genesis 9:1-7

Meditate: This text suggests that God expects human beings to preserve human life and to cause it to flourish on earth. How can I see this?

Why is human life so valuable in God's eyes (v. 6)? What attitudes toward human life does this suggest we ought to foster? What does this suggest not just about bioethical issues, but about how I regard the people around me?

Clearly, one of the critical questions to address in the area of bioethics is, "Does what we are proposing not only help human life to flourish, but does it also *preserve* human life, or does it *threaten* human life?" What are some of the implications of asking that question?

Journal: Wow! I'm getting into deep water here. I need to talk with some Christian friends about these issues, so, today I'll...

Pray: *"Search me, O God, and know my heart! Try me and know my thoughts!"* (Psalm 139:23).

Day 4: Resisting Mere Expediency and Wellbeing

Pray: *"Do not let my heart incline to evil, to busy myself with wicked deeds in company with men who work iniquity..."* (Psalm 142:4).

Read: Leviticus 20:1-5

Meditate: The essence of Molech worship involved parents sacrificing their children to a false god, so that they (the parents) could keep the god happy and doing good for them. In our day, are "expediency" and "wellbeing" like false gods? How can you see that people are "devoted" to these gods, and would give up just about anything to keep them?

How do these two gods enter into discussions of bioethical issues?

In our text, how did God feel about caving-in to such false gods? What did He threaten when a people are unable to "police" themselves over such issues?

Journal: Do I ever worship at the altars of "expedience" or "happiness?" How would I know? Probably, it would look like...

Pray: *"Keep me from the trap that they have laid for me and from the snares of the evildoers!"* (Psalm 142:9).

Day 5: Life Begins in the Womb!

Pray: *"My frame was not hidden from you, when I was being made in secret, intricately woven in the depths of the earth..." (Psalm 139:15).*

Read: Psalm 51:5; Jeremiah 1:4, 5; Luke 2:39-45

Meditate: According to each of these passages, when does full human life begin?

                How can I relate the teaching of these passages to yesterday's devotional about sacrificing life for mere expediency or happiness?

                Is there a "proper time" for bioethical research? Based on what we have studied in this area, what would I insist are some "improper" uses of this discipline?

Journal: I'd like to know what some of my fellow students think about this issue.
So, today...

Pray: *"Your eyes saw my unformed substance; in your book were written, every one of them, the days that were formed for me, when as yet there were none of them" (Psalm 139:16).*

ENDNOTES

1 Merriam-Webster's online dictionary. <http://www.m-w.com/cgi-bin/dictionary?book=Dictionary&vaethics>

2 David A. Noebel, *Understanding the Times* (abridged version), (Manitou Springs, CO: Summit Press, 1995) 115-118.

3 Francis Schaeffer, *How Should We Then Live?* (Old Tappan, N.J.: Fleming Revell, 1976) 145.

4 Max Hocutt, "Toward an Ethic of Mutual Accomodation," Humanist Ethics ed. Morris B. Storer (Buffalo: Prometheus Books, 1980) 137.

5 David A. Noebel, *Understanding the Times* (abridged version), (Manitou Springs, CO: Summit Press, 1995) 115-118.

6 *Websters' New World Dictionary*, Third College Edition, 1988, 140.

7 Merriam-Webster's online dictionary

8 NAS, *Scientific and Medical Aspects of Human Reproductive Cloning* (National Academy Press 2002) page E

9 Larsen, William, *Human Embryology* (New York: Churchill Livingston, 1997). 20.

10 Carlson, Bruce, *Human Embryology and Developmental Biology* (St. Louis, MO: Mosby. 1994) 3.

11 Ordorico, JS, Kaufman, DS, Thomson, JA. "Multilineage Differentiation from Human Embryonic Stem Cell Lines," *Stem Cells* 19, 193-204; 2001

12 E. Kaji and J. Leiden, "Gene and Stem Cells Therapies," _Journal of the American Medical Association_ February 7, 2001, 547.

13 <www.cmdahome.org Standards 4 Life>

14 <http://ohsr.odinih.gov/nuremberg-php3>

15 <http://www.who.int/dsa/cat98/ethic8.htm-International> Ethical Guidelines for Biomedical Research Involving Human Subjects

16 <www.cmdahome.org Standards 4 Life>

17 Bascom, Paul B. MD, Susan W. Tolle, MD. "Responding to Requests for Physician-Assisted Suicide," JAMA Vol 288 No 1, July 3, 2002.

18 <http://www.pbs.org/wgbh/nova/doctors/oath_classical.html>

19 <www.cmdahome.org Standards 4 Life>

20 David Hoffman, et al. "Cryopreserved embryos in the United States and their availability for research," *Fertility and Sterility* 79 May 2003: 1063-1069.

21 Vatican English language text of "Instruction on Respect for Human Life in its Origin and on the Dignity of Procreation: Replies to Certain Questions of the Day," issued by the *Congregation for the Doctrine of the Faith* As quoted by Glahn and Cutrer, 197. Available at <http://www.vatican.va/roman_curia/congregations/cfaith/documents_/rc_con_cfaith_doc_19870222_respect-for-human-life_en.html.>

22 Stewart, Gary P., "The Sanctity of Human Life," *Dignity* Spring 1999.

Recommended Reading

Key Organizations:

- **The Center for Bioethics & Human Dignity**
  2065 Half Day Road Bannockburn, IL 60015 847.317.8180 www.cbhd.org

Key Books:

Beckwith, Francis. Defending Life: A Moral and Legal Case against Abortion Choice. New York: Cambridge UP, 2007.

Beller FK, Weir RF. *The Beginning of Human Life*. Dordrecht: Kluwer Academic Publishers, 1994.

Cameron, Nigel M. De S., Scott E. Daniels and Barbara J. White. *Bioengagement: Making a Christian Difference Through Bioethics Today*. Grand Rapids, MI: Eerdmans, William B. Publishing, 2004.

Colson, Charles W. and Nigel M. De S. Cameron. *Human Dignity in the Biotech Century: A Christian*

Vision for Public Policy. Downers Grove, IL: InterVarsity Press, 2004.

Colson, Charles W. and Nigel M. De S. Cameron. *The Bioethics Challenge.* Downers Grove, IL: InterVarsity Press. In Press.

Demy, Timothy J. and Gary P. Steward. *Suicide: A Christian Response: Crucial Considerations for Choosing Life.* Grand Rapids: Kregel, 1998.

Foreman, Mark W. Christianity & Bioethics: Confronting Clinical Issues. Joplin, MO: College Pub., 1999.

George, Robert P. The Clash of Orthodoxies: Law, Religion, and Morality in Crisis. Wilmington, DE: ISI, 2001.

Hollman, Jay (ed.). *New Issues in Medical Ethics.* Bristol, TN: Christian Medical and Dental Society, 1995.

Kass, Leon R. *Life, Liberty and the Defense of Dignity: The Challenge for Bioethics.* San Francisco: Encounter Books, 2002.

Kilner, John F. *Life on the Line: Ethics, Aging, Ending Patients' Lives and Allocating Vital Resources.* Grand Rapids, MI: Eerdmans Publishing, 1992.

Kreeft, Peter. A Refutation of Moral Relativism: Interviews with an Absolutist. San Francisco: Ignatius, 1999.

Kreeft, Peter. Back to Virtue: Traditional Moral Wisdom for Modern Moral Confusion. San Francisco: Ignatius, 1992.

Kreeft, Peter. Three Approaches to Abortion: A Thoughtful and Compassionate Guide to Today's Most Controversial Issue. San Francisco, CA: Ignatius, 2002.

Lester, Lane P. and James C. Hefley. *Human Cloning: Playing God or Scientific Progress?* Grand Rapids, MI: Fleming H. Revell, 1998.

Meilaender, Gilbert. *Bioethics: A Primer for Chrisitans. Grand Rapids, MI: Wm. B. Eerdmans Publishing Co.* 2004.

Orr, Robert D., et. al. *Life and Death Decisions.* Colorado Springs, CO: NavPress, 1990.

Prentice, D.A. 2003. "The Present and Future of Stem Cell Research: Scientific Ethical, and Public Policy Perspective," *Stem Cell Research: New Frontiers in Science and Ethics* (Nancy E. Snow, ed.) University of Notre Dame Press: 2003.

Rae, Scott B. and Cox, Paul M. *Bioethics: A Christian Approach in a Pluralistic Age.* Grand Rapids: Eerdmans, 1999, pp.159-165.

Schaeffer, Francis A., and C. Everett Koop. *Whatever Happened to the Human Race?* Old Tappan, NJ: Fleming H. Revell, 1979.

Tada, Joni Eareckson and Nigel M. De S. Cameron. *How to Be a Christian in a Brave New World.* Grand Rapids, Michigan: Zondervan, 2006.

Waters, Brent and Ronald Cole-Turner (eds.). "God and the Embryo: Religious Voices on Stem Cells and Cloning." Washington, DC: *Georgetown University Press,* 2003.

Lesson 17: What Are The Biblical Principles To Wise Financial Planning?

A. American Cultural View of Money (The Naturalist Worldview)

(*Note*: This section is preparation for the *Five Biblical Principles* for sound money management. These are the four predominant messages that our world imposes on us.)

1. Materialism is good.

2. Unsecured consumer debt is OK.

3. Get rich quick.

4. Money equals success.

B. How does God look at money and possessions?

1. What does it mean to be a steward?

   a. A steward is a manager or caretaker. He or she is hired to take care of someone else's property. The reality is that we are managing God's resources for some brief period of time.[1]

   b. Stewardship is the use of God-given resources for the accomplishment of God-given goals.[2]

2. Stewardship 101: Whose stuff is it, anyway?

   a. An examination of our hearts will show our true priorities (Hebrews 13:5).

   b. God thinks that how we handle our money is important as there are more than 2,300 passages in the Bible dealing with money, materials, and possessions.

C. Five Biblical Principles for Financial Success:

1. Principle #1: Generous Giving - II Corinthians 9:6-7

   a. Before the gift of the <u>indwelling Holy Spirit</u>, in Malachi 3, God encourages the <u>Israelites</u> to give 10% (Malachi 3:8-10).

   b. "The principle found in Scripture is that He owns it all. Therefore, whatever He chooses to entrust you with, hold with an open hand, allowing Him to entrust you with more if He so chooses, or allowing Him to take whatever He wants."[3]

2. Principle #2: Flee the Love of Money - I Timothy 6:9-12

   a. Seek <u>God</u> and His <u>provision</u>. This is a trust issue.

   b. You will never build a strong <u>asset base</u> by overspending. What are your long-term goals? (An asset base is a transaction based on a tangible asset.)

   c. Find balance. Enjoy the <u>best</u> in life, but don't be owned by it.

3. Principle #3: Live Within Your Means - Proverbs 30:7-9

   a. Act your wage.

   b. Spend less than you make each month, and do this for a long time. What happens if you do this?

   c. The 80/10/10 Principle. Live off the 80%, give 10% and set aside 10% of what you bring home. This will help you create a surplus, so that you can handle emergencies or unexpected expenses.

4. Principle #4: Planning - Luke 14:28

   a. Establish goals and a written game plan.

      i. God teaches repeatedly in the book of Proverbs that we are to work hard and save money little by little (Proverbs 13:11).

   b. Use the concept of <u>escrow</u> accounts.

      i. Escrow = to set aside a sum of money on a regular basis for the purpose of paying for something in the future.

   c. Don't buy things until you have the funds set aside.

5. Principle #5: Use a Spending Plan

    a. Tracking expenses is the key!

D. Create Your Spending Plan: (Turn to your spending worksheets.)

1. Determine your income.

    a. This would be your take home pay after taxes.

2. Set up spending categories.

3. Set spending targets for each category.

4. Track your expenses.

5. Compare actual spending to targets — adjust and modify as needed.

    a. Once or twice during the month, add up what you've spent and compare it to your target amounts. Adjust as needed by shifting money between categories or reducing spending so that you do not spend more than your take-home pay.

Small Contributions Can Lead to Big Savings

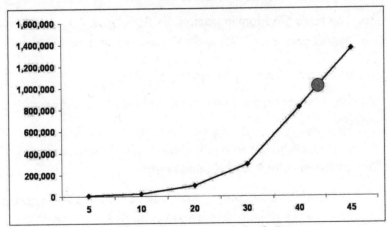

- Start with $100, assume a 10.5% annual compound rate of return.
- Invest for 42 years. Why 42 years?
- How much do I need to invest? $122 per month. At year 42 you will have $1,005,367.

E. Spending Plan Exercise:

1. Assume that you work 20 hours each week and you get paid $9.06 per hour.

2. From here on, we will work with round numbers. This would provide you with $181 per week (20 hrs./wk. X $9.06/hr. or $725 per month. ($181/wk. X 4 weeks)

3. Assume that approximately 25% of this will be paid in both employment (FICA) and income (federal, state & local) taxes. So you only bring home 75% of what you make each month, or $<u>544</u> per month ($725/mo. X 75%). This leaves you with $<u>136</u> per week.

4. Use the worksheets at the end of the chapter to make a guesstimate at how much you might spend in each category.

5. Try actually tracking what you spend for a month to see where the money goes.

6. Don't forget that there are periodic expenses like birthday and Christmas gifts.

F. Principles that work:

1. If you implement the 5 Principles stated above, our position is that you will experience the following outcomes:

   a. You can be <u>debt-free.</u>

   b. You can have your <u>needs</u> met.

   c. You can begin to prudently <u>save.</u>

   d. You can have <u>Kingdom</u> impact.

2. Suggested sources of money for going to college:

   a. Parents, savings from parents, work, scholarships, loans, pay as you go, joining the military

   b. Many students have taken extra time to get through college by working part time and going to college at the same time.

G. Why is debt dangerous?

1. The Definition of Debt

   a. Accelerating <u>future</u> spending into the <u>present</u>

   b. Any monetary <u>value</u> owed to anyone for anything

H. Financial Dangers of Debt:

1. Excessive debt can lead to a bad credit rating.

    a. All Americans are rated on how well they would be able to pay back on loans. This is your credit rating.

    b. If you have late payments, fail to pay debts, or have too many credit cards, your credit rating will go down.

    c. This could affect your ability to get a job, find an apartment, buy a home or car. It can also raise your insurance premiums.

I. Good Debt: (Debt that makes good economic sense.)

1. Home mortgage: Most, but not all, houses tend to appreciate in value.

2. Education: Invest in your earning potential. The more education you have, you typically have a better chance at earning competitive wages.

3. Student loan resources:

    a. <u>Apply for scholarships!</u>

    b. Most every college or university has a financial aid office. Contact them!

    c. Stafford Loans (www.staffordloan.com)

4. Ron Blue, author and financial planner, says that there are four rules to follow regarding debt:[4]

    a. The money borrowed must always earn more than what it costs you to borrow.

    b. Guaranteed way to repay (Income is not the way)

    c. Should not create stress

    d. Get an accountability partner to agree or not agree with your decision to go into debt.

J. Bad Debt: (Foolish Debt)

1. Always bad if for consumptive or depreciating item (for example: clothes, eating out, vacations, computers)

2. Credit cards: If you do not pay it off each month.

3. Car loans (another depreciating item)

4. Payday loans

    a. A payday loan, paycheck advance or cash advance is a small, short-term loan (typically up to $1,500) without a credit check that is intended to bridge the borrower's cash flow gap between pay days.

b. Note, however, that excessive interest rates are charged, usually 10-20% every 14 days! That comes out to an annualized interest rate of 391%.

K. Debt Avoidance Tactics:

1. Commit to only writing checks.

    a. By sticking to a "cash" basis by writing checks, the temptation to overspend is somewhat curtailed.

    b. It is recommended to use checks with the carbon copies for all purchases. The carbon copy makes it very easy to then track expenses onto your spending plan ledger.

2. Use a debit card.

3. Establish a spending plan.

4. Don't buy until cash is on hand.

L. Personal Action Plan:

Write down two or three things you would like to begin working on immediately to help improve your personal financial situation. Set a target date for completion.

	ACTION ITEM	TARGET DATE
1.	Example: Giving Regularly	1 week (next paycheck)
2.	_____	_____
3.	_____	_____

The tools and concepts have now been given to you. Now that you have written down some "Action Items," commit to making a budget and living by it for three months.

Quicken is a great computer program for keeping track of your expenses, saving, taxes, loans, investments, income and much more. You can find it at: www.quicken.com or www.discountshelf.com. Sometimes you can get good deals on Amazon.com.

Spending Plan

Monthly Income & Expenses

High-school Student Worksheet

Notes:

Monthly Income

Income .... $ _____

Less Taxes .... $ (_____)

Net Spendable Income.............$ _____

Monthly Expenses

Giving .... $ _____

Food .... $ _____

Clothing .... $ _____

Automobile/Transportation .... $ _____

Personal .... $ _____

College Tuition .... $ _____

Entertainment .... $ _____

Savings/Investments* .... $ _____

Total Expenses ....$ _____

Income vs. Expenses	Net Spendable Income	-	Total Exp. Expenses	=	Surplus/(Deficit)

Spending Plan

Monthly Income & Expenses

College Student Worksheet

Monthly Income

Income .... $ _____

Less Taxes .... $ (_____)

Net Spendable Income............. $ _____

Monthly Expenses

Giving .... $ _____

Housing .... $ _____

Food.................................... $ _____

Clothing .... $ _____

Insurance/Medical* .... $ _____

Automobile/Transportation .... $ _____

Household/Personal .... $ _____

Entertainment........................ $ _____

Savings/Investments* .... $ _____

College Tuition .... $ _____

Professional Fees/Services .... $ _____

Debts.................................. $ _____

Total Expenses.........................$ _____

Notes:

_____

_____

_____

_____

_____

_____

_____

_____

_____

_____

_____

_____

_____

	Net Spendable Income	-	Total Exp. Expenses	=	Surplus/(Deficit)
Income vs. Expenses					

Lesson 17: What Are the Biblical Principles to Wise Financial Planning?

Small Group Objective:

Your goal is to help the students begin to understand that all of their possessions belong to God. He is the one who pours out blessings by providing for His children. Part of our act of worship is shown through giving back to God what He has given to us. Each of God's children must then be a responsible steward with the remainder of what He has provided to be used in their everyday lives.

✓ Check Points:

☐ Bring 3 x 5 cards for your students to write down any questions they may have which aren't answered during the discussion.

☐ Enlist a student to share a brief personal testimony.

Discussion Questions:

1. Review prayer requests from the week before and ask how the students are doing.

2. Lead a time of discussion, asking the following questions:

(*Note: Work through as many of the following questions as possible. The goal is not to get through all of them, but to encourage each student to participate in the discussion as part of the learning process.*)

   a. What day of the devotional did you find most meaningful?

   b. How did last week's lesson impact your life? Did you share it?

   c. What do you personally struggle with the most when it comes to finances?

   d. Why do so many people spend more money than they make?

   e. How does our handling of money reflect our love for God?

   f. What principles could you use to live as if everything you own is all God's?

   g. What are the dangers of using a credit card?

   h. How does God define success? How do you define it?

   i. What questions, if any, come to mind as a result of this week's lesson?

   j. What is one way you can go out and apply what you have learned at Anchorsaway this week?

Prayer Requests

Student Devotionals written by T.M. Moore

What Are The Biblical Principles To Wise Financial Planning?

Money can be a great blessing or a tremendous stumbling-block. It all depends on how we understand its purpose and use, and whether we use it for God's purposes or our own. In the years to come, lots of money is going to pass through your hand – thousands and thousands, perhaps hundreds of thousands of dollars. Are you ready to deal with it in a way that will please God, bless others, and give you maximum satisfaction and fulfillment?

Day 1: What's More Valuable

Pray: "I love your commandments above gold, above fine gold" (Psalm 119:127).

Read: Psalm 19

Meditate: David lists many benefits of the Law (vv. 7-11 – precepts, rules, etc.). What are some of them?

                    Wait a sec – don't a lot of people I know look to money to give them things like joy, security, and satisfaction in life? In v. 10 David says there's something more valuable than money where these things are concerned. How can that be?

                    I want joy, security, satisfaction in life; should I seek it in pursuit of money, or in obedience to God's Law (Word)? Does that mean even concerning what the Word says about money?

Journal: I'm going to be honest with myself here: Do I feel better when I've just had a really good time in the Word, or when I've just filled my pocket with a wad of cash? Yeah, but...

Pray: "I will give thanks to your name, O LORD, for it is good" (Psalm 54:6).

Day 2: Whose Money is it, Anyway?

Pray: *"O my Strength, I will sing praise to you, for you, O God, are my fortress, the God who shows me steadfast love"* (Psalm 59:17).

Read: Psalm 24

Meditate: According to this psalm, to whom does everything I own belong? Do I *really* believe that? Do I *live my life* as if this were really true?

Even my *money* belongs to the Lord? Does this mean I can't ever spend it? What *does* it mean?

Verse 4 lists some qualities of those who enjoy the presence of God – clean hands, pure heart, truthfulness. Do people who have such qualities show them in the way they use their money? Am I one of those people?

Journal: I need to make sure I'm doing a good job with the Lord's money. How did I do last week? What about the week before that? I think I might need a system for keeping track of this, so...

Pray: *"Lead me in your truth and teach me, for you are the God of my salvation"* (Psalm 25:5).

Day 3: Not My Own

Pray: *"Hear the voice of my pleas for mercy, when I cry to you for help..."* (Psalm 28:2).

Read: Acts 4:32-5:10

Meditate: OK, whom would I rather be like, Barnabas, or Ananias and Sapphira? Why? What motivated Barnabas? What was motivating Ananias and Sapphira?

I can't believe what I see in v. 32. OK, I *believe* it, but, man, it's hard to see how. What would it look like if my friends and I could say this about ourselves?

When urgent financial needs arise in my community, do the leaders generally look to the youth? Why or why not? How might we convince them to turn to us to help when people have financial needs?

Lesson 17: What Are the Biblical Principles to Wise Financial Planning?
- Anchorsaway Worldview Handbook ©

Journal:	I don't know any people my age who live like this. Is this *really* what God expects of us? Maybe I should see if He will really bless me by taking a "Barnabas" attitude toward my stuff. Here's what I'll do...
Pray:	*"Oh grant us help against the foe, for vain is the salvation of man!"* (Psalm 108:12).

Day 4: Stewards All

Pray:	*"Save us, we pray, O LORD! O LORD, we pray, give us success!"* (Psalm 118:25).
Read:	Matthew 25:14-30
Meditate:	What kind of "return" is God expecting of me from the use I make of the stuff and the money He has entrusted to me? How would Barnabas answer that question?
	When I'm getting ready to do something with my money, do I stop and think, "Hey, hold on, this stuff's not yours!"? Should I? Would it make a difference in what I did with my money? How?
	Would I be a better "manager" of my money if I was accountable to someone for how I spent it? Is there anyone I know I could look to for this?
Journal:	I'm not so sure I'm glad about this study. But, wait a minute, I said I wanted to value God's Word more than money. I don't want to be ruined by falling prey to the love of money. I want to use my money...
Pray:	*"With my whole heart I seek you; let me not wander from your commandments!"* (Psalm 119:10).

Day 5: I Need a Plan, Man!

Pray: *"So teach us to number our days that we may get a heart of wisdom"* (Psalm 90:12).

Read: *James 4:13-17*

Meditate: Verse 17: Who gets the blessing? Who ends up living outside God's will?

OK, I need a plan for my money. In v. 15, what has to be the most important part of that plan? How do I make sure that's part of my money plan?

What are some cues that might tell me that I'm beginning to veer away from God's plan for my money, into one that's more designed to make money my god instead of the God of the Bible? If that happens, will I be willing to return to the Lord's plan? How will I do that? With whom should I share my plan for my money?

Journal: Personal Money Plan: Step 1: _____
                                        Step 2: _____
                                        Step 3: _____
                                        Etc.   _____

Pray: *"All your works shall give thanks to you, O LORD, and all your saints shall bless you!"* (Psalm 145:10).

Lesson 17: What Are the Biblical Principles to Wise Financial Planning?
- Anchorsaway Worldview Handbook ©

ENDNOTES

[1] Ron Blue and Judy Blue, *Raising Money-Smart Kids* (Nashville, TN: Thomas Nelson, 1992) 39.

[2] Blue, 39.

[3] Ron Blue, *Master Your Money* (Nashville, TN: Thomas Nelson, Inc., 1986) 22.

[4] Blue, Ron, Judy Blue, *Taming the Money Monster* (Nashville, TN: Thomas Nelson, 1993) 92-102.

Recommended Reading

Key Books:

Blue, Ron and Judy Blue. *Master Your Money.* Nashville, TN: Thomas Nelson Publishers, 1986.

Blue, Ron and Judy Blue. *Raising Money-Smart Kids.* Nashville, TN: Thomas Nelson Publishers, 1992.

Blue, Ron and Judy Blue. *Taming the Money Monster.* Nashville, TN: Thomas Nelson Publishers, 1993.

Burkett, Larry. *Debt-Free Living.* Chicago, IL: Moody Press, 1989.

Burkett, Larry. *Get a Grip on Your Money: A Teen Study in Christian Financial Management.* Gainesville, GA: Christian Financial Concepts, 1996.

Ramsey, Dave, and Sharon Ramsey. Financial Peace Revisited. New York: Viking, 2003.

Richards, Jay W. Money, Greed, and God: Why Capitalism Is the Solution and Not the Problem. New York: HarperOne, 2009.

Schoenfeld, Matt. *Abundant Living: The 5 Biblical Principles for Financial Success.* Oklahoma City, OK: Vibrant Group, 2005.

Schoenfeld, Matt. (A small group Bible study tool): *Achieving Holiness Together.* Oklahoma City, OK: Vibrant Group, 2005.

Toler, Stan. *Cycle of Victorious Giving.* Kansas City, MO: Beacon Hill Press, 2004.

Towns, Elmer. *Fasting for Financial Breakthrough.* Ventura, CA: Regal Books, 2002.

Lesson 18: How Can I Become A Leader Who Influences Culture For Christ?

A. What is leadership?[1]

1. Leadership is the art of influencing others and creating change.

2. Virtually everyone influences other people and creates change, we are all potential leaders.

3. There are two kinds of leaders:

   a. Positional leaders:

   b. Situational leaders:

4. Seeking leadership positions is a good idea, but not necessary for making a difference in our culture for Christ.

5. Cultures are changed at the grass roots by situational leaders.

B. Power vs. Authority Leadership

1. "Power Leadership: The ability to force or coerce someone to do your will, even if they would choose not to, because of your position or your might."[2]

2. "Authority Leadership: The skill of getting people to *willingly* do your will because of your personal influence."[3]

C. The credibility factor

1. People will follow you only if they believe they can trust you.

2. Credibility, comes from Latin "credo," which means "to have faith or trust in."

3. In their book, *Credibility*, James Kouzes and Barry Posner note that "Credibility is the foundation of leadership."[4]

D. Characteristics of an effective leader:

1. Humble

    a. Christian humility is knowing that without Christ we are nothing. It is calling us to think of others greater than ourselves.

        i. 1 Peter 5:5-6

    b. Being a good listener.

        i. James 1:19, Proverbs 15:22

2. Teachable

    a. The popular term for wise counselor is 'mentor,' the name Homer gave Odysseus' spiritual guide and caretaker of Odysseus' son in *The Odyssey*. It refers to a close companion or guide who helps a person make wise decisions about life.

    b. Mentoring is essential to success.

    c. Be willing to accept wise counsel wherever you find it. Prepare a list of questions for you to ask your mentor.

3. Honorable

    a. Some people want to be leaders because they don't want to have to answer to anyone else. Such leaders always fail.

    b. Honor is, according to Scott Turansky and Joann Miller, "treating others as special, doing more than what's expected, and having a good attitude."[5]

    c. Whether you're in class or in a campus group, whether you're with professors or with fellow students, others will assume that what you do as a Christian is what Christ would do if He were in your place.

    d. There is no substitute for acting honorable, even if the other person is not doing so.

4. Credible

    a. *Jesus said, "Let your yes be yes and your no be no"* (Matthew 5:37). Your followers need to know that you will act truthfully, that you won't tell lies, that you won't hide the truth, and that you won't gossip.

    b. Honesty also means speaking the truth when it hurts.

    c. A leader must be above reproach—not perfect but authentically filled with the fruit of a clean conscience. When your followers see that you act in a way that builds respect and demonstrates responsibility, you'll find yourself in demand as a leader.

d. What happens if I have lost my credibility? Restore credibility by:

    i. Identify all the people who have been offended by your actions.

    ii. Contact each person and apologize, without offering excuses.

    iii. Seek someone to hold you accountable so you don't make the same mistake twice.

    iv. Develop a plan for change. Be repentant and determined to do what is right.

5. Persevering

a. Scripture encourages good hard work (Galatians 6:3-5, Proverbs 6:6-11).

b. Hard work, perseverance, a strong will and a vision of the goal that lies ahead are essential components of a successful leader.

c. Hard work in and of itself is of little value. In order for hard work to pay off, you've got to stay sharp spiritually. The Bible says, *"Unless the LORD builds the house, its builders labor in vain"* (Psalm 127:1).

6. Giver

a. All leaders should be leader developers.

b. The great leadership "guru," Warren Bennis said, "Leadership is not so much the exercise of power itself as the empowerment of others."[6] This means that in every leadership situation you have two choices. You can say, "I will lead, you walk with me," or you can say, "Here is an opportunity for you to lead, I will walk with you." The first person gets things done. The second person gets things done and also equips a whole generation of leaders.

c. As soon as you learn a leadership principle, find someone to whom you can pass it.

d. **Is it possible that God wants you to become the most influential student at your school?** Build into the lives of others. That's how it happens.

Can one person make a difference?

Many college students wonder how they can possibly make a difference on a campus of hundreds or thousands or even tens of thousands. Is it really possible that a small number of enlightened people can actually have an influence? Yes. As Bill Brown says, "One person sincerely committed to a cause is more valuable than a thousand who are merely interested."[5]

Make no mistake. The life of leadership is not an easy life. Leaders make sacrifices that pave the way for later generations to succeed. Some years ago, political activist, Gary Bauer, published the following essay to call to mind the sacrifice America's early leaders made:

> Have you ever wondered what happened to the 56 men who signed the Declaration of Independence? Five signers were captured by the British as traitors and tortured before they died. Twelve had their homes ransacked and burned. Two lost their sons serving in the Revolutionary Army; another had two sons captured. Nine of the 56 fought and died from wounds or hardships of the Revolutionary War. They signed and they pledged their lives, their fortunes, and their sacred honor.
>
> What kind of men were they? Twenty-four were lawyers and jurists. Eleven were merchants, nine were farmers and large plantation owners; men of means, well educated. But they signed the Declaration of Independence knowing full well that the penalty would be death if they were captured.
>
> Carter Braxton of Virginia, a wealthy planter and trader, saw his ships swept from the seas by the British Navy. He sold his home and properties to pay his debts and died in rags. Thomas McKeam was so hounded by the British that he was forced to move his family almost constantly. He served in the Congress without pay and his family was kept in hiding. His possessions were taken from him and poverty was his reward.
>
> These were not wild-eyed, rabble-rousing ruffians. They were soft-spoken men of means and education. They had security, but they valued liberty more. Standing tall, straight, and unwavering, they pledged: "For the support of this Declaration, with firm reliance on the protection of the divine providence, we mutually pledge to each other, our lives, our fortunes, and our sacred honor."[6]

By seeking to influence others and create positive change, we are following in a great tradition of leadership that began long ago and continues with every decision we make. The cause in our lifetime is enormously important. Whole nations are suffering for lack of the truth. It is our calling to learn to lead so that we may bring blessing to all nations of the earth. That is what college is ultimately about for the Christian: not just getting a degree, but preparing for a life mission. In this view, pursuing leadership opportunities is one of the most important things a Christian student at college can do.

Lesson 18: How Can I Become a Leader Who Influences Culture for Christ?
- Anchorsaway Worldview Handbook ©

Small Group Discussion Guide

Lesson 18: How Can I Become a Leader Who Influences Culture for Christ?

Small Group Objective:

The goal is to help the students begin to better understand the concept of becoming godly leaders on the college campus or in the workplace.

✓ **Check Points**

☐ Bring 3 x 5 cards for your students to write down any questions they may have which aren't answered during the discussion.

☐ Enlist a student to share a brief personal testimony.

Discussion Questions:

1. Review prayer requests from the week before and ask how the students are doing.

2. Lead a time of discussion, asking the following questions:

(*Note*: Work through as many of the following questions as possible. The goal is not to get through all of them, but to encourage each student to participate in the discussion as part of the learning process.)

   a. What day of the devotional did you find most meaningful?

   b. How did last week's lesson impact your life? Did you share it?

   c. What is your understanding of a godly leader?

   d. Who is someone that you look up to as a good leader and why?

   e. What is keeping you from being a godly leader, and how might you overcome it?

   f. How important is accountability in your role as a leader?

   g. How has failure in your life helped make you into the person that you are today?

   h. Can you see yourself as a leader, and in what way?

3. Ask for prayer requests and tell students that you will be faithful to pray for them during the week. Encourage students to record the prayer requests in the prayer request section of their handbooks, so they can pray for one another during the week. Begin the prayer time by sharing your own request. Spend the remaining time in prayer.

★ **After the Session**

1. Contact small group members during the week. Ask them about their devotional time, a question they have raised, or how their week is going.

Prayer Requests

Lesson 18: How Can I Become a Leader Who Influences Culture for Christ?
- Anchorsaway Worldview Handbook ©

Student Devotionals written by T.M. Moore

How Can I Become A Leader Who Influences Culture For Christ?

Lead, follow, or get out of the way! As followers of Jesus we are also called to lead others to the truth that can set them free. You may regard yourself as a follower, but God is looking to you to lead others. What can we learn about leadership in order to be more effective in the opportunities the Lord presents to us?

Day 1: Lead From Experience

Pray: *"Turn to me and be gracious to me, as is your way with those who love your name"* (Psalm 119:132).

Read: John 1:35-51

Meditate: What's with Andrew and Philip? Where do they get off leading Peter and Nathanael to Jesus? How much did they know about Him? What made them do this?

They were theologians; they didn't know all the answers. What *did* they know? What do *I* know? Is it enough to lead someone else to Jesus? Why?

Andrew and Philip had this much going for them: they had experienced something – Someone – they wanted their friends to meet. Can I say the same? How can I get a little of that Andrew and Philip in me?

Journal: Man, I'm missing something. I know Jesus, and He's changing my life. But am I leading others to Him? For instance, consider these people I see every week: _____ _____ How might I begin to reach out to them and lead them to Jesus?

Pray: *"O Lord, open my lips, and my mouth will declare your praise"* (Psalm 51:15).

Day 2: The Essential Component

Pray: *"One thing I have asked of the LORD, that will I seek after: that I may dwell in the house of the LORD all the days of my life, to gaze upon the beauty of the LORD and to inquire in his temple"* (Psalm 27:4).

Read: Acts 4:1-20

Meditate: Peter and John were the leaders of the first Christian community. Why were they in trouble (see Acts 3)? Do leaders need to be prepared for such risks? Why?

How would I describe Peter's and John's composure before these angry rulers? What is the one qualification for leadership mentioned in this passage (v. 13)? What did that involve?

Should anybody expect to be an effective leader who doesn't spend time with Jesus? Why or why not? What did being with Jesus do for Peter and John? What could it do for me?

Journal: If I want to be a leader I need to spend time with Jesus, like Peter and John did. I'm already doing that to some extent, but it's clear that I need to improve, so...

Pray: *"May integrity and uprightness preserve me, for I wait for you"* (Psalm 25:21).

Day 3: Made, not Born

Pray: *"Let everyone who is godly offer prayer to you at a time when you may be found"* (Psalm 32:6).

Read: Psalm 18:16-24

Meditate: Here in this, his "testimony psalm," David is recalling all the Lord did to bring him into a position of leadership. With how much of David's experience can I identify? How about what he describes in vv. 16-19? Have I experienced this kind of deliverance?

How did David occupy himself following the Lord's deliverance (vv. 20-22)? Can I say the same thing? Am I proving myself "leadership quality" like this?

David's calling to lead Israel came after much testing. He saw it as God's reward of his faithfulness (vv. 23, 24). What is God calling me to be faithful in at this time? Does it seem a little thing? But is it important? If I'm faithful in this, might not the Lord use it to help prepare me for leadership in greater things?

Journal: What if God is preparing me right now for some greater leadership role in the future. Am I paying attention to what He wants me to be doing right now? Can I say the kinds of things David did? Are there areas in which I'm not paying attention to what God may be calling me to do? I think I need to...

Pray: *"I will thank you forever, because you have done it. I will wait for your name, for it is good, in the presence of the godly"* (Psalm 52:9).

Day 4: Step into the Gap

Pray: *"I will hope continually and will praise you yet more and more"* (Psalm 71:14).

Read: Daniel 2:1-24

Meditate: Daniel's just a kid! What's got into him? What seems to have motivated Daniel to step forward and take the lead in this desperate situation? Was he concerned only for himself?

Daniel turned in two directions for help in taking this leadership step. (vv. 17, 18) How do I typically respond to crises? Pressing needs? If I were going to respond like Daniel, to whom would I turn for help?

From where does this kind of courage come? You can't fabricate this "on the spot;" it needs to be built up over time. Am I building myself up to show this kind of courage in the face of a leadership need? Do I need to be doing anything different?

Journal: So I'm sitting in my room, listening to some tunes, and the phone rings. It's one of the leaders of my youth group, and he says something really urgent has come up and they need some people to come out right away and take the lead in a major project for some needy people. I say...

Pray: "Blessed are those whose strength is in you..." (Psalm 84:5).

Day 5: Leaders for the Next Generation

Pray: "I will cause your name to be remembered in all generations; therefore nations will praise you forever and ever" (Psalm 45:17).

Read: 2 Timothy 2:1-7

Meditate: Paul's ministry was coming to its end. He had passed the baton of leadership to Timothy. What was he urging Timothy to do in v. 2? Am I doing this?

Verses 1, 3, 4, 5, and 6 list some essential qualities of effective leaders. What are they? How many of these do I see in my own life?

Am I ready to step into a leadership role for my generation? What am I doing to help make sure there will be leaders when my work is done?

Journal: I have to work harder at making sure I'm ready to lead, and I need to think about encouraging and equipping others for leadership after me, because, if I don't...

Pray: "You, O LORD, are enthroned forever; you are remembered throughout all generations" (Psalm 102:12).

ENDNOTES

[1] Dr. Jeff Myers, Ph.D., contributed much of the information in this lesson and has granted first rights to Anchors Away Ministries, Inc.

[2] James C. Hunter, *The Servant* (Prima Publishing, 1998) 30.

[3] Ibid.

[4] James Kouzes & Barry Posner, *Credibility* (San Francisco: Jossey-Bass, 2003) 22.

[5] Scott Turansky and Joann Miller, *Say Goodbye to Whining, Complaining and Bad Attitudes—In You and In Your Kids* (Shaw Publishers, 2000)

[6] Winston Churchill, address delivered at Harvard University in 1943.

About the contributing author: Dr. Jeff Myers is Associate Professor of Communication Arts at Bryan College and President of the Myers Institute for Communication and Leadership and Passing the Baton International, Inc. He is the developer of six books and four curriculum programs, including <u>Understanding the Times</u>, the curriculum that introduced worldview training to America's Christian schools. His latest program is <u>Secrets of Everyday Leaders</u>. Jeff, and his wife, Danielle, have four children and live in Tennessee. Go to www.myersinstitute.com and www.passingthebaton.org.

Recommended Reading

Key Books:

Barna, George. *A Fish Out of Water*. Brentwood, TN.; Integrity Publishers, 2002.

Copan, Paul. *When God Goes to Starbucks: A Guide to Everyday Apologetics*. Grand Rapids, MI: Baker, 2008.

Habecker, Eugene B. *Rediscovering the Soul of Leadership*. Wheaton, IL: Victor, 1996.

Hyde, Douglas Arnold. *Dedication and Leadership: Learning from the Communists*. Notre Dame, IN: University of Notre Dame Press, 1966.

Kouzes, James M., and Barry Z. Posner. *The Leadership Challenge: How to Keep Getting Extraordinary Things Done in Organizations*. 2nd ed, The Jossey-Bass Management Series. San Francisco: Jossey-Bass, 1995.

Metaxas, Eric. *Amazing Grace: William Wilberforce and the Heroic Campaign to End Slavery*. New York, NY: HarperSanFrancisco, 2007.

Mattson, Ralph. *Visions of Grandeur: Leadership That Creates Positive Change*. Chicago, IL: Moody Press, 1994.

Sanders, J. Oswald. *Spiritual Leadership, Commitment to Spiritual Growth Series*. Chicago, IL: Moody Press, 1994.

Stanley, Andy. *The Next Generation Leader: 5 Essentials for Those Who Will Shape the Future*. Sisters, OR: Multnomah, 2003.

Stanley, Paul D., and J. Robert Clinton. *Connecting: The Mentoring Relationships You Need to Succeed in Life*. Colorado Springs, CO: NavPress, 1992.

Lesson 19: Why Does God Allow Suffering?

A. The Challenge or Problem of Suffering

1. Suffering is ... Misery resulting from affliction; feelings of mental or physical pain; a state of prolonged anguish and privation.[1]

2. John Stott (Christian writer) makes note that suffering undoubtedly constitutes the single greatest challenge to the Christian faith.

3. "Suffering" and "evil" are not synonymous.

B. According to the Bible, suffering and death began in the Garden of Eden.

1. The fall of Humanity: People do evil because they are by nature and by choice sinners. The Christian answer as to why people do evil things centers on the fall of mankind in Genesis, chapters 1-3.

    a. The Curse results from their sin...which brings disunity and separation from God (Genesis 3:8-19) and affects the whole of creation (Romans 8:19-22).

        i. The word here does not imply that Adam would drop over dead the second that he ate the fruit. It literally means "dying you will die" or in other words, "you will begin to die and continue to die until you are dead."

        ii. Human beings, as a result of sin, become sinners both by nature and by choice (Romans 3:23, 5:12). This results in evil acts being committed by these humans. Sin is the cause of conflict between human beings which brings about so much suffering.

        iii. The curse on creation, because of man's rebellion, is also the source of all death and suffering that comes through the natural order like disease, tornadoes, tsunamis and other natural disasters. Before man's rebellion there was no death; death is part of the curse.

2. This provides not only an answer for the reason that people "do" evil, but also the reason that bad things happen to "good" (nice, loving, law abiding) people. ("good" here is typically looked at from a human perspective. <u>The Bible says in Romans 3:9-12, that there is nobody who does good. Nobody is righteous and nobody is seeking God</u>.)

C. God knew we would struggle with the problem of suffering and wrote about it in Scripture.

1. It is as ancient as the story of Job, and as contemporary as today's headlines.

   a. Job suffered greatly

   b. Job 2:10 – "In all this, Job did not sin in what he said."

   c. Job 38:4-39:30 – Notice God did not provide an answer for Job as to why these things were happening.

> "The secret things belong to the Lord our God, but the things revealed belong to us and to our children forever, that we may follow all the words of this law."
>
> Deuteronomy 29:29

2. God knew that man's choice to sin would cause suffering until his physical death and, for the believer, eternal life with Christ in Heaven.

3. Two major causes of suffering:

   a. Suffering caused by human agents (human evil).

   b. Suffering caused by occurrences in nature. Suffering that is the result of earthquakes, fires, floods, diseases and natural disasters of all sorts.

D. What do the different worldviews see as the reason for why people do acts of evil?

E. Suffering and free-will go hand in hand: You can't have one without the possibility of the other.

1. We each have a free-will.

2. All true love relationships are the result of choice. You cannot force a person to love someone or something.

3. Free-will/choice is necessary for life to have any real meaning, for things like love and good deeds, and evil and evil deeds.

F. Is suffering always evil?

1. Pain and suffering seem to be associated with evil. This does raise another question, evil is evil by definition, but: Is suffering always evil? Can good come from suffering?

   a. Suffering is often a wake up call.

   b. Often times suffering shows us that sin is the cause of our pain.

2. Suffering can drive us to God when we realize that suffering, both individual and corporate, is linked with sin.

> "Pain insists upon being attended to. God whispers to us in our pleasures, speaks in our conscience, and shouts in our pain. It is His megaphone to rouse a deaf world."
>
> C.S. Lewis[2]

G. God can mold our lives through suffering.

1. It helps us to develop Godly character (James 1:1-6, Romans 5:1-4).

2. It can help purify our faith (I Peter 1:7).

3. Compassion for others in pain can bring about great acts of sacrificial love.

4. We can help others who go through similar suffering (2 Corinthians 1:4).

H. What has God done in regards to suffering?

1. God has not turned His back on us!

2. God has given us moral laws to follow that are found in Scripture.

   a. "Love the Lord your God with all your heart and with all your soul and with all your mind" (Matthew 22:37).

   b. "Love one another" (John 13:34-35).

   c. "Forgiving each other, just as in Christ, God forgave you" (Ephesians 4:32).

3. God, the Holy Spirit, came to live in all believers so that we can walk through the hard times with hope and peace.

I. The Cross of Christ is God's most powerful answer to suffering.

1. To the question, "Why doesn't God do something?" He did!

a. Jesus died in our place for our sins, taking the punishment for our sin and put it upon Himself.

b. Jesus suffered for all humanity in the world (I Peter 3:18). To the complaint, "It isn't fair," Jesus gives the ultimate example of innocent suffering. Isaiah 53 is a great chapter that teaches us about Christ's innocent suffering.

"God has done everything possible, short of suspending the laws of nature or unmaking man and depriving him of free-will."
Hugh Sylvester[3]

---

2. Jesus empathizes with our suffering.

J. How should a Christian respond to suffering?[4]

1. We can trust God because of His character.

2. We can choose to respond to suffering without resentment.

3. Expect Suffering.

a. Suffering is a part of living in a fallen world of free souls. Choices have to have consequences or else they are not choices.

b. Suffering persecution is also a part of walking obediently in the footsteps of Christ (2 Timothy 3:12, Philippians 1:29, I Peter 2:21, I Peter 4:16).

4. Look for the good God can bring out of suffering.

a. Suffering and trials can bring about the good quality of endurance (James 1:2-4 NIV).

b. Suffering can build godly character which leads to perseverance and hope (Romans 5:3-5, 2 Corinthians 4:16-18).

c. Suffering may seem like it will last forever, but from an eternal perspective, the believer realizes that from heaven it will seem different.

5. Let suffering drive you to your knees in prayer to God.

Conclusion

Suffering and death are here because we as human beings are sinners. The curse started back in Genesis when Adam and Eve sinned. The Christian worldview is the only answer that fully explains the world as we see it. As we continue to suffer and observe others in the world around us that are suffering we should remember that someone suffered in our place and provided hope. Jesus Christ is that sacrifice and our hope. He is the only true answer to the problem of suffering. God promises to one day put an end to the suffering and to remake the world the way that it was originally intended (Isaiah 11, 2 Peter 3, Revelation 21).

These Inward Trials
(John Newton, author of "Amazing Grace")

I asked the Lord, that I might grow in faith, and love, and every grace;
Might more of His salvation know, and seek more earnestly His face.

I hoped that in some favored hour at once He'd answer my request,
And by His love's constraining power subdue my sins, and give me rest.

Instead of this, He made me feel the hidden evils of my heart;
And let the angry powers of hell assault my soul in every part.

Yea more, with His own hand He seemed intent to aggravate my woe;
Crossed all the fair designs I schemed, blasted my gourds, and laid me low.

'Lord why is this?' I trembling cried, 'Wilt thou pursue Thy worm to death?'
'Tis in this way,' the Lord replied, 'I answer prayer for grace and faith.

These inward trials I employ from self and pride to set thee free;
And break thy schemes of earthly joy, that thou may'st seek thy all in Me.'[5]

God reveals that, "In the midst of suffering, I AM."

Small Group Discussion Guide

Lesson 19: Why Does God Allow Suffering?

Small Group Objective:

The goal is to help the students begin to better understand why God allows suffering, and to be able to answer, in part, the objections of unbelievers.

✓ Check Points

☐   Bring 3 x 5 cards for your students to write down any questions they may have which aren't answered during the discussion.

☐   Enlist a student to share a brief personal testimony.

Discussion Questions:

1.   Review prayer requests from the week before and ask how the students are doing.

2.   Lead a time of discussion, asking the following questions:

(Note: Work through as many of the following questions as possible. The goal is not to get through all of them, but to encourage each student to participate in the discussion as part of the learning process.)

a.   What day of the devotional did you find most meaningful?

b.   How did last week's lesson impact your life? Did you share it?

c.   What is one way that you saw God apply last week's lesson to your life this week?

d.   Did your understanding of Christianity and how it addresses the problem of suffering change, at all, as a result of this week's lesson? If so, in what way(s)?

e.   Today, we spoke of the problem of suffering from a philosophical framework. In answering the problem of suffering, would you respond differently to a person who was actually suffering, than one who just had intellectual problems with the issue? If so, how?

f.   Has God ever helped you through a time of suffering? Explain.

g.   When you are suffering, how would you like people to respond to or help you?

h.   Does the Bible say that people are responsible for their moral choices?

i.   If people are not responsible, because their "environment" (genetic and social) determines their choices, why do we punish criminals for the crimes they commit?

j.   What does this say about human beings? Are they free agents or biologically determined machines?

k. Does this elevate or devalue human life?

3. Ask for prayer requests and tell students that you will be faithful to pray for them during the week. Encourage students to record the prayer requests in the prayer request section of their handbooks, so they can pray for one another during the week. Begin the prayer time by sharing your own request. Spend the remaining
time in prayer.

★ After the Session

1. Contact small group members during the week. Ask them about their devotional time, a question they have raised, or how their week is going.

Lesson 19: Why Does God Allow Suffering? - Anchorsaway Worldview Handbook ©

Prayer Requests

Student Devotionals written by T.M. Moore

Why Does God Allow Suffering?

The issue of suffering, and of evil generally, has vexed theologians and philosophers in every age. No attempt to answer the questions concerning the reasons or sources of evil and suffering has ever been satisfactory. And yet they are a daily fact of our existence. The challenge to us is to understand God's view on such matters, and to have His wisdom in knowing how to respond and grow through them.

Day 1: The Purpose for Suffering

Pray: *"Why, O LORD, do you stand afar off? Why do you hide yourself in times of trouble?"* (Psalm 10:1).

Read: John 9:1-38

Meditate: Why did Jesus say this man had been allowed to suffer all these years (v. 3)? What does that mean? Can that still be a purpose for suffering today?

How did this man respond to having his suffering relieved? Do I see any bitterness in him at all? What, then? Were the "works of God" "displayed" in him during this entire situation? How?

My sufferings may not be as severe as this, but I still experience suffering from time to time. What is God trying to do by allowing me such experiences? How should I respond to them?

Journal: All around me I see people suffering in various ways. Do I care? In the face of suffering, God might be wanting to display His works in me. Therefore, whenever I see or hear about suffering, I...

Pray: *"My soul thirsts for God, for the living God. When shall I come and appear before God?"* (Psalm 42:2).

Day 2: Responding to Suffering

Pray: *"How long, O LORD, will you forget me forever? How long will you hide your face from me?"* (Psalm 13:1).

Read: Job 1:13-22; 2:1-10

Meditate: How many ways did Job suffer in these passages? How would I respond to such a sudden, heavy load of suffering?

                     What role did Job perceive the Lord as having in these sufferings (vv. 1:21, 2:10)? Can that really be so? Here we surely come up against profound mystery, but keeping in mind Romans 8:28, can I see how Job could respond the way he did?

                     Job will later lament his suffering – entirely appropriate (cf. chapter 3). He will even go on to resent God – not for allowing him to suffer, but for not making clear to him the reason for his suffering (chapter 31). However, at all times during his ordeal, his eyes are set on finding the Lord. What can I learn from Job about what I should be doing in the midst of suffering?

Journal: My strategy for responding to suffering must always include...

Pray: *"But I have trusted in your steadfast love; my heart shall rejoice in your salvation. I will sing to the LORD, because he has dealt bountifully with me"* (Psalm 13:5, 6).

Day 3: The Reason for Suffering

Pray: *"For it is you who light my lamp; the LORD my God lightens my darkness"* (Psalm 18:28).

Read: 1 Peter 1:3-9

Meditate: The churches in Asia Minor (1 Peter 1:1) were enduring persecution and suffering because of their faith. Why did God allow this (v. 7)? What would that have looked like back then?

                     Peter emphasized looking to Jesus, even though they could not see Him. How can I do that? As I thus "see" Him, what should that lead me to do (v. 8)? How will that affect my faith (v. 9)?

                     Am I or my friends persecuted for our faith in any ways? How do we typically respond?

Why does God allow such "testings" to come to us? How does He want us to respond (see also 1 Peter 2:20-23)?

Journal: I want to be an example to my friends in how to respond to the various kinds of persecution we experience from time to time. I need to talk to them about this, so...

Pray: *"When I am afraid, I put my trust in you. In God, whose word I praise, in God I trust; I shall not be afraid. What can flesh do to me?"* (Psalm 56:3, 4).

Day 4: Dealing with Affliction

Pray: *"Before I was afflicted I went astray, but now I keep your word. You are good and do good..."* (Psalm 119:67, 68).

Read: Psalm 119:65-72, 89-96, 105-112

Meditate: How did the Lord use affliction in the psalmist(v. 67?) The psalmist found the Word of God a source of much help in affliction (vv. 50, 92). How does that work? How does the Word – such as the Scriptures we have examined thus far this week – help us to deal with affliction?

How did the psalmist regard His afflictions (v. 71)? Why?

Given the ways affliction can benefit me (1 Peter 1:3-9; Psalm 119:67, 71), what should be my "first line" response to any affliction (Philippians 4:6, 7)? Why? What use should I make of the Word in the midst of affliction or suffering of any kind?

Journal: Usually, when trials, afflictions, or sufferings beset me, my first line of response is...

From now on, I intend to deal with my afflictions by...

Pray: *"Look on my affliction and deliver me, for I do not forget your law"* (Psalm 119:153).

Day 5: Through Suffering to Glory

Pray: *"Let not the downtrodden turn back in shame; let the poor and needy praise your name"* (Psalm 74:21).

Read: 2 Corinthians 4:7-18

Meditate: We are but frail vessels – "jars of clay." So we're maybe a little fragile. But what power fills and sustains us (v. 7)? How great is that power?

How did Paul regard his trials (vv. 8-11)? For what two purposes did he willingly endure such sufferings (v. 15)?

He said that, in the midst of his suffering, he did not "lose heart" (v. 16). Rather than fixate on his sufferings, to what did Paul look (vv. 17, 18)? What are some of those "unseen things" that I need to pay more attention to when suffering or affliction comes? How can I do that?

Journal: I really believe in the unseen things of Jesus, all that...

And so, I really want to concentrate on that beautiful world when suffering comes. Here's what I'll do:

And here's how I'll help a friend who is suffering:

Pray: *"This is my comfort in my affliction, that your promise gives me life"* (Psalm 119:50).

ENDNOTES

[1] Online Dictionary <http://www.answers.com/topic/suffering>

[2] C.S Lewis, *The Problem of Pain* (New York: Macmillan Publishing Co, 1978) 93

[3] Hugh Sylvester, *Arguing With God* (Downers Grove, IL, NavPress, 1972)

[4] These ideas are taken, with slight modifications from Hugh Sylvester's work, *Arguing with God* chapter 9.

[5] J.I. Packer, *Knowing GOD* (Downers Grove, Ill., InterVarsity Press, 1973) 229

Recommended Reading

Key Books:

Bridges, Jerry. *Trusting God: Even When Life Hurts.* Colorado Springs: NavPress, 1988.

Craig, William Lane, and Greg Koukl. *Answering the Problem of Evil.* Available from Stand to Reason Ministries, www.str.org.

Hansel, Tim. *You Gotta Keep Dancin': In the Midst of Life's Hurts, You Can Choose Joy!* Colorado Springs, CO: David C. Cook, 1998.

Johnson, Patricia R. *Journey into God's Presence.* Mobile, AL: Gazelle, 2004.

Keller, Timothy. *Walking with God through Pain and Suffering.* N.p.: n.p., n.d.

Lewis, C.S. *The Problem of Pain.* New York: Macmillan Publishing, 1978.

Piper, John, and Justin Taylor. *Suffering and the Sovereignty of God.* Wheaton, IL: Crossway, 2006.

Sylvester, Hugh. *Arguing With God.* Downers Grove: NavPress, 1972.

Wenham John, W. *The Goodness of God.* London, England: InterVarsity Press, 1974.

Yancey, Philip. *Disappointment With God.* Grand Rapids: Zondervan, 1988.

Yancey, Philip. *Where Is God When It Hurts.* Grand Rapids, MI: Zondervan Pub. House, 1977.

Zacharias, Ravi. *Deliver Us From Evil.* Nashville, TN: W Publishing Co., 1998.

Zacharias, Ravi K., and Vince Vitale. Why Suffering?: Finding Meaning and Comfort When Life Doesn't Make Sense. N.p.: n.p., n.d.

Lesson 20: How Do I Make Good Life Choices?

⚓ **Anchor of the Week: All human life is sacred to God.**

I. How much does God value life?

John 10:10 *"'The thief comes only to steal and kill and destroy; I have come that they may have life, and have it to the full.'"*

    A. He created each of us in His own image (Genesis 1:27).

    B. We should value all human life, as well (Proverbs 24:11-12; 31:8; I John 2:2).

II. Our Declaration of Independence values life.

    A. The framers of the Constitution support the value of each person's life.

    B. The Declaration of Independence states, "We hold these truths to be self-evident, that all men are created equal, that they are endowed by their Creator with certain unalienable Rights, that among these are Life, Liberty and the pursuit of Happiness."[1]

III. The logical consequences of devaluing human life:

    A. If we support abortion, what is next? Where does it lead?

    B. If we choose to eliminate human life at any point on the life cycle, whether in the womb or on the deathbed, how do we determine when, and if, someone's life should be taken?

    C. Who is Dr. Peter Singer, and why is he significant?

A. Adolf Hitler came to power in 1933 and lost power in 1945 – only 12 years.

B. During that time, over 6 million Jews were killed. Also killed were millions of gypsies, homosexuals, mentally and physically handicapped...

C. The atrocities in Nazi Germany did not come about overnight, they happened over a long, gradual period of time.

V. The history of abortion in our culture

A. The history of abortion

1. Abortion was legalized in 1973 in the Supreme Court case, *Roe v. Wade*.

a. What were the real truths surrounding the case?

b. Does *Roe v. Wade* support the idea that Satan is a liar?

B. <u>A baby is aborted (killed) every 25 seconds in America.</u>[2]

1. From 1973-2016, over 59 million babies have been killed in the United States, and the number is growing.[3] (www.numberofabortions.com)

2. Around the world, over 40 million babies are killed *every year*.[4] Where is the outrage?

4. Where is the outrage for this atrocity?

VI. Addressing our Struggles

A. Dealing with the consequences of sexual sins:

1. Broken relationships

2. Spiritual dryness and distance from God

3. Venereal diseases

    a. A person infected with an STD is more likely to become infected with HIV.

    b. One out of four adults will have an STD.

    c. One out of five will have an HIV infection.

    d. Every 65 seconds, someone in this country is infected with genital herpes.

    e. Common symptoms: discharge, burning or discomfort, swelling, blisters, open sores, rash or warts.

    f. Often appear as flu-like symptoms: fever, headache, muscle aches, swollen lymph glands.

    g. STD symptoms can easily be overlooked and may occur weeks, to many years, after infection.

    h. The possible consequences to a baby infected by the mother while in utero, or at birth, include: stillbirth, blindness, deafness, meningitis, hepatitis, permanent neurological damage, pneumonia, blood sepsis (infection), or death.

Common STDs[5]	Cause	Cure?	Complications
AIDS/HIV	Viral	NO	Debilitates immune system; ends in death
Chlamydia	Bacteria	YES	PID, sterility in men and women
Gonorrhea	Bacteria	YES	PID, sterility in women
Genital Herpes	Viral	NO	Sterility in women, babies can die
HPV	Viral	NO	Warts, risk of cancer, babies can die
Syphilis	Bacteria	YES	Seizures, blindness, heart and blood vessel problems, deafness, and neurological systems
Trichomoniasis	Parasite	YES	Low birth weight babies
Scabies/lice	Mite	YES	Severe itching
Vaginal Infections	Bacteria	YES	PID, sterility, risk of HIV

4. Pregnancy

   a. What are the responsibilities of someone getting pregnant out of wedlock?

   b. Why do so many teens avoid telling their parents? Why would it be better to let them know right away?

   c. What does a sonogram tell you about a 12-week-old baby?

5. Abortion

   a. What is simple or easy about an abortion?

   b. What does a girl have to go through with an abortion?

c. What does a guy have to go through when his baby is killed through an abortion?

d. What are the emotional, spiritual and physical ramifications of an abortion?

6. Adverse affect of sexual sin on eventual marriage relationship and family

7. Sexual addiction

8. Men and women both struggle

"Guys Only": Getting Real

A. In what areas do guys struggle?

1. Pride – It is difficult to be vulnerable with others and admit weaknesses.

2. Image – What is the world telling us we should look like, who we should be?

3. How does this issue affect guys? What does the world say about what it means to be a man?

4. Lust – Does lust have a grip on us? This craving can be after anything (money, gambling, drugs, sex, women...) and can become a driving force in our lives if left unchecked. If we let it, it will drag us down.

5. Sex/Oral Sex – How can we learn to treat women with the kind of respect they deserve?

6. Drinking – How does this issue affect our desire to be accepted? What is it about drinking that makes it so appealing? What does God think about this issue?

7. Drugs – Are we honoring God with our bodies as the "temple" He designed them to be? (1 Corinthians 6:19-20).

8. Language – Are we watching what comes out of our mouths? (Ephesians 5:4; James 1:26, 3:3-12).

B. What does it mean to be a godly man?

1. If we are to overcome these areas of struggle, we must cast a vision for our lives of who God wants us to be.

2. God has given us many examples in His Word of both people and principles that exemplify godliness (Psalm 112:1; Psalm 119:9, Philippians 2:3-7, John 13:34-35).

3. How does a godly man interact with females?
   a. Promote godliness and the spiritual growth of the women in your sphere of influence.
   b. Be a leader.
   c. Guard a woman's heart (Proverbs 4:23).
   d. Set appropriate boundaries in friendship and dating relationships.

4. Be a servant – look out for others first.

5. Pursue purity.

> **Do not lose sight of God's "Big Picture;" who does God want us to be in light of His covenant relationship with us?**

C. What can we do to move from where we are in our struggles to where God wants us to be in a place of freedom?

1. Keep your eyes pure (Job 31:1; Hebrews 12:2; Matthew 6:22).
2. Keep your mind sharp and focused on the right things (Romans 13:14; Philippians 4:8).
3. Do not try to be a "Lone Ranger," and try to do it all on your own.
4. Use "The Buddy System." Be a band of brothers! (Ecclesiastes 4:9-10, 12).

D. Accountability – How important is it and how do I do it?

1. Accountability is one of the most important disciplines of the Christian life.

2. Jesus gave us a model (Luke 10:1).

3. If you do not have an accountability partner or group, find one. It will be critical as you face the many challenges of life after high school.

4. Find someone who is willing to challenge you in your faith, not just someone who says what you want to hear.

5. Commit to being honest with one another in the areas of struggle.

6. Encourage one another and be there to pick one another up when you fall.

E. There is hope! You are not alone in your struggles.

1. God is always there to help you to provide a way out (I Corinthians 10:13).

2. There are other guys that are there to help, as well.

3. You can start fresh. **God is the God of second chances!** (I John 1:9; Isaiah 1:18).

A. In what areas do girls struggle?

1. Image/eating disorders - What is the world telling us we should look like, who we should be? How do we contribute to those messages?

    a. How does this issue affect girls?

        i. Mentally

        ii. Spiritually

        iii. Physically

    b. When it comes to image, where should our focus be?

2. Fear (worship) of men instead of fearing God – How often do we put a guy up on a pedestal, looking to him to have our needs met? Where does God fit?

3. Sexual temptations – What are we looking for that we think sex will provide?

4. Drinking – What makes drinking so appealing? What does God think about this issue?

5. Drugs – Are we honoring God with our bodies as the "temple" He designed them to be? (1 Corinthians 6:19-20).

6. Gossip – Do we let our words cut others down? Are we keeping a tight rein on our tongues? (James 1:26, 3:3-12).

7. Do we give into the temptation to be accepted?

B. What does it mean to be a godly woman?

1. If we are to overcome these areas of struggle, we must have a vision for our lives and who God wants us to be.

2. Scripture provides us with many examples of both people and principles that exemplify godliness.

a. Godly women: Ruth, Hannah, Esther

b. Godly principles:

    i.   Psalm 112:1; Psalm 119:9, Philippians 2:3-7, John 13:34-35

    ii.   What principles might help us become godly women?

3. How should a godly woman interact with males?

    a. Promote godliness and the spiritual growth of the men within your sphere of influence.

    b. Challenge the men to be leaders.

        i.   Demand respect from them.

        ii.   Do not settle for being treated in ways that are disrespectful or demeaning.

    c. Guard the heart – Your own and his.

    d. Promote purity

        i.   Remember: Men are more visually stimulated. Is the way you are dressing, or acting, helping or hurting a man's struggle with lust?

        ii.   Set firm physical boundaries. Do not lose sight of God's "Big Picture." Who does God want us to be in light of His covenant relationship with us?

C. What can we do to move from where we are in our struggles to where God wants us to be in a place of freedom?

1. Matthew 22:37-39, Jesus replied: "'Love the Lord your God with all your heart and with all your soul and with all your mind.' This is the first and greatest commandment. And the second is like it: 'Love your neighbor as yourself.'"

    a. Love is not a feeling, love is a choice.

    b. Obedience to God is not a feeling, it is a choice.

c. Satan wants you to think that faith in God and His commandments are feelings.

d. Acting out our faith is a matter of choice, not a matter of feeling like it.

e. Once we choose to ignore our feelings of wanting to sin, and choose to obey what we know God wants us to do, then God often times sends, through the Holy Spirit, confirmation in the way of peace.

f. Satan will try to convince you that sin is fun and has no consequences.

g. Remember: We choose to sin, but God chooses the consequences.

2. "Keep your eyes on the prize." Pray and read Scripture (Hebrews 12:2; Matthew 6:22).

3. Keep your mind sharp and focused on the right things (Romans 13:14; Philippians 4:8).

D. How important is accountability and how do I do it?

1. Living the Christian life is not easy. There are hard choices to make every day. Our flesh, the world, and Satan constantly try to pull us away from God and do what pleases us. Having accountability is an effective way of dealing with these issues.

   a. How do I incorporate accountability into my life?

      i. Find a person who is not necessarily a friend or someone your own age.

      ii. Find a Christian who tries to live the Christian life.

      iii. Find someone who is willing to speak hard Truth to you when needed, not just someone who says what you want to hear. Find someone who is willing to ask the tough questions.

      iv. Commit to meeting regularly (weekly, bi-monthly, monthly...) in order to share your lives and struggles with one another.

      v. Only through honesty and confession will you find true healing (James 5:16).

E. What if you have already made serious life mistakes?

1. <u>There is hope</u>! You are not alone in your struggles.

2. God is always there to help you to provide a way out (I Corinthians 10:13).

3. There are other girls that are there to help, as well.

4. You can start fresh. **God is the God of second chances!** (I John 1:9; Isaiah 1:18).

Prayer Requests

Student Devotionals written by T.M. Moore

How Do I Make Good Life Choices?

All of life is sacred. At the same time, those who have been set apart for God – made sacred unto Him – are called to work at realizing the sacredness of life by pursuing holiness and working out our salvation in fear and trembling (2 Corinthians 7:1; Philippians 2:12, 13). Our devotionals this week will help to equip us for this ongoing struggle in an age of sin and death.

Day 1: Gird Up Your Mind!

Pray: *"I will ponder the way that is blameless. Oh when will you come to me?"*
          (Psalm 101:2).

Read: Hebrews 2:5-18

Meditate: Why did God make us (vv. 6-8)? But the writer of *Hebrews* says he did not see this happening in his day (v. 8b). What did he see as he looked around at culture and society? In what ways are we still seeing this?

          "But," the writer continues, he saw something eminently beautiful. What did he see? Why is this a vision worth contemplating day and night?

          To what is He bringing us (v. 10)? What does that mean? What does it mean that we are "sanctified" (v. 11)? Do I experience this sanctification? In what ways?

Journal: I see Jesus, and I have been called to be sanctified, as He is sanctified. Today I will work especially hard to...

Pray: *"I will walk with integrity of heart within my house..."* (Psalm 101:2).

Day 2: The Wages of Sin

Pray: *"For the LORD knows the way of the righteous, but the way of the wicked will perish"*
                 (Psalm 1:6).

Read: Romans 6:15-23

Meditate: Why should we not sin? Am I a slave to sin or to righteousness? What would my friends
                 say?

                 How do I try to "present your members as slaves to righteousness leading to
                 sanctification" (v. 19)? Are any of my "members" (bodily parts) still rebelling against
                 God, still slaves to sin? In what ways?

                 To what does sin lead? Is this merely physical and terminal, or may it take other
                 expressions in our lives? Such as?

Journal: Sin is trying to enslave me every day. I will resist it, however, by...

Pray: *"Blessed is the man who walks not in the counsel of the wicked, nor stands in the way of sinners,*
                 nor sits in the seat of the scornful..." (Psalm 1:1).

Day 3: Fighting Against Sin

Pray: *"But for you, O LORD, do I wait; it is you, O Lord my God, who will answer" (Psalm 38:15).*

Read: James 1:12-18

Meditate: Who is the blessed person? Are trials and temptations alike in any ways? How?
                 Where does temptation come from? To what temptations am I particularly vulnerable?
                 How do I try to fight against them?

                 God "brought us forth by the word of truth" (v. 18). Does it make sense that, having
                 been "born" of the Word of truth, I should try to live by it? How do I do that?

Journal: I want the Word of Truth to be my sword against the onslaughts of temptation.
                  So, today...

Pray: *"Do not forsake me, O LORD! O my God, be not far from me! Make haste to help me, O Lord,
                  my salvation!"* (Psalm 38:21, 22).

Day 4: One Anothering

Pray: *"Behold, how good and pleasant it is when brothers dwell together in unity"* (Psalm 133:1).

Read: Hebrews 10:19-31

Meditate: What does it mean to "draw near" to Jesus? Why is this good advice?

                  Why is it important, in an age of sin and death, to "hold fast the confession of our hope
                  without wavering?" How do I try to do that?

                  My brothers and sisters need me to "stir them up" to love and good works. How do I try
                  to do that? Who encourages me in this way?

Journal: "Draw near," "hold fast," "stir up"... whew! That's a tall order. Today, I'm going to give
                  special attention to...

Pray: *"...when brothers dwell together in unity...there the LORD has commanded the blessing, life
                  forevermore"* (Psalm 133:1, 3).

Day 5: Confessing Sin

Pray: *"Against you, you only, have I sinned and done what is evil in your sight..."* (Psalm 51:4).

Read: 1 John 1:5-10

Meditate: Does my life consistently reflect the "light" of God? In what ways? Am I still making
                  room for "darkness" in my life? How?

Why must I not ignore or deny the sins I commit? Does my sin affect my fellowship with Jesus? With His people?

What does it mean to confess my sins? Why should I do so? When?

Journal: I need to keep alert to any sins in my life, and be ready to confess my sins when God brings them to mind. I'm going to make a concerted effort...

Pray: *"Create in me a clean heart, O God, and renew a right spirit within me"* (Psalm 51:10).

ENDNOTES

[1] "The Declaration of Independence: A Transcription," *The National Archives Experience* 30 April 2005 <http://www.archives.gov/national_archives_experience/charters/declaration_transcript.html>.

[2] This statistic comes from *The Voice of the Pregnancies Centers of America,* 30 April 2005 <http://www.crisispregnancy.org>.

[3] "Abortion in the United States: Statistics and Trends," *National Right to Life* 2 May 2005 <http://www.nrlc.org/abortion/facts/abortionstats.html>.

[4] Conversation with Dan Steiner, President and Executive Director of Central Indiana Crisis Pregnancy Center, 1 May 2005.

[5] Adapted from the chart for "The Most Common STDs," <u>Columbia County Health Department</u>, Florida Department of Health 6 May 2005 <http://www.doh.state.fl.us/chdcolumbia/stdchart.htm>. Other information came from Ed Fitzgerald, M.D. of Indianapolis, Indiana.

Recommended Reading

Key Books:

Alcorn, Randy. *ProLife Answers to ProChoice Arguments – Expanded and Updated.* Sisters, OR: Multnomah Publishers, 2000.

Arterburn, Stephen, Fred Stoeker, and Mike Yorley. *Every Man's Battle: Every Man's Guide to Winning the War on Sexual Temptation One Victory at a Time.* Colorado Springs, CO: Waterbrook Press, 2000.

Cochrane, Linda. *Forgiven and Set Free: A Post-Abortion Bible Study for Women.* Grand Rapids, MI: Baker Book House, 1996.

Cochrane, Linda and Kathy Jones. *Healing a Father's Heart: A Post-Abortion Bible Study for Men.* Grand Rapids, MI: Baker Book House, 1996.

"The Declaration of Independence: A Transcription." *The National Archives Experience* 30 April 2005 <http://www.archives.gov/national_archives_experience/charters/declaration_transcript.html>.

Etheridge, Shannon. *Every Woman's Battle: Discovering God's Plan for Sexual and Emotional Fulfillment.* Colorado Springs, CO: Waterbrook Press, 2003.

Fitzpatrick, Elyse. *Love to Eat, Hate to Eat: Breaking the Bondage of Destructive Eating Habits.* Eugene, OR: Harvest House Publishers, 1999.

Harris, Joshua. *Boy Meets Girl.* Sisters, OR: Multnomah Publishers, Inc., 2000.

Harris, Joshua. *I Kissed Dating Goodbye.* Sisters, OR: Multnomah Publishers, Inc., 1997.

Harris, Joshua. *Not Even a Hint: Guarding Your Heart Against Lust.* Sisters, OR: Multnomah Publishers, 2003.

Klusendorf, Scott. *Pro-Life 101: A Step-by-Step Guide to Making Your Case Persuasively.* Signal Hill, CA: Stand to Reason Press, 2002.

Long, Mike. *Teenagers: Everyone is NOT Doing It.* Ottowa, IL: Jameson Books, Inc., 2000.

Ludy, Eric and Leslie Ludy. *When God Writes Your Love Story: The Ultimate Approach to Guy/Girl Relationships.* Sisters, OR: Multnomah Publishers, Inc., 2004.

McCorvey, Norma. *Won by Love: Norma McCorvey, Jane Roe of Roe v. Wade, Speaks Out for the Unborn as She Shares Her New Conviction for Life.* Nashville, TN: Thomas Nelson Publishers, 1998.

"The Most Common STDs." <u>Columbia County Health Department</u> Florida Department of Health 6 May 2005 <http://www.doh.state.fl.us/chdcolumbia/stdchart.htm>.

O'Neill, Jennifer. *You're Not Alone: Healing Through God's Grace After Abortion.* Deerfield Beach, FL: Faith Communications, 2005.

Peretti, Frank E. *Tilly.* Rev. Ed. Wheaton, IL: Crossway Books, 2003.

Proctor, Robert N. *Racial Hygiene: Medicine Under the Nazis.* Cambridge, MA: Harvard University Press, 1988.

Shaver, Jessica. *Gianna: Aborted...and Lived to Tell About It.* Minneapolis, MN: Bethany House Publishers, 1999.

"Statement on the Hiring of Peter Singer." <u>Princeton Students Against Infanticide (PSAI)</u> 30 April 2005 <http://www.geocities.com/Athens/Agora/2900/psai3.html>.

Stenzel, Pam. *Sex Has a Price Tag.* Grand Rapids, MI: Zondervan, 2003.

St. James, Rebecca. *Wait For Me: Rediscovering the Joy of Purity in Romance.* Nashville, TN: Thomas Nelson Publishers, 2002.

The Voice of Pregnancy Centers of America. 30 April 2005 <http://www.crisispregnancy.org>.

Welch, Edward T. *Blame It On The Brain?: Distinguishing Chemical Imbalances, Brain Disorders, and Disobedience.* Phillipsburg, NJ: P & R Publishing, 1998.

"Who was Martin Niemoller and why should you care?" <u>Golden Gate University Library</u>. 30 April 2005. <http://internet.ggu.edu/university_library/if/Niemoller.html>.

Winner, Lauren F. *Real Sex: The Naked Truth About Chastity.* Grand Rapids, MI: Brazos Press, 2005.

Lesson 21: What Are The Keys To Building Healthy Relationships?

⚓ **Anchor of the Week: Healthy relationships have God in the center.**

I. The Significance of Relationships

A. God is a relational God.

B. We are created for relationships – with God and others.

C. Analogy of the cross (a visual reminder of our relationships):

    a. Vertical beam – represents our relationship with God.

    b. Horizontal beam – represents our relationships with others.

II. The Two Greatest Commandments focus on this idea of relationships (Matthew 22:37-40).

III. A relationship with God should be our highest priority, shaping all of our other relationships in life: family, friendships, dating relationships, and marriage.

IV. Building healthy friendships

A. Your friendships will affect you – they will either build you up or drag you down.

    1. You will become like your friends (Psalm 1:1; I Corinthians 15:33).

B. Surround yourself with the right kind of friends – pursue relationships with the kinds of people who will build you up spiritually, emotionally and intellectually.

    1. How can you do that as a college student?

C. To find a friend, be a friend. In order to surround yourself with the right kind of people, you need to be the right kind of person.

D. Practice accountability by finding other Christians who can provide moral support, encouragement, and accountability for you at college.

E. The most important thing is to stay focused on who God wants us to be in our friendships with others.

F. What do healthy guy/girl relationships look like?

1. Understand the unique differences between men and women.

2. Respect for each other: Guys and girls should both be demonstrating godly character in their lives as they interact together.

3. Learn to be friends.

V. Keeping dating relationships healthy

A. Like friendships, in order to find the right person, you must be the right person. – What does this idea mean?

B. There is no hurry.

C. Guard the heart (Proverbs 4:23).

1. What does it mean to "guard the heart?" Dating brings with it a whole mix of feelings, emotions, and responses. We must tread carefully if we are to honor that other person before God.

   a. How might a guy guard the girl's heart? And a girl...the guy's heart?

   b. Pursue purity – *"But among you there must not be even a hint of sexual immorality, or of any kind of impurity..."* (Ephesians 5:3).

2. Plan ahead. How might you plan ahead in pursuing purity?

3. Set your boundaries before you are in the middle of temptation and hold firmly to them. Once you have crossed a physical boundary, it is much easier to do it again. It is nearly impossible to reestablish a boundary that has been crossed.

4. How far is too far? If there is a question or concern, always take the high road – you will never regret it.

D. Marriage

1. What are some issues that we need to be thinking about before we marry?

VI. Accountability is key!

A. Keys to becoming accountable to another person:

1. Seek out other Christians who can provide moral support and encouragement and accountability for you at college or in the workplace.

2. You choose a friend who will stand with you in choosing to be righteous. Accountability begins with you.

3. Have one that will ask tough questions. Scripture repeatedly highlights this principle of the "Buddy System" (Luke 10:1; Ecclesiastes 4:9-12; Proverbs 27:17).

4. Letters of accountability

5. Be willing to be completely honest.

6. The first order of accountability is between you and God.

7. No one can rely on someone else to direct their spiritual activities.

8. An accountability partner, or coach, encourages you to continue on in the good choices you have made and to alert you when you start to stray.

9. You must make the effort to be in contact with your partner regularly.

Love Note

Everyone longs to give themselves completely to someone,
To have a deep soul relationship with another,
To be loved thoroughly and exclusively. But God says to a Christian:
"No, not until you are satisfied, fulfilled, and content with being loved by Me alone.
With giving yourself totally and unreservedly to Me,
With having an intense personal and loving relationship with Me alone.
Discovering that only in Me is your satisfaction to be found.
Then you will be capable of the perfect human relationship
that I have planned for you. You will never be completely united with another
until You are united with Me; - exclusive of anyone or anything else,
- exclusive of any other desires or longings. I want you to have the best.
PLEASE allow Me to give it to you. I want you to stop planning and
stop wishing and allow Me to give you the most thrilling plan existing,
one that you cannot imagine. I want you to have the best so just keep watching Me,
expecting the greatest things and listen and learn the things I tell you.
You just wait — That's all. Don't be anxious. Don't worry.
Don't look around at things others have received or that I've given them.
Don't look at things you THINK you want. Just keep looking to Me
or you'll miss what I want to show you. And then, when you're ready,
I'll surprise you with a love far more wonderful than any you could dream of.
You see, until you are ready, and until the one I have for you is ready,
(and I am working even at this moment to have both of you ready at the same time).
Until you are both satisfied exclusively with me and the life that I have prepared for you,
you won't be able to experience the love that exemplifies your relationship with Me,
and this is the PERFECT love. And dear one, I want you to have this most wonderful love,
I want you to see in the flesh a picture of your relationship
with Me and enjoy materially and concretely the everlasting union of beauty,
perfection and love. Know that I love you.
I am God. Know it and be satisfied!"

- Author Unknown

Choices of Grace

We are often faced with tough choices. It would be nice if our choices got easier as we got older, but unfortunately, with maturity also comes responsibility. Think wisely about the choices you make when you sin against God, and the choices you will then have to make as the consequences of those sins.

Listen to what Dannah Gresh has to say about the consequences of sin:

> "Let me first say there is no escaping the consequences of sin. Adam and Eve, because of their sin, were kicked out of the garden. Adam had to work hard to feed his family, and Eve would experience great pain in childbirth. Even the snake lost his legs. The consequences were tough.

> King David truly sinned - he had sex with another man's wife (Bathsheba). Then, because he got her pregnant, he ended up killing her husband to hide his sin...

> Yes, the consequences of sin can last a long time and be very painful, but does that mean that God no longer wanted David to be in a loving, lasting relationship with him?... When David was confronted, he repented, and Nathan immediately said, 'The Lord has taken away your sin'" (2 Samuel 12:13).

Repentance is not always easy. Sometimes we can feel like we do not deserve to come before God, believing that our sin is too great. But Psalm 103 says, "*The Lord is compassionate and gracious, slow to anger, abounding in love. He will not always accuse, nor will he harbor his anger forever; he does not treat us as our sins deserve or repay us according to our iniquities. For as high as the heavens are above the earth, so great is his love for those who fear him; as far as the east is from the west, so far has he removed our transgressions from us*" (Psalm 103:8-12).

Although we do not deserve God's grace, He showers it upon us, and He longs to have a personal, intimate relationship with us. God said to Paul, "*My grace is sufficient for you, for my power is made perfect in weakness*" (2 Corinthians 12:9).

Solomon, the wisest man to ever live, said something very significant related to the stories we have heard. "*Do not arouse or awaken love until it so desires*" (Song of Songs 8:4). *The Wycliffe Bible Commentary* says the following about that verse, "Love should not be stirred up before its proper time, because the love relationship, unless carefully guarded, may cause grief instead of the great joy it should bring to the human heart."

"*But the fruit of the Spirit is love, joy, peace, patience, kindness, goodness, faithfulness, gentleness and self-control. Against such things there is no law. Those who belong to Christ Jesus have crucified the sinful nature with its passions and desires. Since we live by the Spirit, let us keep in step with the Spirit*" (Galatians 5:22-26).

Relationships

Whether God has called you to be single or in a relationship, the most important relationship you will have is with Jesus Christ.

- "One of the saddest tendencies of dating is to distract young adults from developing their God-given abilities and skills. Instead of equipping themselves with the character, education, and experience necessary to succeed in life, many allow themselves to be consumed by the present needs that dating emphasizes." – Joshua Harris

- *"The Lord does not look at the things man looks at. Man looks at the outward appearance, but the Lord looks at the heart"* (1 Samuel 16:7).

- "A string of uncommitted dating relationships is not the gift! God gives us singleness—a season of our lives unmatched in its boundless opportunities for growth, learning, and service—and we view it as a chance to get bogged down in finding and keeping boyfriends and girlfriends. But we don't find the real beauty of singleness in pursuing romance with as many different people as we want. We find the real beauty in using our freedom to serve God with abandon." – Joshua Harris

- *"There is a time for everything, a season for every activity under heaven"* (Ecclesiastes 3:1).

- "Many people realize too late that we do not arrive at contentment as a destination as much as we develop contentment as a state of mind... And in Philippians 4:11 he [Paul] writes, *"'I have learned to be content whatever the circumstances.'"* Could you be content if God called you to be single?

- "The guy or girl you will one day marry doesn't need a girlfriend or boyfriend... What that person needs is someone mature enough to spend the season before marriage preparing to be a godly wife or husband." – Joshua Harris

- "Self-pity is a sinful response to feelings of loneliness. We don't sin when we feel lonely or admit a desire for companionship, but we do sin when we use these feelings as an excuse to turn from God and exalt our own needs." – Joshua Harris

- *"For God is greater than our hearts, and he knows everything"* (1 John 3:20).

- "I feel very strongly that marriage is not a higher calling than the single state. Happy indeed are those people, married or single, who have discovered that happiness is not found in marriage but in a right relationship with God." – Gary Chapman (1 Corinthians 7)

- *"Above all else, guard your heart, for it is the wellspring of life"* (Proverbs 4:23).

- "You can only see the outward man [or woman] from today's perspective. God sees men's [and women's] hearts from the perspective of eternity. With His perspective, He can see much better what you need."

- "Ponder this: Every unbelieving marriage partner arrived as an unbeliever on the first date. As trite as it may seem, every date is a potential mate. Avoid dating an unbeliever."

"Biblical masculinity is neither passive nor rudely aggressive. God calls us [men] to be servant initiators—firm, but gentle; masculine, yet caring; leaders, yet servants. We're called to be protectors, not seducers."

"God created lines of authority in order for his created world to function smoothly. Although there must be lines of authority, even in marriage, there should not be lines of superiority. God created men and women with unique and complementary characteristics. One sex is not better than the other. We must not let the issue of authority and submission become a wedge to destroy oneness in marriage. Instead, we should use our unique gifts to strengthen our marriage and to glorify God." – Joshua Harris

Lesson 21: What Are the Keys to Building Healthy Relationships? - Anchorsaway Worldview Handbook ©

Small Group Discussion Guide

Lesson 21: What Are the Keys to Building Healthy Relationships?

Small Group Objective:

Your goal is to help the students better understand the importance of relationships, and, in particular, how to develop healthy friendships and dating relationships. The ultimate goal is to help them build a strong relationship with God, which will influence their other relationships in life.

✓ **Check Points:**

☐ Bring 3 x 5 cards for your students to write down any questions they may have which aren't answered during the discussion.

☐ Enlist a student to share a brief personal testimony.

Discussion Questions:

1. Small group activity: Each student writes him/herself a personal letter.

(*Note:* The first 10 minutes of your small group time should be spent having students write a personal accountability letter to themselves. The template for this accountability letter can be found on the Resource CD-ROM. It should include areas of their lives where they need growth and discipline, such as their prayer life, Bible reading, getting involved in a Christian group, their thought life, and sexual purity. Some students may want to include some money in their envelopes, since they know they will have none the next year! (No change, please!!!) Next year, the letter will be sent to them at school.

After the students have had time to write their letters, have them address an envelope. In the return address section, have them include their current address **and phone number**. Ask them to include their names in the mailing address section, and their school address, if they know it. If not, leave it blank. When everyone is finished, collect the letters. Some students want to take them home to finish, but they rarely return them. If they want to write more, have them write another letter and ask their parents to mail it.)

2. Review prayer requests from the week before and ask how the students are doing.

(*Note:* Have students give names of juniors that they would like to be invited for next year's Anchorsaway class. Give names to the administrator.)

3. Lead a time of discussion, asking the following questions:

(*Note:* Work through as many of the following questions as possible. The goal is not to get through all of them, but to encourage each student to participate in the discussion as part of the learning process.)

    a. What day of the devotional did you find most meaningful?

    b. How did last week's lesson impact your life? Did you share it?

    c. Who is your accountability partner for next year?

d. What did you learn this week about building healthy relationships?

e. How essential are healthy relationships?

f. How can we keep from allowing relationships to define who we are?

g. Which do we seek more: To gain from them or to invest in them?

h. When you have messed up, how do you get right with God?

i. Do you feel it is important to live out your worldview in your relationships? Why/why not? If you can't live out your worldview in a relationship, what does that say about the value of that particular friendship?

j. Do you want to continue the relationships in this group by emailing each other next year?

4. Ask for prayer requests and tell students that you will be faithful to pray for them during the week. Encourage students to record the prayer requests in the prayer request section of their handbooks, so they can pray for one another during the week. Begin the prayer time by sharing your own request. Spend the remaining time in prayer.

★ After the Session

1. Contact small group members during the week. Ask them about their devotional time, a question they have raised, or how their week is going.

Prayer Requests

What Are The Keys To Building Healthy Relationships?

God has called us to relationships of devoted love, expressed in mutual service and edification. This week, let's think about what this requires of us.

Day 1: The Greatest of These

Pray: *"Blessed are those whose strength is in you, in whose heart are the highways to Zion"* (Psalm 84:5).

Read: 1 Corinthians 13

Meditate: If I had to rate myself, on a scale of 1 to 5 (5 being the highest rating), on each of the terms Paul uses to explain what love is, how would I do? What areas especially do I seem to need some work on?

Typically, do I reach out to others with the love of Jesus, or do I wait for others to reach out to me? What does love require of me? Why?

Why is love "the greatest of these?"

Journal: I need to take the initiative in loving others. So, today...

Pray: *"O LORD God of hosts, hear my prayer; give ear, O God of Jacob!"* (Psalm 84:8).

Day 2: Committed to Serving

Pray: *"As for the saints in the land, they are the excellent ones, in whom is all my delight"* (Psalm 16:3).

Read: John 13:1-15

Meditate: Why did the disciples not take up the task of washing one another's feet? Am I more like them or more like Jesus?

I won't be washing anyone's feet today, but what can I learn from the example of Jesus about serving others? What kinds of needs do they have?

What would I most like someone to do for me? What does the "Golden Rule" require? How can I put that into practice?

Journal: Jesus needed a towel and a basin to serve the needs before Him. If I'm going to serve the needs of those around me today, I'll need to...

Pray: "I have set the LORD always before me; because he is at my right hand, I shall not be shaken" (Psalm 16:8).

Day 3: Encouraging Others

Pray: "I love you, O LORD, my strength" (Psalm 18:1).

Read: 1 Thessalonians 5:1-11

Meditate: The Lord is coming back soon, even though we don't know when. What should I be doing in the meantime (vv. 6, 8, 11)?

How can I encourage others to "be sober" and to "put on the breastplate of faith?" How would this help to build them up in the Lord?

What's keeping me from being more of an encourager to my fellow Christians?

Journal: To "encourage" is to "instill courage in." Hmmm...That's what I want to be known as, an encourager. So, today...

Pray: "This God – his way is perfect; the word of the LORD proves true; he is a shield for all those who take refuge in him" (Psalm 18:30).

Day 4: Watch That Tongue!

Pray: *"Set a guard, O LORD, over my mouth; keep watch over the door of my lips!"* (Psalm 141:3).

Read: James 3:1-12

Meditate: Why does the tongue have so much power? Does my tongue send out any burning stings or poisonous words? Like what?

                Why is it so hard to "tame" the tongue? Does the culture in which I travel encourage me to use my tongue in a godly or ungodly manner?

                What does it mean for the tongue to be a "blessing?" How can I make my tongue more of a blessing to others?

Journal: I think I need to be more careful about how I use my tongue. I want to build others up and encourage them, not "burn" or "poison" them with my words. So, today...

Pray: *"Do not let my heart incline to any evil, to busy myself with wicked deeds..."* (Psalm 141:4).

Day 5: To Comfort Others

Pray: *"The LORD is my shepherd; I shall not want..."* (Psalm 23:1).

Read: 2 Corinthians 1:3-7

Meditate: How has God comforted me lately? Has He used someone else to comfort – or encourage – me? How?

                What is God trying to make me able to do (v. 4)? Am I willing to do that? Do I know anyone who needs that from me? Who?

                Do I ever "suffer" because of my faith in Jesus? If I did, where would I turn for comfort? Do my friends ever suffer for Him? Would they turn to me for comfort if they did?

Journal: But what does it take to comfort others, or to encourage them? I need to find out. Today, I'm going to ask some friends, like...

Pray: *"Even though I walk through the valley of the shadow of death, I will fear no evil, for you are with me; your rod and your staff, they comfort me"* (Psalm 23:4).

Recommended Reading

Key Books:

Arterburn, Stephen, and Fred Stoeker (with Mike Yorkey). *Every Man's Battle*. Colorado Springs, CO: Waterbrook Press, 2000.

Burns, Jim, and Doug Fields. Getting Ready for Marriage: A Practical Road Map for Your Journey Together. Colorado Springs, CO: David Cook., 2015.

Burns, Jim, and Doug Fields. Getting Ready for Marriage Workbook. Colorado Springs, CO.: David C Cook, 2015..

Chapman, Gary. *The Five Love Languages*. Chicago, IL: Moody Press, 1996.

Clarke, Jeremy. *I Gave Dating a Chance: A Biblical Perspective to Balance the Extremes*. Colorado Springs, CO: Waterbrook Press, 2000.

Cloud, Henry, and John Townsend. *Boundaries*. Grand Rapids, MI: Zondervan, 1992.

Cloud, Henry, and John Townsend. *Boundaries in Dating*. Grand Rapids, MI: Zondervan, 2000.

Curtis, Brent, and John Eldredge. *The Sacred Romance: Drawing Closer to the Heart of God*. Nashville, TN: Thomas Nelson Publishers, 1997.

DeMoss, Nancy Leigh. *Singled Out for Him*. Buchanan, MI: Life Action Ministries, 1998.

Eldredge, John. *Wild at Heart: Discovering the Secret of a Man's Soul*. Nashville, TN: Thomas Nelson Publishers, 2001.

Harris, Joshua. *I Kissed Dating Goodbye: A New Attitude Toward Romance and Relationships*. Sisters, OR: Multnomah Publishers, 1997.

Ludy, Eric and Leslie. *When God Writes Your Love Story: The Ultimate Approach to Guy/Girl Relationships*. Sisters, OR: Multnomah Publishers, 2004.

Vander Laan, Ray. "That the World May Know," video series, Focus on the Family 12 May 2005 <http://www.family.org/webextras/a0023460.cfm>.

Appendix A

Anchorsaway Resource Charts

Comparison of World Religions Resource Chart © Anchorsaway®

Comparison of World Religions

This chart is adapted from Kenneth Boa, *Cults, World Religions and the Occult*

Christian Doctrine	Hinduism	Buddhism	Islam	Judaism
Jesus Christ John 1:1-3, 14; 8:58; Col. 1:16-20	No recognition of any kind given to Christ.	No recognition of any kind given to Christ.	Jesus Christ is nothing more than a prophet of god.	Rabbinic teaching holds that there must be two Messiahs: Son of Joseph, who would die, and Son of David, who would establish the kingdom on earth.
Tri-Unity Luke 3:21-22; 1 Peter 1:2; Matt. 28:19; John 15:26	God is an "it" in Philosophical Hinduism, and in Popular Hinduism there are great multitudes of gods. In a sense: man is god.	No recognition of the Tri-Unity. Most Buddhist sects are polytheistic, pantheistic or atheistic.	There is only one god and that is Allah.	There is only one God and that is Yahweh.
Everyone has an eternal spirit Matt. 25:46; Dan. 12:2; Eccl. 2:7; Rev. 20:11-15	Yes, and it continues through many incarnations.	Guatama, founder of Buddhism, claimed that men have no souls.	Yes	Yes
Born a lost soul Ps. 51:5; James 1:15; Romans 5:12-21; 1 Cor. 15:21-22	No recognition of sin and moral guilt. Sin is an illusion.	Guatama claimed that men do not have souls.	No	Judaism rejects the doctrine of original sin, saying that sin is an act, not a state.
Salvation John 3:14-17; Acts 16:31; Rom. 3: 21-30; 10:4, 9-10; Gal. 2: 16	Hinduism is a works system. Forgiveness of sin does not fit into the picture of karma (cause and effect). Each person has many lives in which to reach salvation.	Theravada Buddhism: salvation by self-effort. Mahayana Buddhism: salvation of one dependent on the grace of others.	After the resurrection, each man's deeds will be weighed to determine his destiny -heaven or hell.	Man does not need redemption. Repentance (turning back to God) is all that is needed when one fails to live according to the law.
Sacred Books (Authority) The Holy Bible	Sruti-revealed script. Smriti-tradition. These groups of books contain many contradictions.	Buddhist scriptures and sayings attributed to Gautama were written about four centuries after his death, and there is no way to be certain they are really his words.	Koran -most important, Tauret, Pentateuch of Moses, Zabur (Psalm of David), Injil (Evangel of Jesus).	The Torah , The Old Testament, The Talmud
Suggested approaches for presenting the Christian faith	Address the Hindu argument that all religions are the same. Emphasize the unique claims of Jesus. No other religion offers a real solution to the problem of sin. Books of the Bible are harmonious; Hindu scriptures contradict one another. Man is born as a lost human headed for hell because he inherited the sin of Adam.	Give a positive and clear exposition of the claims of Christ and His victory over sin and death. Christ offers salvation; Buddhism does not. Each person must work out his own salvation. Adjust and accommodate for the manner in which Buddhism has become embedded in the culture. Make a strong case for the Bible - archaeology, history and prophecy.	Christians must focus on the problem of sin, contrasting what God of the Bible has done about it, with what Allah has not done. Ask questions to determine views. Muslims have no personal relationship with god. Focus on the true deity of Jesus Christ, the lost nature of man, and the salvation offered by Jesus. Point out the error of works righteousness.	Original Christians were all Jews. Note that a Jew does not have to give up his Jewishness to become a Christian. Christianity is not a Gentile religion. NT was written by Jews (except Luke) and Jesus was a Jew. Emphasize Isaiah 53 as prophetic of Jesus' coming.

Five Major Worldviews

It sometimes seems as if there are more philosophical and religious views than any normal person could ever know. Indeed, there are more than six thousand distinct religions in the world today. However, some people are surprised to find that the world's religions and philosophies tend to break down into a few major categories. These five worldviews include all the dominant outlooks in the world today. This chart is adapted from *Christianity: The Faith That Makes Sense* by Dennis McCallum.*

	REALITY	MAN	TRUTH	VALUES
Theism Christianity Neo-Christianity Judaism Islam (heresy)	An infinite, personal God exists. He created a finite, material world. Reality is both material and spiritual. The universe had a beginning and will have an end.	Humankind is the unique creation of God. People were created "in the image of God," which means that we are personal, eternal, spiritual, and biological.	Truth about God is known through revelation and the Bible. Truth about the material world is gained via revelation and the five senses in conjunction with rational thought.	Moral values are the objective expression of an absolute moral being.
Naturalism Atheism Agnosticism Existentialism	The material universe is all that exists. Reality is "one-dimensional." There is no such thing as a soul or a spirit. Everything can be explained on the basis of natural law.	Man is the chance product of a biological process of evolution. Man is entirely material. The human species will one day pass out of existence.	Truth is usually understood as scientific proof. Only that which can be observed with the five senses is accepted as real or true.	No objective values or morals exist. Morals are individual preferences or socially useful behaviors. Even social morals are subject to evolution and change.
Postmodernism	Reality must be interpreted through our language and cultural "paradigm." Therefore, reality is "socially constructed."	Humans are nodes in a cultural reality – they are a product of their social setting. The idea that people are autonomous and free is a myth.	Truths are mental constructs meaningful to people within their own cultural paradigm. They do not apply to other paradigms. Truth is relative to one's culture.	Values are part of our social paradigms, as well. Tolerances, freedom of expression, inclusion, and refusal to claim to have the answers are the only universal values.

Five Major Worldviews Resource Chart © Anchorsaway®

	REALITY	**MAN**	**TRUTH**	**VALUES**
Pantheism Hinduism Taoism Buddhism Much New Age Consciousness	Only the spiritual dimension exists. All else is illusion, Maya. Spiritual reality, Brahman, is eternal, impersonal, and unknowable. It is possible to say that everything is a part of god, or that god is in everything and everyone.	Man is one with ultimate reality. Thus man is spiritual, eternal, and impersonal. Man's belief that he is an individual is illusion.	Truth is an experience of unity with "the oneness" of the universe. Truth is beyond all rational description. Rational thought as it is understood in the West cannot show us reality.	Because ultimate reality is impersonal, many pantheistic thinkers believe that there is no real distinction between good and evil. Instead, "unenlightened" behavior is that which fails to understand essential unity.
Spiritism and Polytheism Thousands of Religions (including Wicca and Witchcraft)	The world is populated by spirit beings who govern what goes on. Gods and demons are the real reason behind "natural" events. Material things are real, but they have spirits associated with them and, therefore, can be interpreted spiritually.	Man is a creation of the gods like the rest of the creatures on earth. Often, tribes or races have a special relationship with some gods who protect them and can punish them.	Truth about the natural world is discovered through the shaman figure who has visions telling him what the gods and demons are doing and how they feel.	Moral values take the form of taboos, which are things that irritate or anger various spirits. These taboos are different from the idea of "good and evil," because it is just as important to avoid irritating evil spirits as it is good ones.

* Dennis McCallum, *Christianity: The Faith That Makes Sense* rev. ed. (Wheaton, IL: Tyndale House Publishers, 1997) 36-37.

Cults and the Occult*

Many times people are confused by the difference between a Cult and the Occult. This chart will make some of those distinctions a little more clear. There are over 5,000 cults in the U.S. While the specifics for each Cult differ, the underlying concepts are the same. If you will learn the biblical concepts in each of these areas, you will be able to defend the Scriptures against these attacks. You will then be able to provide answers to hurting people in need of the true Savior.

Christianity	Mormonism	Jehovah's Witnesses	Scientology[1]	Wicca[2]
God	Once a man as we are now. He is now an exalted man. Literally our heavenly father. He and his many wives have sex to produce spirit babies that eventually become the human race.	One person god, called Jehovah. There is no other name for god. Jesus is not God, he is the first thing that Jehovah created.	Does not define god or supreme being, but rejects the biblical God. Everyone is a "thetan," an immortal spirit with unlimited powers over its own universe, but all are not aware of this.	The supreme being is called the goddess, sometimes the goddess and god, or goddess and horned god. The goddess can be a symbol, the impersonal force in everything, or a personal being.
Jesus Christ John 1:1-3, 14; 8:58 Colossians 1:16-20	Jesus Christ, spirit brother of Lucifer, received a body of flesh and bone and is now elevated to deity. He is referred to as our "elder brother," one of many gods.	Jesus is a god, not God the Son. He is represented as the first creation of Jehovah. Before his incarnation he was Michael, captain of Jehovah's hosts.	Jesus is rarely mentioned. Jesus was not Creator, nor was he an "operating thetan" (in control of supernatural powers, cleared from mental defects). Jesus did not die for our sins.	Jesus is either rejected altogether or sometimes considered a spiritual teacher who taught love and compassion.
Tri-Unity Luke 3:21-22, I Peter 1:2 Matthew 28:19 John 15:26	Mormon theology is henotheistic. It exalts one god (the father - god) above the other gods in the universe. The Holy Spirit is a spiritual impersonal "force."	The doctrine of the Tri-Unity is denied emphatically. The deity of the Holy Spirit is denied—he is likened to a radar beam.	The doctrine of the Tri-Unity is denied. The Holy Spirit is not part of their belief.	The doctrine of the Trui-Unity is denied. The Holy Spirit is not part of their belief. Some Wiccans may refer to "spirit" as a kind of divine energy.
Everyone has an eternal spirit Matthew 25:46 Daniel 12:2 Ecclesiastes 12:7 Revelation 20:11-15	Yes	They argue for painless extinction, indicating man does not possess an immortal soul, just a combination of breath and flesh. That is, unless you become part of the Organization or the 144,000.	There are no particular human incarnations of god, as the universal life force (Theta) is inherent in all. All humans are immortal spiritual beings (thetans), capable of realizing a nearly godlike state.	Values are part of our social paradigms, as well. Tolerance, freedom of expression, inclusion, and refusal to claim to have the answers are the only universal values.

Cults And The Occult Resource Chart © Anchorsaway®

Christianity	Mormonism	Jehovah's Witnesses	Scientology[3]	Wicca[4]
Born a Lost Soul Psalm 51:5 James 1:15 Romans 5:12-21 I Corinthians 15: 21-22	Mormons deny the doctrine of original sin and teach that the fall of man was a good and necessary thing. There is no imputed sin nature.	Adam's sin imputed to mankind, as federal head of the race. However, a sin nature apparently not inherited by the race.	No sin and no need to repent. Hell is a myth. People who get clear of "engrams" become operating "thetans.".	Definitely not.
Suggested Approaches For Presenting The Christian Faith	1. Confront with the "pillars" of Mormonism: god, works, salvation. 2. Compare beliefs with Bible. 3. The archaeology of the New World refutes the Book of Mormon.	1. Present a clear biblical case of Christ's and Holy Spirit's deity. 2. Present the case of the Tri-Unity. 3. Challenge them to look at the whole of Scripture.	1. Ask why they think the world is in such a mess? 2. Ask how they know for sure that what they believe is true. 3. Present the gospel and the gift of eternal life.	1. Wicca is an occultic "nature religion." Explain the origins of this belief. 2. Ask them how they know that there is no God who loves. 3. Share with them the gospel of eternal life.
Other Beliefs	No alcohol, tobacco, coffee or tea. Baptism on behalf of the dead. Two year missionary commitment encouraged. Extensive social network.	Known as the Watchtower Bible and Tract Society. Meet in Kingdom Halls. Do not observe holidays or birthdays. Forbidden to vote, salute flag, work in military.	Highly controversial. Publication of *Dianetics*. Organizations related: Narconan, Criminon, Way to Happiness Foundation, WISE, Applied Scholastics.	Wiccans practice divination and spell-casting, with most rituals performed in a circle. Many Wiccans are part of a coven. Extremely occultic.

* Boa, Kenneth, *Cults, World Religions and the Occult.* (Wheaton, IL: Victor Books, 1990)
1 Rose Publishing, <u>Christianity, Cults & Religions</u> chart. Compares 17 religions and cults
2 Ibid.
3 Ibid.
4 Ibid.

Urban Cults and the Occult

Christian Doctrine	Kemetic Science	Yoruba	Nation of Islam	Black Hebrew Israelite
Jesus Christ John 1:1-3, 14; 8:58; Col. 1:16-20	Without recognition of any kind given to Christ.	Without recognition of any kind given to Christ.	Jesus Christ is nothing more than a prophet or messenger of god.	Hebrew Israelites believe Jesus Christ (although they use a different name - "Yahshuah" - or some other name) was a black man.
Tri-Unity Luke 3:21-22; 1 Peter 1:2; Matt. 28:19; John 15:26	Recognizes many gods and goddesses. Gods can and do manifest as distinct individuals.. Consciousness is "prima materia," it is all, The One.	Olodumare is the most important "state of existence." It is regarded as being all-encompassing, distant creator. Worship to a pantheon of orishas.	There is only one god and that is Allah. Allah also empowers the black man to be god.	Hebrew Israelites are usually part of the Sacred Name movement: they believe you must refer to God as "Yah" (or some other name).
Everyone has an eternal spirit. Matt. 25:46; Dan. 12:2; Eccl. 2:7; Rev. 20:11-15	Yes	Yes	Yes	Yes
Born a Lost Soul Ps. 51:5; James 1:15; Romans 5:12-21; 1 Cor. 15:21-22	No, but all must adhere to the 42 Laws of Maat.	No	No	Reject the doctrine of original sin, saying that sin is an act, not a state.
Salvation John 3:14-17; Acts 16:31; Rom. 3: 21-30; 10:4, 9-10; Gal. 2:16	After death is the judgment. and are hearts will be weighed on the scales of Maat. If our heart is lighter than Maat's feather then we will have a opportunity to go to Aaru(heaven). If not then the neteru will allow a monster to eat us alive.	There is no focus on salvation. There is a good and bad heaven. Most desire reincarnation. Reincarnation is believed to be possible in three different forms which are: ipadawaye (ancestor's rebirth), akudaaya (die and reappear) and abiku (born to die).	Requires conforming to a standard of righteousness: living in truth, shunning immorality, detesting theft and slavery, practicing justice, worshipping Allah, and taking on one of the names of Allah.	Believe "Edomites" (white people) can't be saved. They are destined to be killed or slaves for Hebrew Israelites after the Messiah returns. Others believe ("Gentiles") can be grafted into the Kingdom if they keep the law and submit under the authority of a black man.
Sacred Books (Authority) The Holy Bible	The Book of the Dead, Papyrus of Ani, Pyramid Texts, Coffin Texts	The Book of Diagnosis in Ifa Divination	Koran	The Old Testament, The Apocrypha
Suggested approaches for presenting the Christian faith.	Emphasize the unique claims of Jesus. No other religion offers a real solution to the problem of sin. Man is born as a lost human headed for hell because he inherited the sin of Adam. They have no security in knowing they will go to heaven.	The opportunity to have a relationship with a personal God. Give a positive and clear exposition of the claims of Christ and His victory over sin and death. Christ offers salvation. Each person must work out his own salvation. Make a strong case for the Bible - archaeology, history and prophecy. Similar to Santeria, Voodoo, Candomble, Shango, Obeah.	Christians must focus on the problem of sin, contrasting what God of the Bible has done about it, with what Allah has not done. Muslims have no personal relationship with God. Focus on the true deity of Jesus Christ, the lost nature of man, and the salvation offered by Jesus. Point out the error of works righteousness. Exemplify life in the spirit and the fruit of the spirit.	NT was written by Jews (except Luke) and Jesus was a Jew. Emphasize Isaiah 53 as prophecy. Remember, it's not just knowledge they need; the Hebrew Israelites need to see authentic love, joy, peace, kindness, goodness, gentleness, faithfulness, self-control and patience. If you are going to converse with them, ask the Lord for a double-dose of the last one – patience.

Messianic Prophecies:

Old Testament References and New Testament Fulfillment
(List Is Nat All-Inclusive)

Topic:	Old Testament:	New Testament:
Messiah to be of the seed of the woman	Genesis 3:15	Galatians 4:4
Messiah to be of the seed of Abraham	Genesis 12:3, 18:18	Matthew 1:2; Luke 3:34; Acts 3:25; Galations 3:16
Messiah to be of the tribe of Judah	Genesis 49:10	Matthew 1:2; Luke 3:33
Messiah to be of the seed of Jacob	Numbers 24:17, 19	Matthew 1:2; Luke 3:34
Messiah to be of the seed of David	Psalm 132:11; Isaiah 11:10; Jeremiah 23:5-6; 33:15-16	Matthew 1:6; Luke 1:32-33; Acts 2:30; Romans 1:3
Messiah to be the Son of God	Psalm 2:7; Prov. 30:4	Matthew 3:17; Luke 1:32
Messiah to be raised from the dead	Psalm 16:10	Acts 13:35-37
The crucifixion experience	Psalm 22, Psalm 69:21	Matthew 27:34-50; John 19:28-30
Messiah to be betrayed by a friend	Psalm 41:9	John 13:18, 21
Messiah ascends to heaven	Psalm 68:18	Luke 24:51; Acts 1:9
Homage and tribute paid to Messiah by great kings	Psalm 72:10-11	Matthew 2:1-11
Messiah to be a priest like Melchizedek	Psalm 110:4	Hebrews 5:5-6
Messiah to be at the right hand of God	Psalm 110:1	Matthew 26:64; Hebrews 1:3
Messiah, the stone which the builders rejected, became the head cornerstone	Psalm 118:22-23; Isaiah 8:14-15, 28:16	Matthew 21:42-43; Acts 4:11; Romans 9:32-33; Peter 2:6-8, Eph. 2:20
Messiah to be born of a virgin	Isaiah 7:14	Matthew 1:18-25; Luke 1:26
Galilee to be the first area of Messiah's ministry	Isaiah 9:1-8	Matthew 4:12-16
Messiah will be meek and mild	Isaiah 42:2-3, 53:7	Matthew 12:18-20, 26:62-63
Messiah will minister to the Gentiles	Isaiah 42:1, 49:1, 8	Matthew 12:21

Topic:	Old Testament:	New Testament:
Messiah will be smitten	Isaiah 50:6	Matthew 26:67, 27:26, 30
The Gospel according to Isaiah: (The suffering Messiah brings salvation.)	Isaiah 52:13-53:12	The Four Gospels
The New and Everlasting Covenant	Isaiah 55:3-4; Jeremiah 31:31-33	Matthew 26:28; Mark 14:24; Luke 22:20; Hebrews 8:6-13
Messiah, the Right Arm of God	Isaiah 53:1, 59:16	John 12:38
Messiah as Intercessor	Isaiah 59:16	Hebrews 9:15
Two-fold mission of the Messiah	Isaiah 61:1-11	Luke 4:16-21
Messiah will perform miracles	Isaiah 35:5-6	Matthew 11:3-6; John 11:47
Messiah is called "The Lord"	Jeremiah 23:5-6	Acts 2:36
Time of Messiah's coming	Daniel 9:24-26	Galatians 4:4; Ephesians 1:10
Bethlehem, the Messiah's birthplace	Micah 5:2	Matthew 2:1; Luke 2:4-6
Messiah will enter the Temple with authority	Malachi 3:1	Matthew 21:12
Messiah will enter Jerusalem on a donkey	Zechariah 9:9	Matthew 21:1-10
Messiah will be pierced	Zechariah 12:10; Psalm 22:16	John 19:34, 37
Messiah to be forsaken by His disciples	Zechariah 13:7	Matthew 26:31, 56
Coming of the Holy Spirit in the days of the Messiah	Joel 2:28	Acts 2:16-18
Opposition to the nations	Psalm 2:2	Revelation 19:19
Messiah's final victory over death	Isaiah 25:8	1 Corinthians 15:54; Revelation 7:17, 21:4
The glorious Messiah	Isaiah 63:1	Revelation 19:11-16
Messiah as King	Psalm 2:6-9	Revelation 19:15-16
Submission of nations to Messiah	Isaiah 2:4; Micah 4:1-4	Revelation 12:5
Gentiles shall seek Messiah of Israel	Isaiah 11:10	Romans 11:12

Messianic Prophecies Resource Chart © Anchorsaway®

Jesus is Yahweh.

> "'I and the Father are one.'" John 10:30

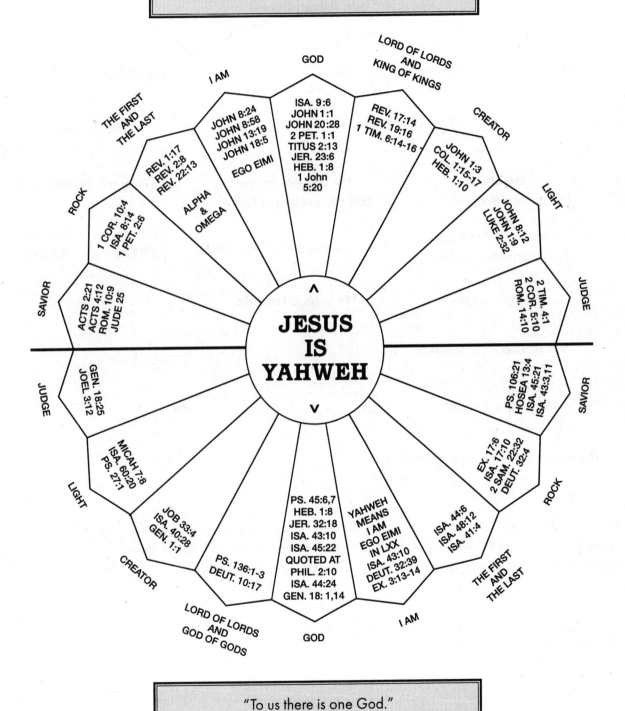

The central diagram "JESUS IS YAHWEH" with surrounding sections:

GOD — ISA. 9:6, JOHN 1:1, JOHN 20:28, 2 PET. 1:1, TITUS 2:13, JER. 23:6, HEB. 1:8, 1 John 5:20

I AM / EGO EIMI — JOHN 8:24, JOHN 8:58, JOHN 13:19, JOHN 18:5

THE FIRST AND THE LAST / ALPHA & OMEGA — REV. 1:17, REV. 2:8, REV. 22:13

ROCK — 1 COR. 10:4, ISA. 8:14, 1 PET. 2:6

SAVIOR — ACTS 2:21, ACTS 4:12, ROM. 10:9, JUDE 25

JUDGE — GEN. 18:25, JOEL 3:12

LIGHT — MICAH 7:8, ISA. 60:20, PS. 27:1

CREATOR — JOB 33:4, ISA. 40:28, GEN. 1:1

LORD OF LORDS AND GOD OF GODS — PS. 136:1-3, DEUT. 10:17

GOD — PS. 45:6,7, HEB. 1:8, JER. 32:18, ISA. 43:10, ISA. 45:22 QUOTED AT PHIL. 2:10, ISA. 44:24, GEN. 18:1,14

I AM — YAHWEH MEANS I AM EGO EIMI IN LXX, ISA. 43:10, DEUT. 32:39, EX. 3:13-14

THE FIRST AND THE LAST — ISA. 44:6, ISA. 48:12, ISA. 41:4

ROCK — EX. 17:6, ISA. 17:10, 2 SAM. 22:32, DEUT. 32:4

SAVIOR — PS. 106:21, HOSEA 13:4, ISA. 43:3,11

JUDGE — 2 TIM. 4:1, 2 COR. 5:10, ROM. 14:10

LIGHT — JOHN 8:12, JOHN 1:9, LUKE 2:32

CREATOR — JOHN 1:3, COL. 1:15-17, HEB. 1:10

LORD OF LORDS AND KING OF KINGS — REV. 17:14, REV. 19:16, 1 TIM. 6:14-16

> "To us there is one God."
> 1 Corinthians 8:6

Is Jesus liar, lunatic or God?*

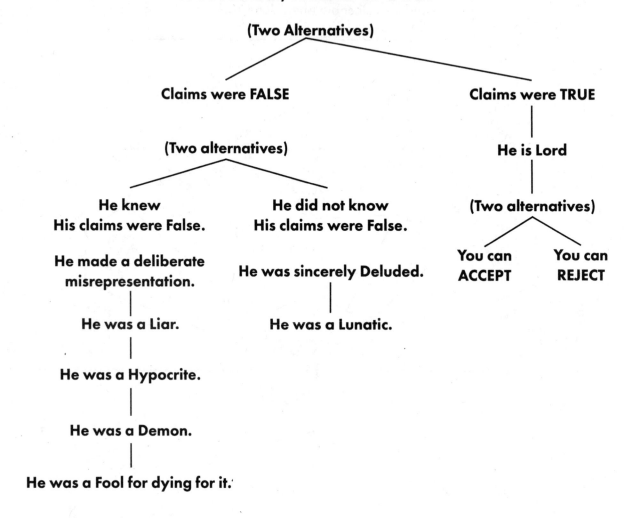

(Two Alternatives)

Claims were FALSE

Claims were TRUE

(Two alternatives)

He is Lord

**He knew
His claims were False.**

**He did not know
His claims were False.**

(Two alternatives)

**He made a deliberate
misrepresentation.**

He was sincerely Deluded.

**You can
ACCEPT**

**You can
REJECT**

He was a Liar.

He was a Lunatic.

He was a Hypocrite.

He was a Demon.

He was a Fool for dying for it.

Some speak of Jesus Christ as a great man. To some He was the founder of a new religion. Others consider him a prophet. But Jesus himself claimed that He was God. If this claim were not true, He could not be called even a good man, but would be an imposter and a liar.

* This diagram comes from Josh McDowell, *Evidence That Demands a Verdict*, vol. 1 (1979; Nashville, TN: Thomas Nelson Publishers, 1999) 104.

Jesus' Claims To Be God Resource Chart © Anchorsaway®

Creator vs. Macro-evolution

	Biblical Creation	Macro-evolution
Person	Creator ("God") – Genesis 1	No Person
God	Revealed – Genesis 1 ("In the beginning God")	Does not exist
Process	Orderly process – Genesis 1	Random process
Uniqueness	Each unique – Genesis 1 ("fearfully and wonderfully made".)	Each an accident
Man Special?	Man special – Genesis 1 ("made in our image")	Man not special
Man and time	Man created near the BEGINNING of time – Genesis 1	Man evolved near the END of evolutionary time
Origin/Offspring	Living things (organisms) after own "kind" – Genesis 1	Living things (organisms) after same single cell
Distinctness	Each thing created distinct - Genesis 1	Each thing from same origin
Temperature	Cool ("water") – Genesis 1	Initially hot, then cooled
Environment	Life sustaining – Genesis 1	Initially harsh
Morality	Defined by creator God – Exodus 20	Defined by masses and power
Rights	Come from God – Exodus 20	Come from government
Races	Single race, created in God's image – Genesis 1& 8	Some 'races' more evolved
Who's involved	God's involved and cares -Genesis 1, John 3:16	Government involved
Involvement	Personal God – John 3:16	Impersonal chance
Love	Loving God (agape) "God so loved the world" – John 3:16	"Love" defined by society/culture - [eros/phileo]
Life approach	Positive approach [life after physical death] – John 3:16	Negative approach [death is the end]
Complexity	Decreases over time - Genesis 1	Increases over time
Change	Limited – Genesis 1	Unlimited
Death	Entered via one man's sin (Adam) Genesis 1	Entered via random upward progression
Information Source	Source & provider – Genesis 1	No provider
Purpose	Purpose to fulfill – Matthew 28:18-20	No purpose to fulfill
Realm	Spiritual and physical – Genesis 1	Physical only
Foundation	Love -John 3:16 ("For God so loved the world...")	Racist (Darwin)
Creation	Created mature - Genesis 1	Single cell, then more complex
Sustained	All things sustained by Jesus Christ "in Him all things hold together" - Colossians 1:17	All things in random motion
Glory to...	God to receive glory and honor Revelation 4:11	Science and man to receive glory and honor

The Four Deadly Questions

These are effective questions to use when your ideas are being attacked, and/or when you wish to point out the errors in someone else's views.[*]

#1. What do you mean by that? The true weakness of an argument lies in the fuzzy definition of terms used. When someone makes a truth claim, ask this question.

#2. How do you know that is true? Surprisingly, most people believe things for which they have absolutely no evidence. Try this question out on someone with strong opinions and be ready for a fascinating discussion.

#3. Where do you get your information? When someone makes a radical claim, you should always ask detailed questions about how they know what they know. Before long you will get to the end of their knowledge and will be on even terms in the discussion.

#4. What happens if you are wrong? It is one thing to claim a belief and yet another to stake your life on it. The most important question that can be asked in life is, "Where do you go when you die, and what happens if you are wrong?"

[*] Thanks to Andrew Heister, Jeff Myers, & Mark Cahill for the four deadly questions which have been used for many years in the teaching at Summit Ministries (Colorado Springs, CO). As a frequent educator at Summit, Mark Cahill effectively explains these penetrating questions in this book. Mark Cahill, *One Thing You Can't Do In Heaven* (Bartlesville, OK: Genesis Publishing Group, 2004) 139-146.

The Four Deadly Questions Resource Chart ®